'Mike Ross has thought hard
here are the considerable frui
essential to church health and ....p....... p....... .. p....... .
that is Christological, churchly, missiological, doctrinal and ethical. Not
many books on church revitalization these days see preaching as crucial,
at least not expository preaching. So it is both a relief and blessing to
listen to wise, tested counsel from a minister of the Word who has put his
method into practice in two local churches over the course of many years of
ministry, and who has seen the hand of God's blessing on his labors. '

J. Ligon Duncan III,
Senior Minister, First Presbyterian Church, Jackson, Mississippi
President, Alliance of Confessing Evangelicals

'A clarion call on the need for biblical preaching by a seasoned and effective
preacher designed to encourage preachers to preach better, to God's glory
and with a view to seeing the Holy Spirit pour forth blessing. I highly
recommend it as vital reading for every preacher.'

Derek W. H. Thomas,
John E. Richards Professor of Systematic and Practical Theology,
Reformed Theological Seminary, Jackson, Mississippi
Editorial Director, Alliance of Confessing Evangelicals

'In this excellent book, Michael Ross argues that church revitalization can
never take place and be maintained unless it is the product of vital expository
preaching. His combination of rigorous biblical argument with empirical
evidence of Reformation and Puritan preaching, persuasively argues the
case. His style is scholarly yet accessible, rich in illustration and practical
elucidation of principles. His concern to guard against emotionalism and
nostalgic hagiography, allow Scripture and history to speak for themselves.
The result is a sobering and inspirational wake-up call to the churches.
As evangelicals, have we lost confidence in pulpits, preachers and preaching,
reducing the proclamation of the living Word of God to mere explanation?
Do we need to re-emphasise and recover the primacy of preaching, having
consciously or subconsciously given primacy to what are important but
secondary issues? The bottom line is that the revitalizing of the Church
necessitates first a revitalization of preaching. We either heed the call or
drift.'

Robin Sydserff,
The Proclamation Trust, London

'Michael F. Ross in Preaching for Revitalization promotes a return to Puritan preaching with its priority, content, characteristics, and expository style. I once heard John Stott urge preachers to read at least one substantial book on preaching a year. For more than a dozen years I have worked along side Mike. This book is not just theory; it is a description of Mike's pulpit ministry. I recommend Preaching for Revitalization be the book all preachers can read with great profit in the coming year.'

Archie Parrish,
President, Serve International

'I am a debtor not only to the grace of God revealed in Christ Jesus, but to Michael Ross for re-affirming the primacy of preaching for the revitalization of the Church. In our day when the majority of churches are in decline spiritually and their pastors are "clueless" as to this malady, Dr. Ross points us back to the power of the pulpit to rekindle our first love, Jesus Christ, modeled by the Puritans. I was especially pleased with his chapter on Missiological Preaching. Invariably, the church in need of revitalization has lost its "outward face" to call sinners to the Savior. Preaching for Revitalization is a long overdue guide to reverse the slide of the Church into spiritual slumber.'

James C. Bland,
Coordinator, Mission to North America, Presbyterian Church in America

'What a privilege to commend to you Preaching for Revitalization by Michael Ross. In this book Michael powerfully sets forth the Biblical basis for confidence in God's commitment to use the preaching of the Word in general, and thoughtful expository preaching in particular to lead as a primary, although not exclusive, means of grace to lead a church back to spiritual health and vitality. His thorough work in the history of expository preaching, as well as the various helpful insights and advise from his personal ministry (and other effective preachers), makes the book both readable and extremely helpful. Finally, while Michael wonderfully affirms Biblical preaching and does not allow cultural fads to diminish our confidence in God's promise to save men and women through the "foolishness of preaching," he does point out the appropriate ways to connect to the culture without being conformed by it.'

Harry L. Reeder, III
Senior Pastor, Briarwood Presbyterian Church, Birmingham, Alabama

PREACHING
FOR
REVITALIZATION

How to Revitalize your Church through your pulpit

Michael F. Ross

MENTOR

Michael Frederick Ross was raised as a Roman Catholic and even studied for the Roman Catholic priesthood, during his high school years, at the Divine Word Seminary, in Perrysburg, Ohio. He was converted in August of 1976 while living and working in Memphis, Tennessee.

He holds degrees from The Ohio State University, Miami (Ohio) University and Memphis State University. His Master of Divinity degree is from the Columbia Biblical Seminary in Columbia, South Carolina(1982) and his a Doctorate of Ministry degree is from Reformed Theological Seminary, Jackson, Mississippi(1997). For ten years, he served as the organizing pastor of the Surfside Presbyterian Church in Myrtle Beach, South Carolina. In 1992, he became the sixth senior pastor of the Trinity Presbyterian Church in Jackson, Mississippi.

Copyright © Michael F, Ross 2006

10 9 8 7 6 5 4 3 2 1

ISBN 1-84550-123-3

Published in 2006
in the
Mentor Imprint
by
Christian Focus Publications Ltd,
Geanies House, Fearn, Ross-shire,
IV20 1TW, Scotland

www.christianfocus.com

Cover design by Danie Van Straaten

Printed and bound by Bell and Bain, Glasgow

Contents

Dedication.. 6
Acknowledgements... 7

Introduction
1. Preaching for Revitalization 11

Part One: Priority and Promotion in Puritan Preaching
2. Preaching and Church Growth.. 29
3. Preaching in The Reformed Heritage................................ 45
4. The Priorities of Preaching 55

Part Two: The Content of Puritan Preaching
5. Preaching With Deliberate Balance 73
6. Christological Preaching 81
7. Ecclesiastical Preaching 87
8. Missiological Preaching... 95
9. Doctrinal Preaching 103
10. Ethical Preaching 119

Part Three: The Characteristics of Puritan Preaching
11. The Puritan Ethos 131
12. Spiritual Preaching 139
13. Romantic Preaching... 145
14. Controversial Preaching... 155
15. Comaraderie in Preaching... 163

Part Four: The Expository Style of Puritan Preaching
16. Expository Preaching Defined.. 173
17. A Brief History of Expository Preaching 179
18. A Workable Method for Expository Preaching................ 193
19. The Expositional Process 211

Epilogue
20. 'A Charge to Keep I Have'... 217

Ten Non Negotiables 227
Fifteen Factors of a Dynamic Church.................................... 229
Bibliography 231

Dedicated to
Jane
My wife and partner in ministry
whose love, encouragement, faith and patience
have strengthened me to preach the Word

and to
Joanna, Abigail, Nathan and Aaron
My children who have been my first parish and
whose love and admiration keep me faithful

Acknowledgements

A sermon and a book are truly joint ventures. I want to thank Dr. J. Ligon Duncan III, the Reverend Derek Thomas, and the Reverend Duncan Rankin, for their help and direction in this dissertation that became the book. Ligon has been a good friend, a faithful co-worker, and a kindred spirit in preaching and pastoral ministry. His guidance in each step of this project has been invaluable. Thanks is also due to Don Malin and John McCarty of the RTS library for their helpful service and many efforts to make the research for this project much easier. Always displayed was their patience and gracious manner. May their servant-like spirit not go unrewarded.

I am profoundly grateful to Dina Plunket, Nancy Benson, Sheila Lester, Cathy Novick and Linda Beard. They typed and retyped, edited and corrected, ran errands and did research, and sent innumerable e-mails in order to turn yellow pages with ink scrawl into a manuscript. My thanks to all these dear ladies for their corrections, comments and contributions to this work. Brent Sadler and Andy Halsey, pastoral interns, did final proof and corrections on footnotes and bibliography. Good work and much thanks!

I am also thankful to four men whose lives have influenced me more than they will ever know and whose ministries have resulted in this book. I will ever be grateful for Dr. James M. Latimer under whose preaching I was converted and called to the ministry. Drs. William J. Larkin, Paul W. Ferris, and Harold E. Burchett taught me Greek, Hebrew, exegesis and homiletics at Columbia Biblical Seminary. What wonderful role models for a young man!

I cannot forget to express my gratitude to the two precious congregations I have pastored these past twenty-four years. Under their love and prayers I learned to preach and to shepherd. I thank the Surfside Presbyterian Church in Myrtle Beach, South Carolina and the Trinity Presbyterian Church in Jackson, Mississippi for helping me become a preacher.

I also thank my four gifts of grace – Joanna, Abigail, Nathan and Aaron. I thank God that every Sunday their honest and hungry eyes look up to me in the pulpit, encouraging me, for their souls' sake, to "rightly divide the Word of truth." Never was there a more precious congregation within a congregation than these four friends.

Finally, I am most indebted to my dear wife, Jane. She has edited this entire project, sometimes staying up all night to do so! She has spent hours in the library, done research, coordinated the editing, typing and dissemination of this manuscript, and made countless incisive and constructive suggestions. She has encouraged me, prayed for me, and inspired me in not only this project but my life's ministry. She has helped me, more than any other person, to preach with integrity, soul, fire and compassion. I must honestly say that without her, I would not be in the pulpit. Second only to Christ Himself, she is the greatest of God's gifts to me (Proverbs 18:22).

Introduction

Chapter 1

Preaching for Revitalization
(The Need for Holy Manna All Around)

In the nineteenth century George Atkins penned the words to a famous hymn, *'Brethren, We Have Met to Worship.'* In the first stanza of that hymn Atkins wrote: *'Brethren, we have met to worship and adore the Lord our God. Will you pray with all your power, while we try to preach the Word? All is vain unless the Spirit of the Holy One comes down. Brethren, pray, and holy manna will be showered all around.'* I am touched by the words to this old hymn, written in 1819, every time I hear it sung. Others are not.

One of my dear friends in the ministry would not sing this hymn. When asked why, he responded that he could not stand the phrase, *'While we try to preach the Word,'* as if somehow we could not just preach the Word whenever we wanted! Such is the way we moderns think. The idea of asking for 'holy manna' from above seems foreign to a generation of preachers reared in an age of Church growth methodology and pragmatic church programming.

When William Moore put Atkins' words to music in 1825, and published the hymn in *The Columbian Harmony,* he chose for his tune title *Holy Manna,* the phrase George Atkins used to end each of his original five stanzas:

Brethren, we have met to worship and adore the Lord our God;
Will you pray with all your power, while we try to preach the
   Word?
All is vain unless the Spirit of the Holy One comes down;
Brethren, pray, and holy manna will be showered all around.

Brethren, see poor sinners round you slumbering on the brink of
woe;
Death is coming, hell is moving, can you bear to let them go?
See our fathers and our mothers, and our children sinking down;
Brethren, pray and holy manna will be showered all around.

Sisters, will you join and help us? Moses' sister aided him;
Will you help the trembling mourners who are struggling hard
with sin?
Tell them all about the Savior, tell them that He will be found;
Sisters, pray, and holy manna will be showered all around.

Is there a trembling jailer, seeking grace, and filled with tears?
Is there here a weeping Mary, pouring forth a flood of tears?
Brethren, join your cries to help them; sisters, let your prayers
abound;
Pray, Oh pray that holy manna may be scattered all around.

Let us love our God supremely, let us love each other, too;
Let us love and pray for sinners, till our God makes all things
new.
Then He'll call us home to Heaven, at His table we'll sit down;
Christ will gird Himself and serve us with sweet manna all
around.

Little is known about the background of this hymn, its author or
the one who set it to music. In fact, we know of no artist rendition
or photo of either George Atkins or William Moore. But we can
speculate a bit about the nature and intent of this hymn. Because we
know it was written in 1819 and put to music in 1825, we know that
this hymn may well be categorized as one of America's revival hymns.
For it was authored during the middle years of America's Second
Great Awakening.

In its words the American evangelical theology is well rehearsed:
the idea that God will work through human agency to bring man to
salvation in Christ and to renew a slumbering, sin-sick Church. Its
five stanzas reflect a straightforward, innocent and even simplistic
approach to religion. God works through His ordinary means of

grace with extraordinary power when these normal means of grace are baptized with the unction of the Holy Spirit. Worship, preaching, prayer and fellowship can be empowered by God the Spirit so that sinners are converted, the lethargic are enlivened in soul and the Church is revived.

Atkins' prayer reflects a man who sensed that a great work of God was needed in the Church and who sensed that God was on the brink of doing just such a work of spiritual awakening, both in England and in America. George Atkins' hymn-prayer was answered in the longest and most profitable revival in the history of Christianity in the Western world.

In their book *Firefall: How God Has Shaped History through Revivals*, Malcolm McDow and Alvin L. Reid chronicle the results of this Second Great Awakening from 1787 to 1843:

Great revival always leads to significant *evangelism and church growth*. From 1800 to 1830 Presbyterians grew fourfold, from about 40,000 to 173,329. Baptists grew from 872 churches and 64,975 members in 1790 to 7,299 churches and 517,523 members in 1836. The Methodist Church, after rapid gains in the latter eighteenth century, actually lost some 11,000 members from 1793–95. But phenomenal growth in the Second great Awakening resulted in 1,323,361 members by 1850.

The most significant impact of the awakening was the rise of *societies and agencies*, many of which still minister. The New York Missionary Society was founded in 1796 by Presbyterians, Baptists, and Dutch Reformed to reach the Indians. The Congregationalists formed the Missionary Society of Connecticut in 1798 to establish new churches in frontier areas. The Massachusetts Society, founded in 1799, supported 224 missionaries by 1824.

By the turn of the century, such enterprises literally exploded. The American Board of Commissioners for Foreign Missions began in 1810. Two of the first missionaries, Adoniram Judson and Luther Rice, became Baptists while enroute to Burma. Rice formed the General Missionary Convention of the Baptist Denomination in the United States for Foreign Missions in 1814.

Samuel Mills itinerated three thousand miles through the western frontier on mission work. His work was influential in the beginning of the American Bible Society. In 1817 Mills helped form the American Colonization Society. He died at sea while returning from Africa, where he discovered a location for returning freed American slaves. Magazines began which promoted missions endeavors: *Connecticut Missionary Magazine, Missionary Herald, Evangelical Intelligence*, and *The Analytical Repository*.

The American Bible Society and the American Education Society came along in 1816; the American Colonization Society in 1817; the American Tract Society in 1825; and the American Home Missions Society in 1826. In 1791 the first Sunday school union was formed in Philadelphia. The New York Sunday School Union was established in 1816. The American Sunday School Union was organized in 1824 to establish a unified effort for the growing Sunday school movement.

Social effects were felt as well. One cannot underestimate the impact of the great awakenings on the cultural fiber of America, particularly in the nation's formative years.... Some of the new societies were directly aimed at social reform: the American Temperance Society in 1826; the American Peace Society in 1828; and the American Antislavery Society in 1833. The Young Men's Christian Association (YMCA) began as an evangelistic outreach. It also became known for its positive influence on society as a whole....

Education was renewed as well. By the end of the awakening, the colleges in that nation were operated, 'from boards of trustees down to senior tutors, by ministers and devout laymen.' The beginning of the modern seminary movement is traced to Andover Theological Seminary in 1808, although earlier prototypes like the Log College had existed. One reason for the need of such schools was the rise of ministers out of the college revivals.

Princeton Seminary began in 1812; Yale Divinity School in 1822; and Hampden-Sydney established a theological library for ministry students. The first Baptist seminary was Newton Theological Seminary, begun in 1824. Oberlin Seminary, later led by Finney, opened in 1835. In 1780 there were nine schools of higher education in America. By 1861 there were 182. Only 27 of these were founded by states or municipalities. The Presbyterians had 49; Methodists, 34; Baptists, 25; Episcopal, 11; and Congregationalists, 21.[1]

It does appear that as the saints sang *Brethren, We Have Met to Worship* God indeed scattered all around the *holy manna* Atkins sought in prayer and in song: the fruit of the preached Word.

Could it be that the old hymn of George Atkins should be sung and prayed again by churches in America, the United Kingdom, Europe and the Western world? No student of History or observer of the modern church scene can doubt that we need reformation and revival in the old world of Christendom. Although the words may appear sentimental and overly passionate for those reared on a spiritual diet of Maranatha music and historic hymns, the fact remains: We need holy manna once again. Jesus told us, 'Man shall not live on bread alone, but on every word that proceeds out of the mouth of God' (Matt. 4:4, quoting Deut. 8:3; NASB). This is still the truth today.

Manna came from God, sent by His providence and grace, gathered in faith and obedience, and able to sustain life with energy and strength indefinitely. It came as a mysterious gift from heaven – arriving each evening, while Israel slept, and disappearing with mid-day sun. If not used as God designed and demanded, it would sour and putrefy. In the age of the Puritans 'holy manna' was a symbol for the life-giving strength of the preached Word, endued with spiritual power from on high, and received by faith and in obedience.

Anyone who regularly attends church in Europe, England or America can attest to the dismal state of preaching; the poor and paltry diet being fed to the people of God week after week. Little wonder then, that many are calling for, and calling upon God to give, a new great awakening, a revival of the Christian religion in the world. There are those who believe that such a revival is no longer possible in the west. Joel A. Carpenter, in his book *Revive Us Again: the Reawakening of American Fundamentalism*, makes the observation that the modern hope for a great awakening is ill-found in our postmodern times.

> Had a national revival come? In the busyness and cultural diversity of mid-century America, it was doubtful that anything like a great Awakening could command national or even local interest for very long.... The revivalists, however, often seemed more reluctant than the secular press to call this new interest in religion a full-blown revival. Edwin Orr thought that the nation was on the verge of a

third great Awakening, but he insisted that it had not yet 'reached the pitch of effectiveness of either of its predecessors.' Real revival would amount to more than what was going on just then, insisted evangelist Fred B. Hoffman. It would 'regenerate the whole life of America' and would be manifest 'in every church, in every city and town and village and rural community' of the nation. Here was a mythic understanding of revival that could never be fulfilled across a vast and variegated modern nation like the mid-century United States.[2]

I am afraid that many others see George Atkins' hymn as nothing more than pining after a *'mythic understanding of revival that could never be fulfilled across a vast and variegated modern nation'*. Yet, the fact remains: There is a famine in our land for the Word of God, a dying hunger for 'holy manna' (Amos 8:11). And it is the duty of godly preachers to seek to do something about that lack of holy manna, that preaching of the Word that reforms religion, revives the Church and regenerates dead souls.

I believe that kind of preaching, by God's grace and the Spirit's enabling, is possible once again. It is just the kind of preaching that brings revival and that revival brings to the Church. Iain Murray speaks of such preaching when he states:

> The twentieth century has seen a more widespread and enduring defection from historic Christianity in the English-speaking world than has been witnessed in any period since the Reformation. This defection has occurred through the removal of the foundation to all Christian teaching, namely that the words of Scripture are so given of God that the teaching they contain is entirely trustworthy and authoritative. The Bible stands supreme above all human wisdom and religious tradition. It alone is the Book which God has given for the salvation of men. If, therefore, Scripture loses its true place in the church nothing remains certain.
>
> Protestant churches came to depart from belief in Scripture not so much by outright denial as by acceptance of the claim, made in the name of scholarship, that 'theories' about the divine inspiration of the Bible are unnecessary. Further, it was argued that Christianity would gain wider acceptance if it ceased to require submission to all that Scripture teaches.

In confronting the consequences of this rejection of biblical authority, which occurred on both sides of the Atlantic, there have been those who have labored to defend Christianity with apologetics and other forms of scholarship. ...But while accepting a measure of value in such endeavours, it has to be said that neither in the eighteenth century nor in the twentieth could the tide be turned by these means. Unbelief is primarily a moral rather than an intellectual problem, and apostasy comes from a sinful bias against God, not merely from mistaken thinking. Accordingly the only effective means for the restoration of reverence has to be the action of God in changing man's moral nature. ...God himself must authenticate the truth to make it real to us....

This being true, it inevitably follows that every period which has seen a widespread restoration of faith has always been a period when the convicting and regenerating work of the Holy Spirit has been manifest. Apologetics may modify conditions for the better but it is only under the powerful preaching of the gospel that unbelief is scattered as mist before the sun. In this respect, as in others, revivals have brought a repetition of what happened when the gospel confronted the wisdom of men in the apostolic age.[3]

The question arises: Does such 'Holy Manna preaching' come from man's efforts or from God's reviving grace? The answer is both! In all times of spiritual declension men must work for and promote reformation while they wait and pray for revival. It is the pastor's duty to seek for the revitalization of a declining congregation and to seek to lead in this revitalizing work through the primacy of the pulpit.

Pastors must themselves awaken to the real challenge of revitalizing the Church through the use of the means of grace, and primarily through the preaching of God's Word accompanied by prayer for holy manna (Acts 6:4). It is to this subject of 'Preaching for Revitalization: The Need for Holy Manna All Around' that we now turn our attention.

In recent years a new buzzword has appeared upon the American church scene: Revitalization. Unlike other buzzwords that come and go with trends, this word carries with it substantive meaning and great impact for the church. Though difficult to define in a comprehensive manner, the idea of revitalization of the church (or local congregation) carries with it the hope of renewed vigor; redirected purpose; restoration of healthy growth, qualitatively and quantitatively; reformed beliefs and practices; and the refreshment of the Holy Spirit over the entire life of the church. Revitalization of the church has become a major concern for the evangelical and Reformed movement in America.[4]

There is a developing genre of literature devoted to the subject of revitalization and touching the various aspects of ministry that periodically need purposeful efforts at renewal (e.g. leadership, preaching, evangelism, etc.). For example, in 1986 Roger S. Greenway edited a book entitled *The Pastor-Evangelist: Preacher, Model and Mobilizer for Church Growth*. In that book's fourteen chapters and two hundred pages, only one chapter was written on 'Revitalizing a Dying Church'. In that chapter Harry L. Reeder III addresses the issue of churches in need of revitalization. The book treats that subject almost as an added thought, a digression from the mainstream of church growth. However, since the publication of Greenway's book, the realization of the vast need for revitalized churches has grown. Reeder defines that need succinctly:

> 'Revitalize a dying church!' In other words, be an instrument in the hands of God to breathe spiritual life back into a body before it becomes a corpse.... The method is twofold. First is an expositional public ministry of the Word that is faithful to the Scriptures, clear, and applicatory. Second is the occupation of discipling leaders who will multiply our ministry as they disciple others, who in turn disciple still others.[5]

What was a new idea, a buzzword a couple of decades ago, has now become a major concern for local churches all across this land. In 1995 the Presbyterian Church in America formed the office of 'Evangelism and Church Revitalization' with Archie Parrish as its director. Other American denominations have taken similar action to ensure that along with evangelism, church planting, and church growth, emphasis is also given to church revitalization.

The writer, on becoming pastor of Trinity Church in Jackson, Mississippi, devoted himself to the study and pursuit of church revitalization, particularly as it is related to the pulpit and its preaching ministry. Therefore, the point of this study shall be 'Preaching for Revitalization and the Implementation of Principles for Such in the Pulpit Ministry'.[6] In pursuit of that end, certain definitions, delimitations and distinctions must be explained, and the purpose of the study with certain hypotheses must be set forth.

True church revitalization can never take place and be maintained unless it is the product of a biblical pulpit. Churches in need of revitalization more than likely need revitalized pulpits. The purpose of this study will be to examine historic and contemporary preaching to assess what changes in approaches to preaching are necessary to help produce church revitalization.

Therefore, this study will incorporate four related aspects of the subject of preaching. Each of these aspects will be discussed in the following chapters:

1. An <u>analysis of preaching</u> from the perspective of the Scripture, the Reformers and Puritans, and contemporary models of preaching.
2. An examination of the <u>weaknesses in the pulpit</u> that have caused a need for revitalization.
3. An analysis of four major areas of Reformed and Puritan preaching: its <u>priority</u>, its <u>content</u>, its <u>ethos</u> and its <u>style</u> (the four hypotheses of this study).
4. Some practical approaches to assist preachers in preparing to preach for revitalization.

This study pursues this avenue of investigation due to the great need existing for revitalized churches and ministries and the part preaching will play in that process. Particular emphasis will be given to Reformation and Puritan preaching because of their revitalizing effect upon the church.

Statement of the Problem
Luder Whitlock, former president of Reformed Theological Seminary, stated in a doctor of ministry course on evangelism and church growth in 1987, that '<u>more than likely every growing and effective church will have an above-average pulpit ministry</u>'. A great

many churches, however, are not experiencing either growth or effectiveness in ministry. In fact, recent statistics show that numerical growth among evangelical churches, liberal churches and Catholic churches is in decline. Over the last twenty years, and in general since the mid-1930s, church membership has dropped.[7] Likewise, church attendance has leveled to 40–42% of the population since 1939.[8] The writer proposes that part of the problem in the loss of members and the stagnation of church attendance is the result of poor preaching. For effective church growth and revitalization, the pulpit must again rise to pre-eminence. A pastor's leadership in revitalizing the church begins with his role as a preacher.[9]

The problem addressed in this study is the lack of revitalizing influence in pulpits. The writer proposes that practical steps can be taken to revitalize the local church through the ministry of revitalized preaching. How this can be accomplished is set forth in the following hypotheses:

1. Certain *priorities* of revitalizing preaching that will positively affect the interest shown by others toward a minister's preaching can be deduced from Reformation and Puritan preaching.

2. A certain *content* to revitalizing preaching that will positively affect the growth experienced from one's preaching can be deduced from Reformation and Puritan preaching.

3. Certain *characteristics* of revitalizing preaching that will positively affect the ethos of one's preaching can be deduced from the study of Reformation and Puritan preaching.

4. A certain style of *revitalizing* preaching that will positively affect the impact of one's preaching can be deduced from Reformation and Puritan preaching.

Each hypothesis will be set forth in the following chapters. The priority of preaching will be examined in chapters two through four. The content of preaching that revitalizes will be studied in chapters five through ten. The characteristics of Puritan preaching used by the Lord to revitalize churches will be explored in chapters eleven through fifteen. Finally, an expository style of preaching will be proposed and explained in chapters sixteen through nineteen.

Definition of Terms

Throughout this study, certain words distinctive to the topic of preaching for revitalization will be used. These are hereby explained in the writer's own terminology. The precise usage and understanding of these terms are critical to this study and its application due to the general manner in which this study may be used.

1. *Revitalization*: The process whereby a church is refocused on its mission of both evangelism and nurturing, and renewed in its efforts to minister to others so that numerical, spiritual and organizational growth occur and are sustained.

2. *Revival*: The visitation of the Holy Spirit that causes a church to experience the power, purity and presence of Christ in such a way that the church is renewed, empowered and purified for more effective use in ministry and mission.

3. *Awakening*: The movement of the Holy Spirit over a wide area, a country or an entire culture, causing great numbers of conversions and the restoration of biblical faith and values to all institutions.

4. *Qualitative Growth*: The spiritual growth of Christians or a church in discipleship and holiness.

5. *Quantitative Growth*: The numerical growth of a church by conversions, transfer of members from other churches and the enfolding of the unchurched.

6. *Organic Growth*: The organizational and administrative development and refinement of a church.

7. *Reformation*: A word used in two ways in this study: 'Reformation' or 'the Reformation' (capitalized), referring to the sixteenth century Protestant movement to return to Pauline theology, restructure the polity of the church for New Testament purity, and break with the Roman Catholic Church (Luther, Calvin, Zwingli and others are thus 'Reformers'); 'reformation' (not capitalized), referring to the process of returning the church to its historical, theological and biblical foundations rooted in the Reformation.

8. *The Reformed Faith*: That theological system of the Protestant Reformation and Puritan experience of faith, best summarized in the *Westminster Confession of Faith and Catechisms*.

9. *The Doctrines of Grace*: The kingpin doctrines of salvation known and defined as 'the doctrines of grace' as expressed in Calvinism. (The acrostic T.U.L.I.P.)

10. *T.U.L.I.P.*: The doctrines of the total depravity of man, unconditional election of God, limited atonement of Christ, irresistible grace of the Holy Spirit, and perseverance of the saints as expressed in the acrostic T.U.L.I.P.

11. *Expository*: That method of preaching systematically through texts of Scripture.

12. *The Puritans*: The grandchildren of the Reformation known as 'the Puritans', men who sought both the total reform of ecclesiology and worship, and the application of the Reformed Faith to all aspects of life. Generally speaking, the Puritans dominated the evangelical church in England and America during the sixteenth to the eighteenth centuries.

13. *Church Growth Movement*: That approach to the numerical growth of the organized church by biblical, managerial and sociological efforts.

14. *Revivalism*: That approach to revival that grew out of the Second Great Awakening and the ministry of Charles G. Finney which believed revival could be secured through the use of proper 'methods'. Revivalism has characterized crusade evangelism and personal witnessing in America since the mid nineteenth century. Revivalism and Revival are not the same phenomenon.

Revival and Revitalization

A clear and definite distinction must be drawn between the content of 'Revival' and that of 'Revitalization'. Although the two may often experience an overlap, they are not necessarily synonymous; nor are they always coincidental. Revival and revitalization are different both in origin and in effect.

Revival is a supernatural work of God, and God alone. It is, as Richard Owen Roberts defines it, 'an extraordinary movement of the Holy Spirit producing extraordinary results.'[10] These extraordinary movements of God have been seen repeatedly in church history, from Old Testament times to modern times. Yet it remains a fact of history that only God can send revival. Andrew W. Blackwood Sr.

writes about God's preeminence and power in controlling when and how revivals come upon the church:

> Both in the hearts of believers and in the life of a congregation there come times that correspond somewhat with the ebb and the flow of the tides. Also in the growth of an oak tree there comes a season of waiting for growth again to begin. But all such analogies fall short of the truth about revivals. A man who knows the ways of the waves, or of an orchard, can judge fairly well what will follow after the present stage. On the contrary, nobody but God can begin to tell when a long-awaited revival will begin, what form it will assume, or how long it will continue at the crest. ... As a rule the movement bursts out all at once, sweeps across its field like a prairie fire, and everywhere leads to a deepened sense of sin. Then comes an outburst of joy through assurance of pardon and cleansing, with peace of heart and eagerness to serve. As a consequence of such a revival believers begin again to 'possess their possessions' in the form of doctrines dear to the heart of God. There also comes a transformation in the morals of persons and congregations whose hearts have been touched with cleansing fire from above.[11]

Preparation for revival can be made, and in fact, should be made by those who sense the church's need for renewal and by those who love the name of Christ and want to see it promoted and professed.[12] But the trap of falling into 'revivalism' while seeking and praying for revival must certainly be avoided. In his book devoted to the history of that subject, Iain H. Murray defines for us the difference:

> American history was shaped by the Spirit of God in revivals of the same kind as launched the early church into a pagan world. Until 1858, innumerable authors understood events which they had themselves seen in this way.... What they had in common was the conviction that God is always faithful to his Word, that Christ is risen and that the Holy Spirit has been given to ensure the advancement of his kingdom. But it may come as a surprise to find that these men were equally opposed to what was merely emotional, contrived or manipulated. They believed that strict adherence to Scripture is the only guard against what may be wrongly claimed as the work of

God's Spirit. They foresaw the danger of revivalism long before it became a respected part of evangelicalism, and they would have had no problem in agreeing with the criticism which has since discredited it. What is needed now is to get back to the authors of the eras *before* the whole meaning of revival was confused.[13]

Thus, 'Revivalism' is the Charles Finney approach to using the 'right means' to effect the 'right changes' upon one's audience – the church – in order to produce desired results of 'decisions for Christ' and so-called conversions. A distinction is made here because much of the church growth movement and many efforts for revitalization border on revivalistic methodology. The reader must see that a genuine revival is a sovereign act of God, while genuine revivalism is a planned and programmed effort by man.[14] Andrew S. Blackwood Sr. says, 'As for the present-day term, "revivalism," let it serve as a stigma, non-biblical and reprehensible.'[15]

Revitalization is the effort to bring purpose, passion, purity and proper priorities back to the life and ministry of the local congregation, but it is not an attempt to produce a revival by means of revivalistic techniques. Revitalization originates with men who cooperate with God in applying biblical principles to church life, ministry and growth, but these efforts cannot guarantee revival. Today it is common to hear of 'revival happening somewhere' when in effect revitalization ministry is merely yielding its fruits.

It can thus rightly be said that genuine revival from God will always lead to true revitalization in the form of biblical purposes, proper priorities, fruitful ministry, missiological focus, and well-rounded growth in every aspect of church life, i.e. qualitative, quantitative and organic growth. But revitalization will not yield genuine revival without the sovereign grace of God. Simply put, one can never have revival without revitalization, but one can often have revitalization without revival.

This distinction must be clearly made so that the reader does not misinterpret revitalization efforts for revivalism or genuine revival. Hopefully, the reader now understands these crucial distinctions about like-sounding and related concepts.

Donald McGavran gives a reminder that, 'Under certain conditions revival may be said to cause growth. Under others, its relationship to church growth is so distant that apparently revival occurs without growth and growth without revival. Careful consideration of the subject is necessary if we are to understand the function of each in God's purpose of redemption.[16] The reader has been forewarned.

ENDNOTES

1. McDow and Reid, 1997, 247-49.
2. Carpenter, 1997, 231-32.
3. Murray, 1998, 170-75.
4. Greenway, 1986, v-vi.
5. Reeder, 1986, 162. Reeder then identifies three types of pastoral ministry in the church today: organizing pastoral ministry, continuing pastoral ministry and revitalizing pastoral ministry (p. 163).
6. Such a vast subject as preaching relating to the vast problem of the need for revitalization will need to be limited in scope. The study of preaching for revitalization was limited to the context of a local congregation within the confines of the Presbyterian Church in America. Although there will more than likely emerge transferable concepts for preaching in general, the study was limited to that of preaching by pastors of local churches within a Reformed and Presbyterian denomination. This study was done in the context of the culture of the Deep South of the United States, a fact that may have some bearing upon the approach to preaching taken in this study. Finally, study and experiences are in the context of a genuinely evangelical congregation and not one of Neo-orthodoxy, Pentecostalism or opposition to the Reformed Faith or Presbyterian Polity.

The church the writer now pastors did not need to be revitalized by laying a foundation of biblical truth. For the most part, the preceding pastors (and particularly those two who immediately preceded the writer for a combined total of sixteen years) were men faithful to the Scriptures and the basics of the Reformed Faith. Trinity Presbyterian Church, although a church in need of revitalization, was by no means antagonistic to or unfamiliar with biblical truth or spiritually dead.

Therefore, this study was done in the context of a conservative, biblical and reformed congregation; in a conservative, biblical and reformed denomination; in a conservative southern culture; in a city influenced greatly by the Presbyterian Church in America and the Reformed Theological Seminary. These factors surely make the process of revitalization unique in this specific context.

7. Gallup, 1989, 30.
8. Bezilla, 1993, 42.
9. McNair, 1980, 45.

10. Roberts, 1982, 16-17.
11. Burns, 1909, 10,12.
12. Stephens, 1961, 30-42.
13. Murray, 1994, xx.
14. Lloyd-Jones, 1987, 98-100.
15. Burns, 1909, 8.
16. McGavran, 1970, 163.

Part One

Priority and Promotion
in Puritan Preaching

Chapter 2

Preaching and Church Growth

The study of preaching for revitalization begins by inquiring into the priority preaching has historically had in the church compared with its present place in modern philosophy of ministry. In doing this, the first hypothesis will be tested: certain priorities of revitalizing preaching that will positively affect the interest shown by others toward a minister's preaching can be deduced from Reformation and Puritan preaching. Naturally, this interest must first be shown by the minister before the congregation will display genuine interest. In other words, preaching must become the chief duty of the minister if his preaching is to be taken seriously or attended with God's blessing of revitalization.

As this first hypothesis is examined, the following three things will be observed: (a) Chapter Two will consider how modern communication theory and the church growth movement have caused preachers to focus more on style than on content; (b) Chapter Three will show that biblical and Reformed convictions about preaching, shared by the Puritans, led preachers and people alike to hold a much higher view of the pulpit than is customary today; (c) in Chapter Four the four steps to the recovery of interest in preaching on the part of both the preacher and his listeners will be examined: planning sermon series, promoting sermon series, constructing worship services where the preaching of the Word is pre-eminent, and protecting adequate time for the preaching of the Word.

These four simple steps will revolutionize the way people evaluate the place of preaching in the life of the church. Frankly, the premise is quite simple: If the minister treats the sermon series as the most important, deliberate, protected and well-developed aspect of the church's life, it will not be long until others come to hold that same conviction. Revitalization begins with a commitment to the priorities of preaching: the priority of planning, promotion, preeminence and protection. To prove this point, a careful study of the primacy of preaching from a number of viewpoints – Scripture, the Reformers and Puritans, and contemporary models – ensues.

Preaching in an Age of Confusion

Today in the minds of many ministers there is much confusion about their primary role in ministry. There exists today a 'prevailing uncertainty among ministers, both to their purpose and their capabilities in a rapidly changing world'.[1] This statement is verified by Schuller, Strommen and Breeke's landmark study, 'Ministry in America.' Their assessment of forty-seven denominations reveals great diversity, confusion and even disparity between laity and clergy concerning both the purpose of ministry and its criteria for success. In their massive study they analyze eleven factors, one being 'Development of Fellowship and Worship'. In this category, as a subset of duties, is the task of 'preaching with competence and sensitivity'.[2] Yet, even in this assessment, preaching takes a back seat to other liturgical and pastoral duties and is judged mainly by how well ministers are 'holding attention while preaching and being well in command of all aspects of the service'.[3] Perhaps most surprising are the countless charts ranking the importance of these eleven factors among the laity and the clergy, denomination by denomination. While assessing the Presbyterian-Reformed churches, Schuller and his associates find that these churches placed higher priority on preaching than other groups did;[4] but when both groups gave preaching a numerical rating of importance, the laity ranked 'competent preaching' higher than the clergy did![5] Overall, preaching ranked sixth on the list of the eleven general factors of ministry behind (1) having an open, affirming style, (2) caring for persons under stress, (3) exhibiting congregational leadership, (4) being a theologian in life and thought, and (5) ministering from personal commitment of faith.[6]

A break exists between the modern and historic priority of the pulpit in ministry. Robert S. Michaelson writes, 'The pulpit has stood at the front and center of the Protestant Church in America – both in practice and in theory; preaching has been by all odds the most important aspect of the minister's work.[7] However, this pre-eminence of the pulpit is now on the wane due to sociological, psychological and political pressures calling for a different set of priorities – counseling, education, community work, and management.[8]

Preaching and Church Growth

This devaluation of preaching is not at all surprising. An examination of a number of leading books on church growth yields a much-expected trend. Church growth techniques give much higher priority and emphasis to location and facilities, small groups, managerial style, laity participation and evangelistic methods of outreach than to preaching.

> The place of preaching has been neglected in church growth literature. Few authors have dealt with the vital significance of the message which a growing church proclaims. While it is generally assumed that the message will be somewhat biblical, few resources have been made available to preaching pastors that will encourage them to recognize the potential of a fresh approach to preaching.[9]

Titles like *Dynamics of Church Growth*, *Modern Strategies for Church Growth*, *Principles of Church Growth*, and *Leading Your Church to Growth* by such church-growth specialists as Arn, McGavran, Wagner, Jensen, Stevens and Towns give little if any place to the primacy of preaching. In one of these handbooks, Reverend Ken Parker lists the seven characteristics of a growing church:

1. A strong commitment to worship (prayer)
2. A strong commitment to outreach (evangelism)
3. A strong commitment to edification (discipleship)
4. A strong commitment to people (love)
5. A strong commitment to growth as a goal (membership)
6. A strong commitment to the possibility of change (flexibility)
7. A strong commitment to sacrifice and faithfulness (commitment).[10]

Yet, in characteristics one and three, where preaching should certainly be preeminent, Parker almost ignores the subject altogether. Other church growth specialists address the subject calling for shorter sermons, less content, more entertainment and 'relevance'.[11] The general viewpoint of most church growth specialists concerning preaching can be summarized by C. Peter Wagner:

> While I know of a few growth pastors who do not handle themselves admirably in the pulpit, I would hasten to say that some pulpit committees overemphasize preaching to the extent that it is virtually the only quality they really look for. Many growth pastors are not golden-mouthed orators, but they understand the function of the pulpit in the broader context of worship, leadership, and group dynamics. Try to make sure that the preacher is receptor-oriented, gearing the ministry to the felt needs of the congregation. Don't confuse communication, which is highly important, with eloquence which is of minimal importance.[12]

While confirming the importance of 'communication' and the nebulous value of 'eloquence', Wagner and other church growth advocates give mixed signals concerning the priority and effect of preaching in churches needing growth and revitalization. When push comes to shove, they shove preaching to the back burner while emphasizing more the marketing and managerial aspects of pastoral ministry.[13]

In reality then, overshadowed by emphases on entertainment, felt needs, psychological approaches, and managerial direction of a multifaceted program of activities for all ages, preaching has diminished in importance in the local church[14]. One wonders whether it is a problem with the chicken or the egg: Did a lack of priority on preaching draw into the ministry men who no longer put it as top priority, or did a multiplication of men in the ministry who cannot preach well lead to the diminishing of the pulpit in power and priority? An examination of textbooks on preaching used in seminaries may give an answer.

Preaching and Seminary Instruction

A sampling of books on preaching and homiletics in many theological seminary libraries will reveal that the pulpit and preaching are indeed in a state of uncertainty and flux. Some notable issues have surfaced in modern times.

Characteristically, books on preaching prior to the twentieth century do not indicate that the pulpit and preaching were either in decline or in question in people's minds. They indicate no problems in the pulpit whatsoever. Rather their emphasis is on the spiritual aspects of preaching: the minister's life and heart, prayer, Spirit-led preparation, the hope of the gospel, and so forth. By the 1930s and 40s, however, a distinct shift in the subject matter of homiletical books occurred. In the following decades titles such as *The Problem of Preaching*, *Crisis in the Pulpit*, *The Recovery of Preaching*, *The Quest for Better Preaching* and *The Empty Pulpit* appeared on library bookshelves.

In *The Problem of Preaching*, Donald MacLeod lists a number of reasons for 'an identity crisis' in the pulpit:

1. Fewer and fewer strong preachers can be found to fill significant pulpits.
2. Preaching has been given a delimited place in the life of the church, mission of denominations, and curriculum in seminaries.
3. A great misunderstanding of the reason for, purpose of, and expectations for the preaching ministry prevails.
4. A growing number of preachers have 'lost their souls' in the ministry and thus their preaching is irrelevant, moralistic, lifeless, uninformed and tedious.[15]

MacLeod summarizes the general consensus of modern observers of preaching when he states:

We have seen that preaching – once the strongest factor in the program of the Protestant Reformation – is in a period of crisis. This is seen in the figure cut by the preacher him- or herself and in the downgrading of the pulpit in the face of new aspects of ministry. Our lay people are hearing bad preaching and are inclined to write the pulpit off. Shortsightedly, many preachers see their role as being caught in a vicious circle of suffering from the law of diminishing returns. No one seems to see preaching in the right perspective – its history, its theology, and its place in the worship and mission of the church.[16]

Chevis F. Horne has analyzed the crisis in preaching in the most comprehensive way. He states that this crisis is a result of a fourfold crisis of faith, the church, authority, and communication.[17] In other words, as the institutional church grows less and less effective in reaching Americans in this secular culture, faith in God's Word and historic theology waivers. The communication of God's message becomes less confident, more confusing, and increasingly ineffective. The writer could quote one author after another on the 'crisis', the 'problem', the 'decline', or the 'death' of preaching, but the point has been made: Something is wrong!

What is fascinating, however, is the *emphasis* of the more modern books on preaching compared to the emphasis of earlier works on the pulpit. Overall, the current works focus most on communication theory and practice – style, SAIs (stories, analogies and illustrations), voice methods and time usage – while earlier works dwell on content, theology, spiritual motivations and the character of the minister. To be certain, these latter concerns are mentioned in modern textbooks, but they are given 'the nod' and then put on the shelf while more 'pragmatic' issues are dealt with. An illustration proves my point. In the book *Quest for Better Preaching: Resources for Renewal in the Pulpit*, Edward F. Markquart lists the 'eleven deadly sins of preaching':

1. Most preaching is too abstract and academic; too theoretical and theological.
2. Sermons contain too many ideas which are too complex and come at the listener too fast.
3. There is too little concern for people's needs.
4. There is too much theological jargon and biblical talk.
5. Too much time is spent describing the past and telling about the 'land of Zion'.
6. There are too few illustrations and these are often too literary and not helpful.

7. In preaching, there is too much bad news and not enough good news, too much diagnosis and not enough prognosis, too much 'what's wrong with the world' and not enough 'this is what we can do to make it better'.

8. Sermons are often too predictable and passionless.

9. Much preaching is moralistic.

10. Preachers don't take quality study time.

11. Preaching too often consists of 'Saturday night notions'. [18]

Although the writer agrees with Markquart in his last four assessments of modern preaching (passionless, moralistic, ill-prepared and trite), he takes issue with his first seven 'deadly sins' and would even challenge Markquart's very premise about what constitutes the key to renewal. He holds forth the hope of revitalized preaching through the use of more SAIs. These he believes are the keys to powerful preaching. Markquart states that these SAIs have the 'power to transform'. Like so many other writers, he relies almost totally on communication theory and skills to solve the pulpit's problems. But this approach is erroneous. The crisis of the American pulpit is not one of communication theory, but rather one of content, conviction and consistency of theology and life. The writer is not the only one who believes this.

Helmut Thielicke indicates that the problem of the pulpit is not mechanics but the man and the message:

> This is the point, it seems to me, where the secret distrust of Christian preaching is smoldering. Behind all the obvious and superficial criticisms – such as that the sermon is boring, remote from life, irrelevant – there is, I am convinced, this ultimate reservation, namely, that the man who bores others must also be boring himself. And the man who bores himself is not really living in what he – so boringly – hands out. 'Where your treasure is, there will your heart be also' – in this case the treasure of the heart seems not to be identical with what it is commending to others. The attractions by which this heart is moved seem to come from some other source. So we miss the very thing that my teacher of theology was talking about: the peculiar, personal tone. For that peculiar tone will be immediately audible if

the speaker himself is in what he says, if he gives of himself and puts his whole heart into it.[19]

Whether it is using more SAIs as Markquart suggests, imitating Black (African-American) preachers as Mitchell proposes,[20] or keying in on better communication theory as Cartier demands,[21] the end result is the same: a preoccupation with methodology rather than with the man and the message. The end result is similar to placing a band-aid on cancer; the root problem is never corrected. There is a crisis in the pulpit because there is a crisis in the parsonage. Many preachers are convinced that preaching is past its day of glory. They believe people want only entertaining 'talks'. A survey of literature about preaching easily demonstrates this fact. And so American students of the pulpit focus on illustrations, 'dialogue in preaching,' and listener responses (feedback), rather than the prophetic nature of their message. There is a danger in this approach as several books demonstrate. Preoccupation with self-disclosure, listening, non-verbal messages and self-esteem results in a redefinition of preaching in terms of sociological and psychological results rather than in terms of biblical content and spiritual impact.[22] A statement like, 'A sermon without illustrations is like a house without windows,'[23] misrepresents what preaching is and emphasizes the style of the message over the soul of the message.

There is wisdom with keeping in mind what one author calls 'the preaching cycle'. Preaching has *always* been 'in trouble', over-analyzed, controversial, and challenged. Over years a cycle occurs that preaching historically must work through: search, discovery, excitement, routinization, boredom, disillusionment, search, etc.[24] Ministers need to be devoted to preaching 'in season and out of season' (2 Tim. 4:1-4). Attention must be given to preparing preachers to preach in all stages of this 'preaching cycle'.

The great need is to rediscover and reemphasize what *content* and *character* issues undergird revitalizing preaching rather than what communication techniques are effective. This is not to say that communication theory and practice are not important, but rather to keep two concepts separate: homiletics and preaching.[25] Good homiletics does not necessarily result in good preaching. Homiletics does not transform the soul; true preaching does!

If revitalization of the church is to be seen, then a revival of the biblical pulpit must occur which necessitates a reformation in preaching. To see this reformation take place, the priority and proper place of preaching must be realized and reasserted by those who preach. H. C. Brown Jr. incisively analyzes the distortions of the preaching ministry that have caused such poverty in preaching.[26] He enumerates five common misunderstandings of ministry and misuses of the pulpit. He labels these shortcomings in colorful terms:

1. The Pulpit Coach: the man busy with activities – unfortunately preaching is not one of them.
2. The Gospel Falsifier: the man who corrupts the biblical message and distorts gospel truth.
3. The Clown in the Pulpit: the man given to entertainment and performance but not prophetic truth.
4. The Madison Avenue Con Artist: the man concerned with public relations, large crowds, and sensationalism.
5. The Psychological Pump-Primer: the man given more to psychiatric jargon and counseling than to preaching.

Brown criticizes shoddy content (preaching) and shabby style (homiletics), believing that the one flows from the other. But, content comes first:

The reason is that Protestant ministers hold inadequate and inferior concepts about the ministry in general and preaching in particular. These inadequate and inferior concepts make impossible the task of creative preaching. Men holding such views have been presenting cheap and shoddy content to starving congregations! For as long as preachers hold to these distortions about the ministry and preaching they will continue to produce sermons deficient in content.... The scarcity of effective preaching procedures – tools for sermonic craftsmanship – exists because preachers have not availed themselves of the known resources of the craft of preaching. Each generation and each man in his generation must exert himself in order to fashion and use for himself the proved creative rules and principles of preaching. No man can be given a ready-made homiletical tool chest any more than he can be given a ready-made predigested theological system. Preaching procedures are poor in the main because preachers simply have not taken the time and energy to master them.[27]

This subject of the content of preaching will be addressed later in the book. For now, the connection between the poverty in the pulpit and the loss of interest in preaching must be understood. When content is shallow, when style is pre-eminent, and when sermons lack an aura of authority and depth, it is difficult, if not impossible, to do three things: promote the importance of preaching, gain primacy for preaching in the church schedule, and convince people they need to be excited about and committed to preaching. This very situation, which exists today, is undergirded by a profound sense of misunderstanding about the true nature of preaching. An illustration will suffice: Years ago, at a luncheon with six Presbyterian ministers of my own denomination, one minister said, 'I find that people remember my illustrations long after I've given them, but they never remember the three points of my sermon. I have come to the conclusion that preaching is far too overrated, and it ought to be less of a priority for us than it is.' Four of the remaining five ministers agreed. The writer alone disagreed, saying, 'They may remember your illustrations for years to come, but your illustrations will not change their lives as God's Word promises to do' (2 Tim. 3:16,17). His remarks were met with silence.

This illustration reflects the greatest cause of the devaluation of preaching: the lack of true understanding of what preaching really is. To gain a true perspective on preaching's necessity and nature, study must be given to what Scripture says about preaching.

Preaching and the Witness of Scriptures

Ian Pitt-Watson summarizes the biblical view of preaching quite thoroughly when he writes:

> Rhetoric and speech communication for the homiletician is not a master discipline of which preaching is a subspecies, the subject matter of which happens to be about God but might equally well be about astrophysics or fishing or George Washington. Precisely because God is the subject of the communication, because preaching

is about God and not about anything else, it is *sui generis* – in a class by itself. Even to call God the 'subject' of the communication or to speak of the communication as being 'about' him is to falsify the situation. For in the preaching event it is not just we who are talking 'about' God, God being the subject of our talk (or for that matter the object of our inquiry). It is God who is the communicator. It is not just we who are communicating truths about him. He is communicating himself. In His divine foolishness God speaks through our fumblings and bumblings in the pulpit Sunday by Sunday – sometimes because of what we have said, sometimes (I suspect) in spite of it. His Word does not return to Him fruitless without accomplishing His purpose (Isa. 55:11). The Word of God comes to us in three ways: first in Jesus Christ, the Word made flesh; second, in the written Word of Scripture as contained in the Old and New Testaments; but third (and this is the divine-crazy absurdity), in the Word preached. The Word preached is part of the 'foolishness of God' that is wiser than we are (1 Cor. 1:25). The Second Helvetic Confession is outrageously specific: *Praedicatio verbi dei est verbum dei* – the preaching of the Word of God is the Word of God. If this is true, then indeed preaching is a communication transaction like no other. This is not to invalidate the importance of communication theory for the preacher. On the contrary, such a high doctrine of preaching should make us passionately concerned to ensure that we have done everything humanly possible to become the kind of people who in the pulpit will facilitate and not obstruct the Word of God that speaks to us and through us. We preachers need more speech-communication skills, not fewer. That is all too obvious. But these speech-communication skills must be subject to theological scrutiny. They must be seen as a vital part of the discipline of homiletics and thus as a subspecies of practical theology. Homiletics employs communication skills but owes obedience to biblical theology alone. Communication theory is an honored servant of the Word but must never presume to be its master.[28]

'The preaching of the Word of God *is* the Word of God.' Could this be true? A study of the Scriptures will indeed verify that this assessment of preaching is accurate. The New Testament Greek uses a beautiful family of words to describe preaching:

1. *didaskw* (to teach or instruct) and *didaskalia* (the teaching, doctrine or instruction).
2. *kathcho*: to communicate systematically content to be learned (hence our English word "to catechize").
3. *paradidwmi*: to pass on tradition or belief (usually orally but perhaps also from oral tradition to written text).
4. *angellw* (and a whole family of related words): to bring tidings, to give a message, to notify or publicly proclaim. The activity of a messenger who speaks for someone else.
5. *euangelizomai* (evangelize) and *euangelion* (gospel): to speak forth the good news that becomes the gospel.
6. *khrussw* (preach), *khrux* (preacher), and *khrugma* (proclamation): the primary family of words used for preaching in the New Testament.[29]

These Greek words tell us that the Word of God and its gospel are to be 'proclaimed' – shouted forth with both authority and confidence. Preaching not only proclaims but also teaches, passes on the traditions of the great and historic faith, and publishes abroad the good news of God's gospel. These Greek words, selected by the Holy Spirit, all communicate a speaking forth with authority and confidence. Time and again the apostles denied their concern with 'cleverly devised tales', or with 'superiority of speech', or even 'peddling the Word of God'. They preached, 'Thus saith the Lord,' and they did so with such great confidence that, irregardless of their stories, analogies and illustrations, the very content of the truth they spoke was so weighty that it 'would take every thought captive to the obedience of Christ'. Here is a confidence that needs to be recovered today. This confidence comes from the very fact that God has chosen men to incarnationally preach His Word.

By preaching is manifested the *logos* which brings to man the eternal life that was promised. God could have made His Word known to men in other ways, but men could not have borne this. Hence God would not have been the *soter* who gives life; His declaration would have spelled death. He thus chose men to be His preachers. By them His Word becomes flesh just as the Son came to sinners in human form. The *kerugma* is the mode in which the divine Logos comes to us.[30]

Because the preaching of the Word is God's way to flesh out His truth in the lives of men, there is a preeminence, a priority, to preaching in the New Testament. Clearly the New Testament writers, especially Paul, make preaching the very foundation of New Testament ministry. Countless references to 'preaching' draw us to this conclusion. The following are especially significant:

Matthew 24:14: 'And this gospel of the kingdom shall be preached in the whole world for a witness to all the nations, and then the end shall come.'

Luke 24:47: 'and that repentance for forgiveness of sins should be proclaimed (preached) in His name to all the nations, beginning from Jerusalem.'

Acts 28:31: 'preaching the kingdom of God, and teaching concerning the Lord Jesus Christ with all openness, unhindered.'

1 Corinthians 1:21: 'For since in the wisdom of God the world through its wisdom did not come to know God, God was well-pleased through the foolishness of the message preached to save those who believe' (cf. 1:23 and 2:1-4).

2 Timothy 4:1-4: 'preach the word; be ready in season and out of season; reprove, rebuke, exhort, with great patience and instruction.'

These few references suffice to assert these conclusions about preaching:

1. The preaching of the message given by God is the mission of the church.
2. The preaching of the Word is the means by which God saves and sanctifies His elect.
3. The preaching of the Word is the sacred trust and duty of the ministers of this gospel.
4. The preaching of the Word is to be done when it is 'in season' (i.e. popular) and 'out of season' (i.e. not popular).
5. The preaching of the Word is essential to the eschatological fulfillment of God's eternal decree.
6. Preaching reveals God's gospel truth to men (Rom. 10:14, 17).

41

Lest it be assumed that the New Testament writers and apostles thought preaching more important than they should, one must be reminded that their view of the Word of God, and the duty of preaching it, was drawn from the example of Christ (and His clear commands) and the legacy of the Old Testament prophets. Both Christ and the prophets gave preeminence to the preaching of God's Word.

Contrary to modern speculation that Christ's ministry was primarily 'disciple making', counseling, healing, or even 'liberating' the poor, oppressed and disenfranchised, the Scripture clearly states that Jesus was 'a preacher' who 'preached'! His ministry opened with a 'preaching' of the gospel of the kingdom (Mark 1:14,15). It is summarized as 'going about all Galilee teaching in their synagogues, and proclaiming (preaching) the gospel of the kingdom' (Matt. 4:23). When pressured to heal more, perform more miracles, and meet a multitude of 'felt needs', Jesus withdrew from such ministry and clearly gave this reason for doing so: 'Let us go somewhere else to the towns nearby, in order that I may preach there also; for that is what I came out for' (Mark 1:38). The hallmark of His ministry was His 'authoritative' preaching that captivated the hearts and minds of Israel (Mark 1:22, 27, 28).

Jesus Christ was the prophet foretold in the Old Testament, and He stands as the last prophet and first apostle, the preaching bridge between the old covenant and the new. Like Christ and His successors (the apostles), the prophets of the Old Testament were pre-eminently preachers. Indeed they did foretell the future, but their foretelling was far less prominent than their forth-telling as the defining aspect of their ministry. 'Thus saith the Lord!' was their paramount message, and their words were sermons directed toward their contemporaries.

Without doubt, the priority of preaching is demanded by the very nature of Scripture – Old Testament, Gospels, and New Testament. Derek Thomas makes the point that the Old Testament prophecies and messages, the psalms and 'writings', the historical stories, the Gospel narratives, parables, and sermons of Christ, the epistles and the preached messages of the apostles in the Book of Acts were *all* written in order to be preached.[31] The written Word was given to become the preached Word. This scriptural testimony to the priority of preaching is the genesis of the Reformed Theology of Preaching. The Word of God is revealed to men in written form (Scripture), human form (Christ), and spoken form (preaching). A Reformed view of preaching clearly reflects this conviction about the pre-eminence and importance of preaching. The Word of God is never more alive than when it is faithfully preached.

ENDNOTES

1. Niebuhr, Williams and Ahlstrom, 1983, 309.
2. Schuller, Strommen and Breeke, 1980, 26.
3. Schuller, Strommen and Breeke, 1980, 41.
4. Schuller, Strommen and Breeke, 1980, 464.
5. Schuller, Strommen and Breeke, 1980, 103
6. Schuller, Strommen and Breeke, 1980, 30-41.
7. Niebuhr, Williams and Ahlstrom, 1983, 280.
8. Niebuhr, Williams and Ahlstrom, 1983, 285-87.
9. Harding, 1982, 13.
10. Parker, 1979, 61-68.
11. Rainer, 1993, 233-34.
12. Wagner, 1984, 170.
13. Means, 1993, 83-92.
14. Wells, 1994, 72-87.
15. MacLeod, 1987, 12-19.
16. MacLeod, 1987, 23.
17. Horne, 1975, 15-27.
18. Markquart, 1985, 21-46.
19. Thielicke, 1965, 9-10.
20. Mitchell, 1977, 11-12.
21. Cartier, 1981, 14-26.
22. Cartier, 1981, 111.
23. Lehman, 1975, ix.
24. Fant, 1987, 30-33.
25. Buttrick, 1987, xi.
26. Brown, 1968, 16-21.
27. Brown, 1968, 16, 21.
28. Pitt-Watson, 1986, 13-15.
29. Brown, 1978, 5:44-68.
30. Kittel, 1976, 3:716.
31. Derek W. Thomas, in a sermon at Trinity Presbyterian Church entitled, 'What is Preaching?'

Chapter 3

Preaching in The Reformed Heritage

Preaching and the Reformers

Martin Luther and Ulrich Zwingli, his Swiss counterpart and contemporary, were key figures in the Protestant Reformation who returned preaching to the centrality of worship, liturgy, and church life. The Protestant conviction of *sola Scriptura* became the foundational doctrine of the new evangelical faith. R. C. Sproul states, 'It has often been noted by the Aristotelian distinction between form and matter that the *formal cause* of the Reformation was the issue of authority (*sola Scriptura*) and that the material cause was the issue of justification (*sola fide*).... The formal cause is the idea, blueprint, or concept the artist uses to "form" his works.'[1]

The Reformers distinguished between various causes of the Reformation. Borrowing from Aristotelian metaphysical philosophy, the Reformers listed five principal causes of the great renaissance of religion in the sixteenth century:[2]

1. *The Formal Cause*: the design or idea or pattern that must be followed. In salvation and religion, Luther believed this to be the Word of God – Scripture alone. (*sola Scriptura*)
2. *The Material Cause*: that out of which something else is made. In salvation and religion, Luther designated faith as the 'substance' of salvation – Faith alone. (*sola Fide*)
3. *The Efficient Cause*: the chief agent causing something to be conceived, made or developed. The efficient cause of salvation and the Christian religion is Christ Himself; Jesus alone saves – Christ alone. (*solus Christus*)

45

4. *The Instrumental Cause*: the means or instrument(s) by which something comes into being. In salvation and faith, God works 'by grace' – Grace alone. (*sola Gratia*)

5. *The Final Cause*: the purpose or end result for which something is made. In salvation and religion, the glory of God is the 'bottom line' for why humans are saved and how they are saved – God's glory alone. (*soli Deo gloria*)

What is important about Luther's and other Reformers' appropriation and usage of these Aristotelian categories of cause is that the Scriptures, the Word of God, became the very heart of any attempt to formulate Christian belief and practice. The entire Reformation swirled around the issue of supreme authority – either the Bible alone (the evangelicals) or Scripture, Tradition and Papal pronouncements (the Roman Catholics). It is no surprise that historically where Scripture has been central in authority, preaching has become preeminent in life and liturgy. Where Scripture has not, the sacraments and extra-biblical formularies have taken precedence. The writer contends that the sole authority of Scripture and the primacy of preaching go hand-in-hand. This is not a partisan Protestant view, but can be born out in the testimony of several who have converted from Reformed-Evangelical backgrounds to Roman Catholic beliefs. Even those who reject the reformed doctrine of *sola Scriptura* acknowledge that the issue of authority still rages at the center of Catholic-Protestant differences.

Elizabeth Altham wrote an article entitled, 'Protestant Pastors on the Road to Rome,' in a special issue of *Sursum Corda* magazine. In the testimonies of four pastors and one missionary who have renounced Protestantism and embraced Roman Catholicism, the authority of Scripture and centrality of the Word was *the* central issue in every case. Here are their own words:

'The most crucial was the issue of the canon of the Scriptures. Who had the authority to define what would be in the canon? It is a foundational question. I became more and more uncomfortable with the Calvinistic view I'd always held; the other views that were out there were filled with holes.'

'But I knew that if I could trust the authority of the Magisterium centered on the See of Peter, then everything else would fall into place.'

'It made me realize that as Protestants we choose our churches according to our own personal doctrine. That makes us the final authority about what's true and what's right. That really struck me: my interpretation of Scripture is the bottom line for truth. I choose my truth. I choose my Christian truth...'

'There was a rightness to the emphasis on the liturgy and the Eucharist as opposed to the sermon.'

'It didn't take long once we were able to work through the authority issue – Scripture versus the Church.'

'Our Lord says in Matthew 18:18 that we should heed the Church. All of the statements about the authority of the Church were not restricted to the Church's Bible-collecting.'

'I saw that the authority of the Church and the authority of Scripture were Siamese twins and that what God had joined together I could not separate. In fact, if I attacked the authority of the Church, the infallibility of the Church, then I was biting the hand that fed me.'

'I came to the conclusion that the Papacy was not only not the Antichrist, but was a salutary institution, historically and theologically. Its unifying character, its ability to speak with one voice, was indispensable in a church that was starting to sound like the Tower of Babel.'[3]

Key words discussed in these accounts should be noted: 'Scriptural authority,' 'the Magisterium,' 'the Canon,' 'sermon' or 'liturgy'. These sound like the issues of the Protestant Reformation, and yet these comments come from neo-Catholics today. Here is contemporary proof that the centerpiece of controversy between Rome and Wittenberg remains as it has always been – *sola Scriptura*. For the purposes of this study, it is crucial to see that when the Scripture is no longer supreme in authority, the sermon is no longer pre-eminent in liturgy; and soon sacramental priorities replace preaching. These 'sacramental' replacements may not just be penance, the eucharist or liturgies to Mary and the saints, but may also include drama, liturgical dance, overemphasis on music and other innovations in worship revealing a lack of confidence in Scripture and a low view of preaching.[4]

Edwin C. Dargan, in his two volume work entitled *A History of Preaching*, has correctly stated that 'Preaching is an essential part and distinguishing feature of Christianity'. Dargan credits preaching with the very advancement of Christianity:

> Preaching is an essential part and a distinguishing feature of Christianity, and accordingly the larger history of general religious movements includes that of preaching. Here, as before, a reciprocal influence must be reckoned with: the movement has sometimes produced the preaching, the preaching sometimes the movement, but most commonly they have each helped the other. Illustrations readily occur. The spread of Christianity, both geographically and numerically, has been largely the work of preaching. The preacher as a missionary has always been the advance herald of the gospel. From the apostolic days, through the long Middle Ages, and even down to present times this has been true. Moreover, the leavening of the nations already reached by the gospel, the adding to the church daily those who are being saved, is, on the human side and to a great extent, the result of preaching. We must not underestimate the value and effect of personal example and suasion, but history forbids that we should assign an inferior place to preaching in bringing men to know Christ as Saviour and Lord, and in training them in the Christian life, doctrine and service. For spiritual life, doctrine and service are the very marrow of the gospel, and therefore of the preaching of the gospel. The message of the true preacher in every age has had to do with these fundamental things.[5]

Others agree that preaching 'is indispensable to Christianity',[6] and that Christianity's very authenticity and mission depend on preaching. The great Reformers of the sixteenth century stood in a line of men who gave supremacy to preaching. It is no matter of coincidence that the Reformation began in Zurich, Switzerland, when Zwingli decided to forsake the Lectionary and began to preach, expositorily and verse by verse through the New Testament, beginning in Matthew, chapter one, verse one. It was not a matter of just personal preference that led John Calvin, on his return to Geneva after a brief exile, to resume preaching on the very text where he had ceased preaching when he was run out of the city. It cannot be considered irrelevant that over a quarter century Luther's persuasive power lay not only in his widely published pamphlets, but also in his expository and plain-spoken pulpit ministry. Dargan describes the Great Reformation as a reformation brought about by preaching:

> We come now to consider the more particular relation of the Reformation to preaching. It is at once apparent how close that relation is. The great events and achievements of that mighty revolution were largely the work of preachers and preaching; for it was by the Word of God through the ministry of earnest men who believed, loved and taught it, that the best and most enduring work of the Reformation was done. And, conversely, the events and principles of the movement powerfully reacted on preaching itself, giving it new spirit, new power, new forms. So that the relation between the Reformation and preaching may be succinctly described as one of mutual dependence, aid and guidance. This applies chiefly, of course, to Protestant preaching, but the Catholic pulpit also was in some degree stimulated and otherwise wholesomely affected by the movement. And thus, in the most general view, a distinctly new epoch in the history of preaching meets us now, and the greatest and most fruitful one since the fourth century.[7]

John A. Broadus calls the Reformation 'a revival of preaching'[8] – biblical, controversial, expository preaching of the doctrines of grace. Not only do Luther and others place Scripture in the prominent place of church life and theology, but they also stress the essential nature of *hearing* the Word *preached*.

> Since the Word of God has entered into the realm of human history in Jesus Christ, Luther felt that it was more profitable to busy oneself in the understanding of this action of God in history. It is in this context that the written and the spoken Word of God holds a prominent place in Luther's theology. God still speaks to people through the (preached) Word. And it is through this Word that He is present with His people and continues to fulfil the work of salvation which He began through Jesus Christ. Luther was firmly convinced

(that) God does not deal with human beings in accordance with His divine majesty but assumes human form and speaks with them 'as man speaks with man.'... Where the preached Word, through which God speaks, is neglected, and the Bible (the written Word which bears witness to Christ and what God has done for the human race) is not taught and interpreted properly how can the church claim that God is still properly worshiped in the church? That was Luther's struggle. For him, the church needs both the oral and the written Word in order to know what God has done through Christ for the salvation of its members. Secondly, the oral and the written Word are the only means chosen and appointed by God to communicate with the human race till the end of the world.... Why must the Word be heard? Is it not enough that one reads the Scripture? Luther would say that by its very nature the Gospel is meant to be heard. Since the origin of the Scripture lies in the act of preaching, the Scripture is conveyed best in oral proclamation. The Word should be returned to its pristine, oral form. Therefore the Word of God must be preached and heard to become fully effective. Further, the Word should be continually heard so that people may not become arrogant and think that they can earn their salvation through their good works. Preaching is a reminder that a Christian is accountable to God who is so graciously merciful to him in spite of continuous human rebellion. Since the task of preaching is to communicate the good news, the preacher is a messenger from God to the people.[9]

This conviction of the early Reformers has become one of the distinguishing marks of the reformed faith – the primacy and protection of the preaching of God's Word.[10] This high view of the pulpit and the supremacy of preaching has been handed down to the modern Reformed church through the legacy of the Puritan Fathers.[11]

Preaching and the Puritans

The Puritan divines, who were masterful preachers,[12] have sometimes been referred to as 'a race of preachers'. In fact, more than one student of the Puritans refer to them as 'the Godly Preachers'.[13] The Puritan preachers themselves preferred this label over all other names used to describe them. Irvonwy Morgan (1965, 10-11) explains how that label was given to the Puritans:

Of all the names used in the sixteenth century to describe the Puritans, names such as 'precisians,' 'disciplinarians,' 'the brethren,' 'the consistorians,' the name which best sums up their character is the 'Godly Preachers.' It was the name used by Bishop Freake of Norwich of the Puritan preachers in his diocese, and found its way into the popular poetic tracts of the period.... The name the Puritan clergy preferred as a description of themselves was the 'godly' or 'painful' preachers, and they chose the name 'brethren' to describe their fellowship.... The essential thing in understanding the Puritans was that they were preachers before they were anything else, and preachers with a particular emphasis that could be distinguished from other preachers by those who heard them. Into whatever efforts they were led in their attempt to reform the world through the Church, and however these efforts were frustrated by the leaders of the Church, what bound them together, undergirded their striving, and gave them the dynamic to persist was their consciousness that they were called to preach the Gospel.[14]

It must not be assumed, however, that the Puritan age was an age of zealous preachers forcing their long 'jeremiad' sermons down the throats of an unwilling church populace. It was quite the contrary. Part of the wonder and beauty of Puritan preaching was the way the congregation took ownership of both the necessity and importance of preaching. In short, Puritan preachers preached to Puritan congregations who realized the value of such preaching. One writer explains how this came to be.

Its much-minimised and now almost forgotten popularity among the people is not difficult to explain for the Puritan preachers, more than any others, made true religion the *possession* of their people. They did not show them the 'Promised Land' from afar but led them into it, pressed upon them its fruits and bade them boldly claim all its territories. Their congregations 'possessed' the sermons: the colloquial style of these was winsome, abounding in similes and metaphors from every-day life and alive with anecdote and illustration, thus bringing home to the meanest capacity truths precious to the humblest soul.[15]

The Puritan preachers' high view of the pulpit led the way for this true appreciation for preaching. The Puritan, William Perkins, in his book entitled *The Art of Prophesying*, first published in 1606, describes what a lofty concept Puritan pastors had of their task in the pulpit:

> Preaching the Word is prophesying in the name and on behalf of Christ. Through preaching those who hear are called into the state of grace, and preserved in it. God has 'given us the ministry of reconciliation.... Now then, we are ambassadors for Christ, as though God were pleading through us; we implore you on Christ's behalf, be reconciled to God' (2 Cor. 5:18,20); 'God from the beginning chose you for salvation, through sanctification by the Spirit, and belief in the truth, to which He called you by our gospel' (2 Thess. 2:13,14); 'The gospel is the power of God to salvation for everyone who believes' (Rom. 1:16); 'Where there is no revelation the people cast off restraint' (Prov. 29:18); 'How then shall they call on Him in whom they have not believed? And how shall they believe in Him they have not heard? And how shall they hear without a preacher?' (Rom. 10:14). [16]

This study will look into Puritan preaching in more detail in future chapters, but it must be realized that a very simple 'law' of preaching took place in the Puritan pulpit yielding it great success. The Puritan preachers truly believed that what they did in the preaching of the Word of God was *the* most strategic thing they were called to do as ministers, *the* most important event in the local congregation's life, and *the* most essential element of a godly, healthy and balanced church life. [17] Because they were excited about and committed to powerful preaching, their congregations soon became excited about the same thing. It is a fact of ministry – what the pastor (preacher) places as the highest priority of his ministry will eventually become the top priority of the local church he serves. [18] A passion for preaching is contagious.

ENDNOTES

1. Sproul, 1995, 67,74.
2. Sproul, 1995, 74.

3. Altham, 1996, 2-13.
4. Wilson, 1977, 10-11
5. Dargan, 1968, 12.
6. Stott, 1982, 15.
7. Dargan, 1968, 366-67.
8. Broadus, 1889, 113-18.
9. Wilson, 1977, 9-11,118.
10. deWitt, 1981, 17-24.
11. Stott, 1982, 28.
12. Lloyd-Jones, 1987, The Puritans: Their Origins.... 374-77.
13. Morgan, 1973, 10-11.
14. Morgan, 1973, 10-11.
15. Lewis, 1977, 19.
16. Perkins, 1996, 7-8.
17. Means 1993, 82-83.
18. Jensen and Stevens, 1981, 62-66,69-71.

Chapter 4

The Priorities of Preaching

Herein lies the first major problem in preaching today: Preachers no longer get excited about preaching and, therefore, neither do their congregations. Ministers have come to seriously doubt the efficacy of the preached Word. They are in serious confusion about their ministry, and thus small groups, counseling, one-on-one discipleship, church growth techniques, drama, dance and music, as well as other secondary and supportive ministries, pre-empt the pulpit and preaching. The solution is simply to get excited about the preached Word and the power of the pulpit and to begin communicating that excitement. This can be done by any pastor who is willing to follow four steps in developing the priority of preaching. The writer has been practicing these four steps for over two decades with consistent success in preaching and a willing response by the congregations to make the pulpit pre-eminent in the ministry and life of the church.

Step One: The Priority of Planning

The first step involves the simple and yet crucial planning of the pulpit, year by year. Those aspects of ministry that are important are worth planning well. Jensen and Stevens remind us, 'We need to have clear-cut objectives – and a sense of purpose – for everything we do. Objectives also must be measurable. Achieving excellence is impossible when people are unsure about why they do things or what they are trying to accomplish. To plan without purpose is futile. Since planning is related to purpose and objectives, a pastor who initiates the management process will spend a good deal of his time thinking about the future.'[1]

The planning of the pulpit is an integral part of pastoral leadership. Donald J. NcNair clearly states: 'The pastor's responsibility for authoritative leadership is expressed in two functions: the function of preaching the Word and the function of discipling members of the congregation. A pastor-teacher has been given gifts to interpret and apply the Word of God (2 Tim. 4:2). As he brings authoritative interpretation of God's Word to the church, he leads the congregation in the way it must go. The ministry of the Word is a ministry of leadership.[2] This leadership through preaching begins where all leadership process begins, in planning.

The late Frank Harrington of Peachtree Presbyterian Church in Atlanta is an advocate of such leadership by pastors through carefully planned preaching.

> My own view is that preaching is the central task of the preacher. All else in ministry radiates from the effectiveness of the man or the woman in the pulpit. The pulpit is your best opportunity to be an evangelist, your best opportunity to be a pastor, your best opportunity to be a prophet. The pulpit sets the tone for the parish. The preacher ought to consider himself as God's chief dreamer in this church – as the standard to articulate the dream God has placed on the heart, so that preacher and people together can make the dream come true. That is the central task of the preaching minister.... I prepare my preaching a year in advance – I know where I'm headed, I know what specific subject, topic and text that I'm going to be addressing on a given Sunday a year in advance. I actually write my sermon three months in advance so that I'm never operating under the pressure of next Sunday.... I will come back to where I began – preaching is the central task of the minister. My own judgment is that we are going to move into a tremendous era of renewal in preaching. I have on my desk right now five folders, several letters there from churches writing me, asking me to recommend them a minister. And those churches range in membership from about 350 to 3,800. All of them have one central issue: recommend someone who is an effective preacher. I think if you can create a caring environment in an uplifting worship environment and have standing at the center of that a person who can articulate the truth of God in relevant terminology, you would be hard-pressed to have a building big enough to hold the people.[3]

Bill Hybels of Willow Creek Community Church, a church quite the opposite of Peachtree Presbyterian in worship style, ministries and mission focus, also attests to the value of planning in preaching. He says, concerning his preaching, 'We have it planned out for about nine months.... The teaching team, a few staff members, and a few lay people will huddle together and spend multiple retreats working out what we sense of the direction of God on that matter. We spend a lot of time discerning the Spirit on the preaching menu.'[4]

For churches desiring revitalization, there is a need to recapture a vision and direction for what a church of Christ should be. Years of ingrown focus, poor leadership, wrong priorities, ineffective ministries, maintenance of the status quo, and unspiritual, unscriptural practices have been undergirded by a weak pulpit with little, if any, direction. Therefore, the planning of the preaching year is critical.

Without preempting the focus of the next chapter concerning the content of preaching for revitalization, the writer must emphasize the necessity of planning for preaching on the very problems and issues causing spiritual decline that have been ignored and avoided. These must be addressed authoritatively, biblically, doctrinally and practically from the pulpit. Subtle ways of avoiding these issues must be purposefully counteracted by deliberate preaching relevant to the issues the church faces. Wiersbe and Wiersbe tell us: 'The Word is profitable for *doctrine* – that's what is right; for *reproof* – that's what is not right; for *correction* – that's how to get right; and for *instruction in righteousness* – that's how to stay right.'[5] To properly teach, reprove, rebuke, exhort and proclaim, the minister must take the time to think through his congregation's needs, the church's weaknesses, and the day's burning issues. Worrying, week to week, sermon to sermon, about homiletical style will not revitalize a dying church. What that church needs is a well-planned, purposeful diet of spiritual truth preached with deliberate intent.

The chart on the following page is the actual planned schedule of preaching followed at the Trinity Presbyterian Church in Jackson, Mississippi, for the years 1992 through 1996. This chart notes the following four characteristics:

1. Many of the sermon series deal with the nature, mission and life of the church and local congregation. (missiological)

THE PREACHING PLAN OF TRINITY PRESBYTERIAN CHURCH

	1992 Morning	1992 Evening	1993 Morning	1993 Evening	1994 Morning	1994 Evening	1995 Morning	1995 Evening	1996 Morning	1996 Evening	
JAN			First Corinthians (Cont.)	Book of Acts (Cont.)	Together God's Way		Apostles' Creed (Cont.)	Ruth (cont.)	Titus	The Songs of Ascent (Pss. 120-134)	W I N T E R
FEB					Genesis 1-11 (Parameters of Life)	Revelation		The Song of Solomon			
MAR							Legacy of Luther (Ps. 46)				
APR											S P R I N G
MAY					The Dynamic Church (Acts 2:37-47)		First John	Genesis 12:25 (Life of Abraham)			
JUN		Book of Acts								Five Smooth Stones	
JUL	First Corinthians								The Prayer of a Man of God (Ps. 90)	Spiritual Depression (Pss. 42-43)	S U M M E R
AUG											
SEP					Apostles' Creed	Lamentations	Philippians		The Lord's Prayer (Matt. 6)	Praying for the Lost (1 Tim. 2)	
OCT						Book of Ruth			Sola Crux (The Theology of the Cross)	The Five Pillars of the Reformation	F A L L
NOV			Together God's Way								
DEC	Advent Series						Advent Series	Misc. Messages			

2. Many of the sermon series deal with basic doctrine and cat-echetical issues. (foundational)
3. Several sermon series deal with issues basic to the Reformed Faith. (doctrinal)
4. The sermon series often focus on revival, reformation, renewal and basic Christianity. (revitalization)

This plan was chosen for preaching because congregations needing revitalization often suffer from decades of not being taught well in either basic ecclesiology, historic doctrines or the call to true discipleship. In short, a congregation must be taught to focus on good doctrine and proper priorities of true ministry.

Preachers often make two fundamental mistakes in preaching. First, they plan only one series at a time, usually a series which either interests them (whatever they are studying) or which focuses on an immediate need or crisis. Second, they often preach topically, week to week, unconsciously touching upon their pet issues and current events, but never addressing root problems and core issues that have caused a need for revitalization. Deliberate planning, for a minimum of one year (twelve months) in advance, will do much to undergird pastoral leadership in preaching. Remember, these are plans and not laws; they can be amended, adjusted or rearranged if needed.[6] This planning should also involve the church officers who should assist the pastor in focusing on certain general areas of need in the church. The preaching plans on the chart indicate that the themes of mission, personal ministry, fellowship, prayer, revival and reformation are general themes the Session of Trinity Church chose to dwell upon during these five years. More will be said about the content of preaching for revitalization in the next chapter.

J. Winston Pearce lists several good reasons for, and benefits of, planning for a year at a time:

1. It facilitates the Holy Spirit's work in and through the preacher.
2. It tends to force preachers to preach in a more balanced way, preaching in the direction of the full gospel.
3. It develops into a teaching ministry.

59

4. It aids in the building of worthy services of worship.
5. It offers both growth and refreshment for the minister himself, keeping him motivated and fresh in the pulpit.
6. It makes for timeliness in preaching.
7. It helps in actual sermon preparation time.
8. It allows for the minister to build his pastoral library in a systematic and balanced manner.
9. It causes better and more concentrated study for sermon series with an accumulative effect over weeks and months.
10. It removes much stress and worry concerning the next sermon or series.
11. It compensates for interruptions and wasted time and helps maximize the preacher's energies.[7]

Those men who will not prepare long-range plans for preaching will more than likely limp along with the same day-to-day problems that contributed to the need for revitalization.

Step Two: The Priority of Promotion

The second step to developing the priority of preaching involves the promotion of preaching – advertising the sermon series. Preaching must be publicly promoted as being exciting and important to elicit interest and support for preaching in the local church.

There may be some who object to the 'commercializing' of the sermon. Certainly Lloyd-Jones objected to such ideas as promoting, excessive planning, and announcing beforehand the text, topic and even titles to sermons. He feared the cheap commercializing of the pulpit that has unfortunately been a result of shallow marketing techniques. He believed this forced the preacher into a set message, robbing him of the freedom of the Spirit needed to preach with freshness and spontaneity. He objected as well to any sort of gimmicks designed to lure people to church. He believed that if a man had an unction to preach, people would come to hear him. Lloyd-Jones believed that to preach the Word was enough – fancy, cute titles, poster boards and flyers, and detailed outlines were not necessary.[8] The writer disagrees – and seldom does that with 'the Doctor'. He believes that these sorts of practices can actually enhance the appeal of preaching. When a church has become used to the pulpit being boring, then colorful flyers, well-planned series, communication of a sense of direction in the pulpit, and visual aids to learning can greatly stir up genuine interest in the preached Word.

The writer maintains that the Reformers and Puritans did promote their preaching! Luther was a genius at the art of writing pamphlets, many of which were his sermons published in 'popular' format – complete with artful wood-cut visuals. Zwingli publicized his debates and discourses and drew hundreds to hear them. The Puritan lectureships used printed materials and posters to advertise lecture series, and they, too, popularly published their sermons for use in newspapers, pamphlets and books of printed sermons. None of this was manipulative or crass commercialism. These Reformers and Puritans simply believed that popular interest in the preached Word was a good and godly thing to develop. The writer believes that same thing.

One of the plagues of a church that needs revitalization is a tedious, unexciting and directionless pulpit. Those ministers who want to reverse this trend must proactively work to convey that something new, something truly exciting, and something spiritually profound *is* going to happen because of the preached Word! If preaching is the most important aspect of church life, then it ought to be given the promotion it deserves. Four impressions are communicated to people when proper promotion takes place:

1. It communicates to people that prayer, planning and preparation have gone into each sermon series, and it challenges the congregation to give as much attention to the series as has the preacher.
2. It informs the congregation concerning the course of the sermon series – its purpose, flow of thought and direction, including:
    a) The theme and purpose for the series.
    b) The organization and relationship of the parts of the series to the whole.
    c) The beginning and completion of the series content and development.
3. It reinforces the main focus and relevance of the series in three ways: schematically (in organization), materially (in written form), and pictorially (in art).

4. It demonstrates the importance of preaching in that creative talent, money, printing materials and much time have gone into the planning, promotion and presentation of the sermon series.

Dr. Joe A. Harding mentions three principal reasons why much of contemporary preaching is ineffective and unappreciated. First, pastors have low expectations for what can be accomplished through preaching and subconsciously convey this to their congregations. Second, a profound confusion exists in many pastors' minds about the purpose and place of preaching in the ministry. Third, careless preparation contributes to low esteem for the pulpit.[9] Harding summarizes the problem this way:

> Preaching has too often been viewed as a dull, deadening monologue. The New Testament, on the other hand, communicates a lofty and inspiring perception of the power of Christian preaching. Vital Biblical preaching opens to today's congregations the great reality of God's forgiveness, healing, and deliverance from defeat and death. A study of Church history illustrates the importance of preaching in the health and vitality of the church. The failure of much contemporary preaching can be traced to low expectations, a confused understanding of preaching itself, and careless sermon preparation. The pastor's attitude toward preaching is of key importance. The result or response to the message will be strongly influenced by the pastor's expectations. As the true nature of preaching is more clearly understood, there is strong motivation for careful disciplined preparation for preaching. The stage is thus set for a new priority for preaching and a transformation in the life of the local congregation.

Since the pulpit often lacks appeal, creativity and hopeful expectations, revitalizing pastors should actively promote and publicize their sermon series to generate a positive sense of direction and hopeful expectation. Creativity in the planning and promotion of sermon series is essential to a sense of excitement about the pulpit. Jay Weener writes, 'Preaching is an artistic expression of a vision of the world, a vision of the extraordinary at work in the ordinary.'[10] This vision of God doing 'extraordinary in the ordinary' certainly needs to be communicated to people in an obvious manner. Part of the biblical expositor's task is to create a sense of excitement and adventure about the preached Word. John F. MacArthur, Jr., one of America's most respected expositors, realizes the importance of communicating an excitement about the sermon series:

> It is also vitally important that they have a sense of adventure. There is a sense in which they must know that I cannot tell them everything about this text. They must expect the text to unfold and explode in their own minds at some point. With every text they should know that there is something beyond the obvious. If the hearers are not really in the text, they will not be able to see it. I am not going to berate what is obvious. I'm not going to hammer away at what they can read for themselves. You know, the average 'expository' preacher I hear reads the text, states the obvious, and tells stories about it. But the text holds some truths and meaning that the average layperson does not have the tools or the time to draw out. I need to unfold those things in a way that will excite the hearer – at least that's the goal. I keep them in the text with the promise that something is going to unfold – something very, very important that they will miss unless they are with me in the text.[11]

This sense of adventure should begin even before the first sermon is preached. It should begin when the preacher begins to build this sense of anticipation by means of creative and tasteful promotion of forthcoming sermon series.

Longer series may be subdivided into a 'series of series' to allow for easier assimilation of information by the congregation and for flexibility in preaching through a major series. These more manageable segments of a longer series might look like the following:

Romans: The Gospel of God

Part 1:   God's Story (1:1-17) (Introduction)
Part 2:   Of Human Bondage (1:18–3:20) (Human Sinfulness)
Part 3:   Men Made New (3:21–5:21) (Justification)
Part 4:   Victory in Jesus (6–8) (Sanctification)
Part 5:   The Mystery of Israel (9–11) (Predestination)

Part 6:   Saved to Serve (12:1–15:13) (Christian Duties)
Part 7:   Friends of the Gospel (15:14–16:27) (Epilogue)

In whatever manner the series is planned, the outline, flow and development of the series must be clear to the people. Proper sermon promotion does not just stir up interest, but also communicates content and truth. In fact, creativity in preaching really aids in effective confrontation in preaching. When people know what is forthcoming they are often more prone to listen with an open mind and teachable spirit.

> Creativity helps enlightenment come in more than merely a gnostic sense. We can become preoccupied with the entertainment dimension of creativity only to have people walk away, having been entertained but thinking 'I've heard nothing from God!' Creativity is something that helps us accomplish a primary purpose of all preaching: confrontation. Whether we are preaching a doctrinal sermon, an evangelistic sermon, or any of the range of sermon types available to the preacher, confrontation remains a primary aim. Christian preaching confronts people with the claims of Jesus Christ in one way or another.... a strong encouragement from the Church Growth Movement urges preachers not to threaten people from the pulpit. A seeker service aims at making people feel comfortable. This strategy raises the subtle danger in some minds to avoid the confrontation and only reinforce the existing prejudices of Baby Boomers. In such a climate, how does one communicate with a contemporary audience and hold their interest so that they will listen to a word from God, and yet still *give* them a word from God? Successful confrontation requires some creativity. We can preach prophetically, yet fail in the confrontation task of helping people see themselves. We can be prophetic but fail to communicate. Creativity can help us in achieving that goal of effective confrontation.[12]

People listen to sermons one at a time, week to week, and seldom connect one to the other. These promotional pieces serve as teaching tools to keep not only the series but also the relationship of several sermons to one another before the eyes of the congregation. This present information age dictates three realities. First, those who advertise (give information) will get people's attention. Second, 'information overload' from a multiplicity of sensory sources often deadens people's response to non-visual sources of information. Third, creativity and variety capture attention and refocus minds toward key messages. There is nothing unspiritual or manipulative about communicating the importance and relevance of the preached Word with summary and organization, word and graphics, and color and creativity.

Step Three: The Priority of Preeminence

A third step in the promotion of revitalized preaching is to ensure that everything in the worship service flows from and reinforces the sermon itself. Worship should augment the preaching of the Word, not compete with it. The tension between 'worship' and 'Word' is a false dichotomy. In fact, in reformed circles, the sermon has generally been considered — and rightfully so — the centerpiece of worship, the climax of worship and that which draws the worship service together. Pearce succinctly explains the dynamic cooperation of worship and Word:

Look further: a planned preaching program *aids in the building of a worthy service of worship*. This is important. The true worship of God is man's highest function and his greatest need. Ideally, people do not attend church to hear a sermon; they come to worship God. A worthy sermon will have a vital place in that experience. The different parts of the service can be carefully chosen and wisely planned in relationship to each other. Calls to worship, responses, prayers, hymns, Scripture reading, anthems, sermons, preludes, postludes, interludes, silence, and meditation can be vital parts of a whole, 'in [which] all the building fitly framed together groweth unto an holy temple in the Lord.' The needs of the people are too great for the sermon to assume full responsibility. There are few discoveries that will bring more comfort to the preacher than the knowledge that the various parts of the service, if carefully planned, earnestly prayed over, and effectively administered, will of themselves minister to the needs of the people. To know that God can, has and will come to his people through these channels is knowledge that is 'more precious than gold, yea than much fine gold.' Every person who has administered hours of worship knows that such a service, such an experience of worship, does not 'just happen.' It cannot be extemporized on the spot in a quickly thrown together 'order of service.' This kind cometh forth only through much prayer, effort, and planning.[13]

The Trinity Presbyterian Church has been blessed to have as its worship leaders and ministers of music associates who understand this biblical dynamic. They use both the sermon plan and the sermon promotion to develop well-designed worship services that blend in with the sermon, reinforce its message, and move people to apply its truth. Churches needing revitalization are usually hindered by dead worship services which follow an unwritten but very definite liturgy, the parts of which usually do not relate to or reinforce one another. Church revitalization comes not only from good preaching, but also from vibrant and deliberate worship. Planned and promoted preaching contributes to purposeful worship experiences.

Step Four: The Priority of Protection

Fourthly, and finally, revitalized preaching wrestles with the issue of time: How long should the sermon be? In a quick-fix, consumer-oriented society geared to customer comfort, the evangelical institution of the twenty-minute sermon is well-promoted. But a careful analysis of historical and contemporary preaching will demonstrate that when preaching revitalizes a church the sermon usually increases in length. Great preachers of the past like Calvin, the Puritans, Spurgeon and Lloyd-Jones were lengthy in their delivery (thirty minutes to an hour or more!). Contemporary preachers with well-respected pulpits, such as John F. MacArthur, the late James M. Boice, Charles Swindoll and Stephen Olford, usually preach on an average of forty-five minutes.

There is no set, sacred and certain length of time that guarantees success and response in preaching. But human nature does evaluate life in measurement of time: People tend to give the most time to those things which they deem most important in life. Preachers need to beware of subconsciously communicating to their congregations that preaching is unimportant and thus should be 'cut off' in fifteen to twenty minutes. Sermonettes make for Christianettes. Homilies cannot replace true biblical sermons. Pastors must communicate the importance of preaching and deliberately develop the congregation's ability to listen longer. Sermons must not be rushed, truncated to please the restless and immature, or shortened to keep people's interest. No doubt longer sermons may cause some to leave the church, but over time they will draw many more who truly hunger for God's Word in its fullness. Serious thought must be given to the time allocated to preaching in comparison to singing, announcements, choir specials and so forth. Whatever receives the lion's share of time in the worship service will be perceived as the most important aspect of the service.

Overview

Let us briefly recap what I have said in chapters two to four. I began by setting forth the hypothesis that certain priorities of revitalizing preaching that will positively affect the interest shown by others toward a minister's preaching can be deduced from Reformation and Puritan preaching. These priorities are rooted in the biblical view of preaching as proclamation of the living Word of God, a Word designed by God to be communicated most effectively in oral form and not primarily in written form. The view of Luther, other reformers and the Puritans bear out this conviction – the Reformation and Puritan movements were essentially great eras of preaching when the church experienced both revival and reformation, i.e. revitalization. And, in the spirit of this heritage, modern preaching should demand and develop that sense of the primacy of preaching that characterized the great preaching movements of the past.

> In view of the New Testament and contemporary theological emphasis on the importance of preaching, it comes as a surprise to discover that preaching is largely in eclipse in the mid-twentieth century. Evidence abounds that preaching is in a deplorable condition and that preachers are seriously confused about their basic responsibility.... In spite of the present low estate of preaching, signs of hope are present which indicate a renaissance of preaching. One sign of this awakening is that preaching is receiving a strong emphasis in American seminaries.... Another sign of an awakening as

to the importance of preaching is that some outstanding preachers dare to lock their office doors in order to pray, to study, and to prepare sermons. They are encouraged to believe that when they find messages from the Lord, people will rejoice to hear those messages. They dare to believe that people will excuse them from many aimless activities which plague the modern preacher if they are busy finding God's message. Another sign of a renaissance in preaching is the heart-hunger of laymen for pastors who preach the Word. Again and again laymen have volunteered their convictions that ministers should pray more, study more, and rightly divide the word of truth.... In view of the prominence of preaching in the New Testament and in the writings of scholars in the field of homiletics, Bible, and theology, and in view of the many encouraging signs pointing to a renaissance of preaching, what should the modern minister do about preaching? *He should re-emphasize the primacy of preaching....* Only when God's chosen servant comes to a true understanding of the nature of preaching and discovers that preaching should be primary in his ministry, will he devote the proper time and attention to it. When he attains this state of understanding and performance, he will walk after the noble example of the prophets, the apostles, and the Lord Jesus Christ.[14]

To accomplish this, contemporary preachers should do the following:

1. To their concern for communication theory, add a concern for the reformed doctrine that 'the preaching of the Word of God is the Word of God'.
2. Recapture the biblical sense of *kerugma* – an authoritative and apostolic body of truth to be learned and then communicated.
3. Plan for the pulpit in a prayerful and purposeful manner, at least a year in advance, so that those issues and concerns that have held back the church and caused a need for revitalization can be systematically addressed, with balance, over a span of time.
4. Promote the pulpit with proper information that will communicate both the excitement and the expectation that the congregation ought to experience from hearing the preached Word.
5. Consciously undergird the preeminence of the preached Word with a well-developed worship service that augments the sermon and seeks its fruit.

6. Deliberately protect a serious and extended time for the proclamation of the Word each time it is preached.

In addition to focusing on the priority of preaching, pastors who want to see true revitalization in their churches will also give attention to the actual content of their preaching. This naturally leads to the second hypothesis and its discussion in the following chapters: 'The Content of Preaching for Revitalization.'

ENDNOTES

1. Jensen and Stevens, 1981, 74, 75.
2. McNair, 1980, 45.
3. Harrington, 1992, 8,13.
4. Hybels, 1992, 8.
5. Wiersbe and Wiersbe, 1986, 66-67.
6. Pearce, 1967, 3.
7. Pearce, 1967, 12-24.
8. Lloyd-Jones, 1971, 244-54.
9. Harding, 1982, 19-24.
10. Weener, 1990, 3.
11. MacArthur, 1991, 6.
12. Poe 1994, 4,6.
13. Pearce, 1967, 15-16.
14. Brown, Clinard and Northcutt, 1963, 8-15.

Part Two

The Content
of Puritan Preaching

Chapter 5

Preaching With Deliberate Balance

Having already emphasized the importance of the pulpit and, therefore, the preeminence of preaching in both the ministry and the life of the church, the writer now turns to the second hypothesis: A certain content to revitalizing preaching that will positively affect the growth experienced from one's preaching can be deduced from Reformation and Puritan preaching. There are many subjects and topics upon which to preach, and there is great effort given by modern communicators to convince modern preachers that 'felt needs' of the congregation should direct the content of one's preaching. But should this approach dictate the subject matter of sermons?

Certainly feedback is necessary, and the minister who does not understand where his people's lives are confronted with struggles and challenges might consistently miss the mark in preaching that 'connects' with his people. One must also assess the times in which he lives, making certain to preach in a manner that addresses the broader issues of the day in addition to people's individual felt needs. And yet in spite of these three dimensions of preaching to modern people about modern issues and problems (i.e. felt needs, feedback, cultural relevance), a major tactical error in one's preaching must carefully be avoided.

Many contemporary preachers automatically assume that the world no longer considers the Word relevant; therefore, the preacher must make it become relevant in his preaching.[1] Nothing could be further from the truth, and nothing could be more damaging to preaching than to assume that preaching God's Word is naturally 'irrelevant'. Ben Patterson speaks of five deadly temptations in the

73

pulpit, the last of which is to try to 'make the Scripture relevant' in one's preaching:

> I offer one last temptation of the preacher. It is the temptation to try to make the Bible relevant, to make it come alive. This particular temptation used to be the sole province of the liberal theological tradition. But in the past few years, it has gained a number of victims in the evangelical community. I succumb to this temptation whenever I feel the Bible needs my help to be believed, that somehow it requires my zinger illustration or my perceptive restatement into thought forms more familiar to my congregation. Most often today those thought forms are the categories and vocabulary of pop psychology. The sin courted in this temptation is the presumption that it is the Bible that is dead and we who are alive. Of course no preacher would admit to that formal proposition. But many act as though they believe it. Is the Bible relevant? Dr. Bernard Ramm once remarked, 'There is nothing more relevant than the truth.' The longer I preach, the more convinced I become that the best thing I can do is simply get out of Scripture's way. The soundest homiletical advice I know is not to try to preach it well but just to try not to preach it badly. This does not mean the preacher should not translate the message of the Bible in words people can understand. But the purpose should always be to help them see the relevance of the Scriptures, not make the Scriptures relevant. In the final analysis, the Word of God authenticates itself through the work of the Holy Spirit, often in spite of, not because of, us preachers.[2]

The Word of God is, in and of itself, always alive and relevant (Heb. 4:12). As a result, the content of the Scripture — its doctrine, history and ethics — is timely for today. In determining what to preach and how to plan a balanced diet of sermons for a congregation, the pastor in the ministry of revitalizing a church must devote himself to preaching the same sort of balance in content that is in the Word of God itself. In other words, he must trust God's Word not only for the inspiration of the particular text and subject, but also for an inspired balance of preaching content that includes teaching, reproof, correction, training in righteousness, exhortation, rebuke, patient instruction and evangelism (2 Tim. 3:16–4:5).

An examination of the content of preaching that revitalizes congregations will reveal five broad categories that should be faithfully blended in a preaching plan to impact dying churches:

1. Christological messages: Sermons on the person and work of Christ.
2. Ecclesiastical messages: Sermons on the nature and life of the church.
3. Missiological messages: Sermons on the mission and ministry of the church.
4. Doctrinal messages: Sermons on the subjects of systematic theology including Gospel messages.
5. Ethical messages: Sermons on the Law, duty and issues that confront believers.

In preaching through the books of the Bible, a preacher will find a divinely planned balance of just such subjects in almost every epistle and most biblical books. This systematic, expository preaching through texts, sections and books of the Bible is the easiest way to ensure that one is preaching the 'whole counsel of God' (Acts 20:27).

The classification of sermons into these five categories needs some explanation. Sermons could be categorized in numerous ways. Usually categories include evangelism, missions, discipleship, theology and so forth. The writer found it more accurate to group sermons by means of their intended purpose. In so doing, the writer arrived at these five categories:

1. *Christological Sermons*: these messages have as their subject the person and work of Jesus Christ. They may or may not be evangelistic in nature, although such is usually the case, but they are primarily sermons about Christ.

2. *Ecclesiastical Sermons*: these messages have primarily to do with the body life of the church including such aspects as church discipline, the Lord's Supper, church government, fellowship, leadership, and so forth.

3. *Missiological Sermons*: these messages have to do with the ministry and the mission of the church – evangelism, outreach, mercy ministry, world missions, spiritual gifts, and so forth.

4. *Doctrinal Sermons*: these messages are on topics of Systematic Theology that should be known by every Christian. Included in these messages are evangelistic messages.

5. *Ethical Sermons*: these messages cover the very broad category of those things Christians should know and do in the context of discipleship and Christian living, such as obeying the commandments, understanding the biblical perspective on abortion, and growing in holiness. These topics include the Law, Christian ethics, contemporary issues, discipleship, spiritual growth and the disciplines of the Christian life.

This deliberate plan and balance in preaching are not of the writer's origin or invention, but rather, are attempts to implement that balance in preaching content found among the Puritan preachers.[3] Naturally, the plan has been modified to address the unique and historic needs of my congregation. While every pulpit should reflect a careful analysis of the theological and ecclesiastical needs of the particular local church, the five-fold balance found in Puritan preaching should be maintained.

The question is naturally forthcoming, 'Why do we need to plan and preach sermon content and themes similar to that of the Puritans?' The answer is obvious: No group of preachers in the history of Christendom has been used more by God to effect Reformation and Revival upon the church and revitalization of the congregation than the men known as the Puritans.[4] The Puritans were, before all others, biblical preachers – not only in content of specific messages, but also in the preaching plan and the mix of spiritual diet they set before their congregations. The writer will demonstrate later that as they followed the legacy of Zwingli and Calvin, dispensing with the lectionary format, and as they expositorily preached through books of the Bible, they naturally maintained this balance of content. Thus, to analyze what they gave themselves to in preaching is of great benefit to preachers today.

James Waddel Alexander, the son of Archibal Alexander and brother of J. A. Alexander, was the son of Puritans. His classic work *Thoughts on Preaching*, first published in 1864, includes a chapter on 'The Matter of Preaching'. In that chapter, Alexander clearly sets forth several guidelines for choosing the subjects, themes or content of preaching. These thoughts include:

1. The Doctrine of God – His work, nature, attributes; and the doctrine of anthropology – man's sin nature and creaturely state (i.e. doctrine).
2. The person and work of Christ as well as man's duty to love, obey and believe on Him (i.e. Christology).
3. Doctrinal Preaching – systematic theology, drawn from Scripture and practically applied to men's lives.
4. Preaching about man's errors and lies and his rightful duty (i.e. ethics).
5. Proper presentation of the Christian religion as opposed to moralism, virtue and worldly works (i.e. evangelism).[5]

Alexander thus exhorts young preachers to devote themselves to categories of preaching similar to those detailed above.

In addition to a systematic approach to preaching all types of Scripture, these Puritan preachers were also great 'physicians of the soul'; they were masters at discovering the cause and effect relationships in matters of spiritual life and death. Thus they diagnosed the spiritual problems of their congregations and preached pointedly at those problems with corrective intent behind their preaching. This use of casuistry was unique and most developed among the Puritans. Even a cursory examination of Richard Baxter's *Practical Works* can establish this truth. Richard Sibbes was known as 'the heavenly doctor' for this very reason.

As the Puritans did, it is both wise and strategic to analyze the errors and negligence of one's congregation: one must discern what nagging problems rob a congregation of the revitalized life Christ desires for each church. In so doing, a pastor will discover false theology, lack of church discipline, unqualified officers, a shame for the gospel, politically-correct thinking, cowardice and unfaithfulness in ministry, and sinful habits in the background and history of the church. William Perkins exhorts ministers to do exactly what the writer is advocating:

Reprove only the errors which currently trouble the church. Leave others alone if they lie dead in past history, or if they are not relevant to the people, unless you know that spiritual danger may still arise from them. This was the situation described in Revelation chapter two when the church at Pergamos was warned to beware of the Nicolaitans whose teaching had already influenced some of them.[6]

When balanced content in the preaching of the church has been neglected over a period of years, there will be a need for preaching with a 'Puritan balance' in the five categories of sermons explained above. The Puritans inherited congregations that were dead, biblically illiterate, and full of both ethical immorality and doctrinal apostasy. Their balance of preaching in these five categories was deliberate and well-planned, and it would be of great benefit to imitate their approach. An insightful analysis of the spiritual problems of a congregation in need of revitalization will reveal the great wisdom of preaching the content of this 'Puritan Mix' for reasons now to be explained.

The Revelation of Saint John (the Apocalypse) is an epistle addressed to seven churches – the seven churches on the old postal route of Asia Minor: Ephesus, Smyrna, Pergamum, Thyatira, Sardis, Philadelphia, and Laodicea. Of these seven churches, five were in need of revitalization. Hence, Christ addressed them with words like 'repent' and 'do the deeds you did before' and 'remember therefore from where you have fallen'. These seven 'words' were five messages to declining churches in need of renewal and reformation and two messages of comfort to faithful churches. The five churches needing revitalization gave indication of five distinct spiritual problems. The amazing fact is this: the five problems these declining churches of Revelation had are the same five problems needing to be addressed by revitalizing preaching! Even a cursory study will show that the churches of Asia Minor were troubled by the following problems that are typical of declining churches:

Ephesus: a church in need of a 'first love' for Christ (Christological problem).

Laodicea: a lukewarm church in need of a holy church life (Ecclesiastical problem).

Sardis: a church without vision or evangelistic growth
               (Missiological problem).
Pergamum: a church of false teachings (Doctrinal problem).
Thyatira: a church of immorality and worldliness (Ethical
               problem).

In examining each of these areas of trouble in declining churches,
insight will be gained from the seven churches of Revelation. There is
strong biblical evidence that these five problems are *generic* to churches
in decline and in need of revitalization![7] The writer will examine
these problems one at a time, giving a chapter to each, and show how
the five categories of sermon content can correct these problems,
beginning with the Christological problem and the corrective nature
of Christological sermons.

ENDNOTES

1. Warren, 1996, 4-6.
2. Patterson, 1986, 155-56.
3. An analysis of several sources gives a clear picture of the balance maintained
by Puritan preachers. A survey of sermons by Richard Sibbes, David Clarkson,
John Owen, Samuel Bolton, Nathaniel Vincent, Thomas Watson, Jeremiah
Burroughs, Thomas Adams, Matthew Mead, George Whitefield and seventy-
five preachers at the morning exercises at churches in London from 1659–1689
(Roberts, 1981) reveals a typical mix in the content of the sermons preached.
Of particular interest were the sermons entitled *Puritan Sermons 1659-1689:
During the Morning Exercises at Crippelgate, St. Giles in the Fields, and in Southwark by
Seventy-five Ministers of the Gospel in or near London.* This group of sermons is of
interest because it gives a good sampling of random messages, preached outside
of a sermon series on a book of the Bible, whereby the ministers preached on
the needs, issues and ministerial concerns of their day.

A total of three hundred ninety-six (396) sermons were surveyed; one
hundred forty (140) belonging to the 'morning exercises' collection. This
sampling of sermons revealed the following percentages in each of the five
categories of content: 10% were Christological; 17% were Ecclesiastical; 8%
were Missiological; 25% were Doctrinal; 40% were Ethical.

When the sermons of the Crippelgate morning exercise series were
tabulated, an even more accurate picture of the balance in content in Puritan
preaching was attained: 8% were Christological;15% were Ecclesiastical; 12%
were Missiological; 31% were Doctrinal; 34% were Ethical.

It was often difficult to place a particular sermon in one of the five categories; many were mixed in type and had a multifaceted thrust. The title, general theme, the text, and the main points of the sermon, together with its application were used to categorize each sermon. Others may classify specific sermons differently, but probably not enough to greatly affect the percentages in each category.

4. Lloyd-Jones, 1987, The Puritans: Their Origins.... 356, 368-70.

5. Alexander, 1988, 194-207.

6. Perkins, 1996, 64.

7. Guthrie, 1987, 71-72.

Chapter 6

Christological Preaching

The first and most fundamental of all the spiritual problems facing troubled churches in need of revitalization is clearly set forth in Revelation 2:1-7. Dying and sick churches have *always* 'left their first love'.

> To the angel of the church in Ephesus write: The One who holds the seven stars in His right hand, the One who walks among the seven golden lampstands, says this: 'I know your deeds and your toil and perseverance, and that you cannot endure evil men, and you put to the test those who call themselves apostles, and they are not, and you found them to be false; and you have perseverance and have endured for My name's sake, and have not grown weary. But I have this against you, that you have left your first love. Remember therefore from where you have fallen, and repent and do the deeds you did at first; or else I am coming to you, and will remove your lampstand out of its place – unless you repent. Yet this you do have, that you hate the deeds of the Nicolaitans, which I also hate. He who has an ear, let him hear what the Spirit says to the churches. To him who overcomes, I will grant to eat of the tree of life, which is in the Paradise of God.'

The loss of vision, of zeal, of 'fire in the belly', of passion for godliness, of love for others, of ministry and mission are always reflective of a loss of love for Christ. Churches that need to be revitalized most assuredly need to be taught their 'first love' once again (cf. Heb. 5:11-14). Because the love for Christ has been neither taught nor modeled in the pulpit, the people have lost that first and fiery love for Christ. There are three symptoms of a congregation that has lost its love for Christ.

First, human personalities begin to take preeminence in the life of the church, over the person and work of Christ. This can easily be seen in I Corinthians 1:10-17 where party strife arose among those loyal to Cephas (Peter), Apollos, or Paul. There is a definite corollary between the first and second chapters of I Corinthians: the loss of love for Christ that makes the cross void (ch. 1) is caused by the lack of 'preaching Christ crucified and nothing else' (ch. 2). Paul's approach to the factionalism in Corinth was to turn their eyes away from men to Christ. His simple questions were penetrating and precisely aimed, 'Has Christ been divided? Paul was not crucified for you, was he? Or were you baptized in the name of Paul?' (I Cor. 1:13).

When Christ is not preached (I Cor. 2:2) then a vacuum is created; people need some leader, some champion, some 'holy man' to cling to other than Christ. Therefore it is essential that preaching be both Christ-centered and devoted to regularly focusing on the beauty and bounty of Jesus Christ.[1]

Certainly, all sermons should major on Christ, focusing on His redemptive and renewing power and purpose for lives, homes, churches, communities and nations. Preaching that ignores Christ is pure moralism and is not preaching at all – 'We preach Christ crucified...' (I Cor. 1:23). But there is also a great need to 'woo' hearers back to the sweetness of the love of Christ again and again. In fact, Richard Sibbes defined preaching in just those terms: 'It is not sufficient to preach Christ, or to lay open all this in the view of others; but in the opening of them, there must be application of them to the use of God's people, that they may see their interest in them; and there must be an alluring of them, *for to preach is to woo*.'[2] Sibbes says in his work entitled *The Bruised Reed*:

> Ministers by their calling are friends of the Bride, and to bring Christ and his Spouse together, and therefore ought, upon all good occasions, to lay open all the excellencies of Christ, and amongst others, as that he is highly born, mighty, One 'in whom all the treasures of wisdom are hid,' Col. ii.3, & c., so likewise gentle, and of a good nature, and of a gracious disposition.... The more glory to God, and the more comfort to a Christian soul, ariseth from the belief and application of these things, the more the enemy of God's

glory and man's comfort labours to breed mispersuasions of them, that if he cannot keep men from heaven, and bring them into that cursed condition he is in himself, yet he may trouble them in their passage; some and none of the worst, Satan prevails withal so far as to neglect the means, upon fear they should, being so sinful, dishonour God and increase their sins; and so they lie smothering under this temptation, as it were bound hand and foot by Satan, not daring to make out to Christ, and yet are secretly upheld by a spirit of faith, shewing itself in hidden sighs and groans unto God. These are abused by false representations of Christ; all whose ways to such being ways of mercy, and all his thoughts, thoughts of love.... It adds strength to faith to consider, that all expressions of love issue from nature in Christ, which is constant. God knows that, as we are prone to sin, so, when conscience is thoroughly awaked, we are as prone to despair for sin; and therefore he would have us know, that he setteth himself in the covenant of grace to triumph in Christ over the greatest evils and enemies we fear, and that his thoughts are not as our thoughts are, Isa. v.8; that he is God, and not man, Hos. xi.9; that there are heights, and depths, and breadths of mercy in him above all the depths of our sin and misery, Eph. iii.18; that we should never be in such a forlorn condition, wherein there should be ground of despair, considering our sins be the sins of men, his mercy the mercy of an infinite God.... Now God dealing with men as understanding creatures, the manner which he useth in this powerful work upon their consciences, is by way of friendly intercourse, as entreaty and persuasion, and discovery of his love in Christ, and Christ's gracious inclination thus even to the weakest and lowest of men.... The main scope of all, is, to allure us to the entertainment of Christ's mild, safe, wise, victorious government, and to leave men naked of all pretences, why they will not have Christ to rule over them, when we see salvation not only strongly wrought, but sweetly dispensed by him. His government is not for his own pleasure, but for our good. We are saved by a way of love, that love might be kindled by this way in us to God again; because this affection melteth the soul, and mouldeth it to all duty and acceptable manner of performance of duty. It is love in duties that God regards, more than duties themselves. This is the true and evangelical disposition arising from Christ's love to us, and our love to him again; and not to fear to come to him, as if we were to take an elephant by the tooth. It is almost a fundamental mistake, to think that God delights in slavish fears, whenas the fruits of Christ's kingdom are peace and joy in the Holy Ghost: for from this mistake come weak, slavish, superstitious conceit.[3]

James I. Packer writes of the 'Christ-centered orientation' of Puritan preaching:

Puritan preaching revolved around 'Christ, and Him crucified' – for this is the hub of the Bible. The preachers' commission is to declare the whole counsel of God; but the cross is the centre of that counsel, and the Puritans knew that the traveler through the Bible landscape misses his way as soon as he loses sight of the hill called Calvary.[4]

The pulpit that revitalizes a church must refocus people on the wonder and glory of the person of Jesus Christ instead of making debilitating comparisons of past to present preachers. The only way for that to happen is to wean people off an unbiblical preoccupation with the popularity of ministers by helping them become 'addicted' to Christ!

A second symptom that a church has lost its love for Christ is that, without a Christo-centric foundation in the hearts of people, the Christian religion soon evolves into a religion of rules and traditions. Pastors must constantly remind their congregations that the key to the Christian life is found in the Pauline phrase 'in Christ' (see Ephesians, chapter one). If all one is and all one does is not done 'in Christ', then it is not Christian.

When the writer came to Trinity Church, the first series preached was that of I Corinthians: 'The Shadow of the Cross.' All of the messages in this series flowed from the first four chapters of this epistle – the cross of Christ being the power, purpose and principle for all Christian life. The mistake was made, however, of too quickly diving into such controversial issues as tongues, divorce and remarriage, marital relationships, and so forth. A much wiser approach was set forth by Dr. J. Ligon Duncan III. Upon assuming the pulpit of the historic First Presbyterian Church in Jackson, Mississippi, he preached his first sermon series on the Epistle to the Colossians: 'The Incomparable Christ' – a pure and winsome Christological thrust. It is better to lay a long and deep foundation in the person of Christ (Eph. 2:19, 20) before delving into doctrinal and ethical issues. When people see the love of Christ and His perfect will behind all they are asked to do, it is easier for them to obey His Word and accept His will.

A third symptom that churches have lost their first love for Christ is that churches in need of revitalization are full of unconverted souls who are merely nominal Christians. More will be said about the need for evangelization in the chapter on 'Doctrinal Sermons', but suffice it to say: dying churches are dying because they are full of spiritually dead people. In the final analysis, a church that needs revitalization is in that condition because neo-orthodox theology, a liberal social-gospel, and cowardly man-pleasing preaching have robbed the congregation of the life-giving, life-changing and life-enriching message of Jesus Christ. When men preach moralistic messages, the law without Christ, the result is that 'doing good' becomes the only challenge offered from their pulpits each Sunday. They preach much about doing good but little about being godly in Christ. Moralism replaces a love for Christ; the church loses its first love. They fail to realize that to preach the law faithfully is to preach Christ fervently. J. W. Alexander states this truth clearly when he writes:

> The effect of preaching the law faithfully, will not be to encourage men to attempt to gain life by keeping it, but to show them their utter inability to keep it, and their hopeless condemnation by it. Convincing them of their ruin, it fills them with a sense of their need of a Redeemer. This is the great central truth of revelation, and the foundation of true religion. For 'other foundation can no man lay.' Therefore, while, as we have shown, God must be set forth, first of all, and above all, in preaching, he must. [5]

The Puritans would preach Christ just for the purpose of calling people to love Him more and rest in Him securely. Nearly one in ten sermons referenced in the Puritan sermons surveyed were 'Christological' in content, thrust and primary focus. When a congregation comes to see Jesus Christ for who He is and what He has done, they again fall deeply in love with Him. This, the writer maintains, is always the first step in revitalization.

ENDNOTES

1. McGrath, 1994, 152.
2. Sibbes, 1977, 5:505.
3. Sibbes 1977, 1: 38-41.
4. Packer, 1990, 286.
5. Alexander, 1988, 207.

Chapter 7

Ecclesiastical Preaching

The Puritan pulpit was regularly devoted to instructions about 'being the church'. What the writer calls 'Ecclesiastical Preaching' constituted a full fifteen percent of Puritan preaching. It was from this emphasis – the desire to 'purify' the church from worldly and extra-biblical influences – that the derisive title 'Puritan' first came.[1] Naturally, then, these Puritans preached, taught and wrote often on such subjects as worship, the sacraments, preaching, liturgy and tradition, fellowship and the body life of the congregation. The strength of the Puritan movement lay in the central place the local church had in the life of the Puritan people. J. I. Packer goes so far as to call Puritanism 'a movement of revival' affecting the Protestant churches more than any movement since the Reformation:

> I define Puritanism as that movement in sixteenth- and seventeenth-century England which sought further reformation and renewal in the Church of England than the Elizabethan settlement allowed. 'Puritan' itself was an imprecise term of contemptuous abuse which between 1564 and 1642 (these exact dates are given by Thomas Fuller and Richard Baxter) was applied to at least five overlapping groups of people – first, to clergy who scrupled some Prayer Book ceremonies and phrasing; second, to advocates of the Presbyterian reform programme broached by Thomas Cartwright and the 1572 Admonition to the Parliament; third, to clergy and laity, not necessarily non-conformists, who practised a serious Calvinistic piety; fourth, to 'rigid Calvinists' who applauded the Synod of Dort, and were called doctrinal Puritans by other Anglicans who did not; fifth, to MPs, JPs and other gentry who showed public respect for

the things of God, the laws of England and the rights of subjects....
This was a clergy-led movement which for more than a century was
held together, and given a sense of identity too deep for differences
of judgement on questions of polity and politics to destroy, by
three things. The first was a set of shared convictions, biblicist and
Calvinist in character, about on the one hand Christian faith and
practice and on the other hand congregational life and the pastoral
office. The second was a shared sense of being called to work for
God's glory in the Church of England by eliminating popery from
its worship, prelacy from its government and pagan irreligion from
its membership, and so realising in it the New Testament pattern
of true and authentic church life. The third was a shared literature,
catechetical, evangelistic and devotional, with a homiletical style and
experiential emphasis that were all its own.[2]

Surely those very things that were central issues of church life in the
sixteenth century are the same controversies of today. This is the age
of debate about drama in worship, hymnody and contemporary music,
Sabbath day observance, women's ordination, expected activities of
ministry in the church, and concern over the loss of 'community' in
the typical congregation. Moreover, with the signing of *Evangelicals
and Catholics Together*, the church is once again forced to deal with
the same issues of Rome and Popery that inflamed the Elizabethan
Church in England in great controversy: transubstantiation,
mariolatry, ecclesiastical union with Rome, and so forth. These
issues, once settled by the Puritan pulpit, have arisen again today.
Any pastor seeking revitalization will, out of necessity, have to deal
with these issues. Many evangelicals are leaving Protestantism for
Rome because they believe that something is lacking in the life of
evangelical churches. The lukewarm, lackluster lifestyle common in
many evangelical circles has caused people to look elsewhere for a
meaningful church family. Lukewarm evangelicalism is a common
problem.

This same problem was found in the church of Laodicea. Although
the concept of poor ecclesiastical church life is not clearly or openly
stated, this was the great issue of the church of Laodicea.

And to the angel of the church in Laodicea write: The Amen, the faithful and true Witness, the Beginning of the creation of God, says this: 'I know your deeds, that you are neither cold nor hot; I would that you were cold or hot. So because you are lukewarm, and neither hot nor cold, I will spit you out of My mouth. Because you say, "I am rich, and have become wealthy, and have need of nothing," and you do not know that you are wretched and miserable and poor and blind and naked, I advise you to buy from Me gold refined by fire, that you may become rich, and white garments, that you may clothe yourself, and that the shame of your nakedness may not be revealed; and eye salve to anoint your eyes, that you may see. Those whom I love, I reprove and discipline; be zealous therefore, and repent. Behold, I stand at the door and knock; if anyone hears My voice and opens the door, I will come in to him, and will dine with him, and he with Me. He who overcomes, I will grant to him to sit down with Me on My throne, as I also overcame and sat down with My Father on His throne. He who has an ear, let him hear what the Spirit says to the churches' (Rev. 3:14-22).

The root problem is a smug sense of feeling 'I'm O.K.,' when in fact Christ stands outside the church's life and fellowship and knocks to enter! A lukewarmness which reflected a lack of zeal, love, passion and concern was devoted to maintaining the status quo and was killing the church of Laodicea. Their problem was obvious to all but themselves. They saw themselves as wealthy, healthy and aware of what was going on around them, while in fact they were poor, sick and blind because their body life was lacking the love and fellowship of Christ. They believed themselves to be theologically sound, lovingly caring and spiritually grounded. In fact, they were diseased and dying as a local church.

Declining churches often feel that they are 'tight-knit' groups. This conception is often the result of a fortress mentality caused by the loss of members which drives the membership into a closed huddle out of a sense of fear and self-preservation. In reality their body life, worship, fellowship, mutual ministry and commitment to one another may be very lukewarm, quite conditional and limited in scope. Christ desires to revive these churches (Rev. 3:20) to bring to them the ecclesiastical joy promised to healthy New Testament churches. These churches need to see themselves accurately. A congregation may think it is warm, friendly and supportive in its body life, but visitors and new members often feel the opposite.

Several needs must be addressed by revitalizing pastors in order to help declining churches begin to understand how a healthy church functions. First, there needs to be basic teaching on the nature and purpose of the church. For this reason, the writer seeks each year to preach a sermon series on the biblical design and purpose of the church. Over the years, sermon series on ecclesiology have been preached: 'The Book of Acts'; 'Together God's Way: Essential Elements of a Dynamic Church'; The Dynamic Church (Acts 2:37-47)'; 'Philippians: Upon This Rock'; 'Titus: The Worldly Saints,' and other series on practical church life.

Such repeated instruction on the church, its body life, and its mission is critical to overcoming the consumerism and self-focus of most evangelical churches.[3] When people see how their congregational life does not reflect the biblical pattern and plan for a local body of believers, the stage is set for positive change.

Churches in need of revitalization, due to poor preaching and teaching, have been reduced to a very nondescript faith the writer chooses to call 'neo-evangelicalism'. It can best be described and understood by an encounter the writer had with one of the older ruling elders of his present charge. When the elder refused to come to church because of the preaching, the writer decided to visit him in his home. Quite irritated at the church, he angrily accused the writer of 'mean-spirited arrogance'. Why was the writer guilty of such a charge? For three reasons: First, the church requires officer training and adherence to qualifications for office derived from 1 Timothy 3 and Titus 1. Second, the church requires attendance at a mandatory orientation class for prospective members. Third, the writer does not consider Roman Catholicism as an acceptable form of biblical Christianity. The writer was informed by this man that 'all God requires of His church is that they believe in God, Jesus and the Bible'. This elder proceeded to tell him that he did not believe 'all that stupid stuff in the Westminster Confession anyway' and that he felt it produced a sort of 'Phariseeism' to focus too much on doctrine and denominationalism.

It should come as no surprise that such a reaction to Puritan preaching surfaces when for years, even decades, souls are taught not much more than to 'believe in God, Jesus and the Bible...and do good!' This neo-evangelical, eclectic and indefinite ecclesiastical mindset is a challenge that sincere pastors of the Reformed Faith must face today.[4] Although it seems highly 'dogmatic' to be concerned with such 'ecclesiastical stuff' as regulative worship, officer training, church discipline and mutual ministry, this is the 'stuff' of which community is made. The point seems always to be missed that churches without distinctives offer a bland Christian experience that may attract many listeners who want easy-believism, but can never help build a community of faith. Who a group of people are and how they behave together are rooted in what they believe.

> Doctrine is there to help the church to be what it is called to be. It shapes the vision of the world associated with the body of Christ. It can be said that doctrine gives Christians a sense of identity, at both the personal and the communal level. It explains what Christianity is all about. But this suggestion is open to a misunderstanding – that doctrine somehow invents a corporate identity. In fact, the Christian church has already been given its identity by the God who called it into being. The Christian church did not come into being of its own accord. It is a response to the calling of God. The initiative lies with God, who has called the church out (the root meaning of the Greek work ekklesia) of the world – called it out of darkness into his wonderful light.[5]

Those pastors involved in revitalization will find the need to preach regularly on what worship, polity and community must look like in a Reformed congregation. The fact that denominationalism is on the wane is not necessarily a good trend.[6] With the loss of denominational distinctives will come a weakening of creedal and confessional doctrine, a lack of accountability to higher ecclesiastical authority, and a forsaking of historical values. Reformed and Presbyterian congregations must be taught what it is to be reformed and presbyterian rather than broadly and in-descriptively evangelical.

91

Preachers should devote pulpit time to ecclesiastical matters because Western culture is experiencing a tremendous loss of community. Homes (marriages) are falling apart. Neighborhoods cease to exist. Racial and ethnic tension tear cities apart. The neighborhood school is gone. Mobility from place to place is more frequent than ever. Distrust for any institution or organization is at an all-time high. These are not easy days to attempt to build a community of faith!

As churches age, begin to decline, live in transitioning neighborhoods, and grow into the generation gaps now present in today's culture, the community life of the church breaks down. In addition, when symptoms of both decline and trouble surface many leave a church and go elsewhere, further discouraging and dissolving attempts to build strong community in a congregation.

And yet, historically, the strength of the Reformed and evangelical movement has been in the vibrancy of the local congregations serving as communities of faith and fellowship.

> At its heart, evangelicalism has a deep-seated awareness of the importance of the Christian community to the tasks of evangelism, spiritual nourishment, teaching and discipling. Evangelicalism rejoices in the Pauline image of the church as the body of Christ, realizing that this points to a corporate rather than individualistic conception of the Christian life. The 'community of Christ' is integral to an evangelical understanding of the Christian life and is of growing importance to evangelical understandings of the tasks of Christian theology.[7]

Protestant churches have historically found doctrinal unity in denominations, conventions or associations, but the strength of their community life lies in the congregation or local church body. The Roman Catholic church, on the other hand, has traditionally held to its supposed unanimity in belief and conformity in liturgy, imposed from Rome as its strength in community. In other words, Protestant congregations must work harder at developing fellowship, mutual ministry, and reciprocal living than Catholic churches do because Catholics usually sense a 'bondedness' by virtue of their traditions, liturgy and canon laws. Biblical fellowship is quite fragile, and for that reason, the writers of the New Testament devote many a paragraph and page to the ideas of living together as God's children, brethren in Christ.

Declining churches are usually failing in their fellowship. They perceive that they are 'warm and friendly' because their shrinking numbers have forced core-group members into a bond: 'We will never leave this church!' Because cliques and self-sustaining groups have, of necessity, become committed to the continuing legacy of a dissolving church, they remain closed to new members breaking into such close circles of friends. As a result, salt is rubbed in the gaping wound. Believing themselves to be 'a supportive fellowship', the members of a declining church have actually become ingrown, suspicious and fearful of even more loss of members. Only those possessing boldness and extroverted personality are able to 'feel at home' in declining churches.

Consequently, pastors of churches in need of revitalization must often speak on such subjects as fellowship, cooperation with church officers, openness to strangers, hospitality, spiritual gifts, reciprocal living, sins of the tongue, mutual ministry, joyful worship, communion of the sacraments, officer qualifications, and the Book of Church Order's position or practice on various issues related to healthy body life. A pastor seeking to revitalize a church cannot just add new members. He must repair the damage done by years of ingrown, self-centered and unfriendly living among the members of the congregation. He must rebuild a healthy community of faith, a supportive church fellowship and spiritual family in which new believers and new members will feel welcomed, loved and undergirded. This is an extremely slow process and an excruciatingly difficult challenge.

ENDNOTES

1. Ryken, 1986, 7.
2. Packer, 1990, 35-48.
3. Beates, 1996, 12-13.
4. McGrath, 1996, 201-02.
5. McGrath, 1990, 53.
6. Schaller, 1996, 20-23.
7. McGrath, 1994, 78-79.

Chapter 8

Missiological Preaching

The third category of sermons with unique content for declining churches concerns the mission of the church. It should come as absolutely no surprise that dying, troubled, struggling churches have lost a sense of mission. When the Puritans sought to revive their congregations in their day, they devoted twelve percent of their preaching to the mission of the church. They often preached on the state of the lost, outreach to the Jews, missions overseas, the cultural mandate and the use of one's spiritual gifts to minister to others. Contrary to popular misconception, the Puritans were concerned with the outreach, evangelistic growth and mission of the church.[1]

Archie Parrish reveals that this problem remains a desperate need for many churches in the Presbyterian Church in America (PCA):

> As we race toward the twenty-first century, the greatest need in the world is revival of the Christian church! There is a growing disparity between the *church of Scripture* and the institution called the church today. The church, once a mission-minded organism, has become a maintenance-minded organization. Nominalism is rampant in local churches today. Nominal Christians are Christian in name only. American churches, on average, spend 96% of their income on themselves. Of the remaining 4%, local and global evangelism receives 3.5% and the unreached people of the earth receive the last 0.5%. The 'edifice complex' – obsession with buildings and the activities that go on in them – causes many churches to borrow large amounts of money to finance immense, elaborate structures. Too often this indebtedness leads to disproportionate time spent in fund raising and the use of techniques that generate funds but are questionable

from a biblical point of view; preferential treatment for the wealthy, selection of officers solely for financial net worth rather than spiritual qualification. Efficient management methods become substitutes for biblical disciplines such as prayer and fasting. The message coming from many pulpits is pop psychology and self-help. Many sermons are eloquent and intellectual but they lack soul. They are powerless because of lack of prayer on the part of both the pastor and his people. Most of the churches of our land are spiritually barren. I studied a group of 1,122 local Bible-believing evangelical churches. More than six hundred of these did not have one addition by adult profession of faith in 1994. The impotency of the church is reflected in the disintegrating American families. Half of all marriages are ending in divorce and in 1990 only 26.3% of families in America were the traditional nuclear family – nearly one quarter of these were blended or step-families. There is improper emphasis on external indicators such as baptisms, budget, buildings, membership, and attendance and the church-gathered activities. The problem is not that Christians are not where they should be: the problem is that they are not what they should be right where they are.[2]

The Scriptures clearly reveal that such an ingrown, worldly, and self-centered loss of world vision and heart for mission was a problem plaguing congregations from apostolic times until now. The church of Sardis was just such a church: 'I know your deeds, that you have a name that you are alive, but you are dead' (Rev. 3:1). Christ then proceeds to call Sardis to an awakening (i.e. revival) because their deeds were not complete (Rev. 3:3). In other words, here was a church that was going through all the religious motions (deeds), many of which were godly and good, but it was 'dead' and barren because new births in Christ through evangelism and missions were not taking place. They were 'dead' because they were not growing by conversions and new members.

And to the angel of the church in Sardis write: He who has the seven Spirits of God, and the seven stars, says this: 'I know your deeds, that you have a name that you are alive, but you are dead. Wake up, and strengthen the things that remain, which were about to die; for I have not found your deeds completed in the sight of My God. Remember therefore what you have received and heard; and keep it, and repent. If therefore you will not wake up, I will come like a thief, and you will not know at what hour I will come upon you. But you have a few people in Sardis who have not soiled their garments; and they will walk with Me in white; for they are worthy. He who overcomes shall thus be clothed in white garments; and I will not erase his name from the book of life, and I will confess his name before My Father, and before His angels. He who has an ear, let him hear what the Spirit says to the churches' (Rev. 3:1-6).

Sardis suffered from a loss of missiological vision, a fact even painfully more obvious when the next church in the biblical text is a church with a great missiological vision. Philadelphia, an outreaching, evangelistic and courageously missions-minded church, is compared to dead Sardis. They were much smaller and weaker than Sardis, yet more faithful in the Great Commission. This remains a telltale sign that a church needs revitalization – the lack of evangelistic efforts, missions emphasis and growth by conversions. Every declining church has lost its vision for missions. As a result, pastors seeking revitalization must often remind and instruct the congregation in this great mission calling from Christ.

The causes of this loss of mission effort can be multifaceted. Churches in need of revitalization often have *ministers who are ashamed of the gospel and neglect it because it is irrelevant to their theology and lives*. These ministers let many into membership of the church who are not converted. When a great influx of these lost souls swells the rolls of a church, it becomes quite difficult to preach the gospel without offending unconverted sensibilities. As a result, gospel-oriented outreach and mission work take a back seat to social programs and mercy ministries that are only tangentially related to Christ and His gospel message.

Another cause of loss of mission vision is *ingrownness* – the tendency to focus on self rather than the world.[3] Most often this is the direct result of a lack of vision and poor representation of the church's purpose. When a congregation grows up focused solely on people's neighborhoods and children, the seeds of ingrown thinking are already sown; in time they will yield the harvest of a lost vision for souls. Often, when a church is formed, it is full of young couples with little children in new homes on the new growth end of town. Within a twenty-year period, trouble can set in: grown children will go off to college, military or careers and do not return to their home church, thus leaving behind a congregation of middle-aged people with an unclear purpose for ministry.

Pastors need to teach their people to think in terms of outreach, a heterogeneous congregation, and a city-wide ministry. This will help prevent a crisis of purpose that can last for a quarter of a century! When pastors preach missiologically from the Book of Acts, the pastoral epistles and other key passages, reminding their people of their chief reason for existence – the Great Commission – then congregations slowly but surely grow to see that reaching the lost is as essential to church life as caring for the nursery, singing in the choir, developing home Bible studies and sponsoring a good youth ministry. In fact, over time, all the normal aspects of congregational life become open to the unchurched and unsaved, and they are used by members as tools to bring people to church and later to Christ.

Preachers of declining churches in need of revitalization must periodically and persistently preach series to remind people of the great mission and calling of the church. The writer has preached series on the evangelistic, missiological and compassionate responsibilities of a healthy church. These series have increased sensitivity to the church's mission and mandate to reach the lost. A warning is given to pastors of 'homogenous', yuppie churches in the suburbs: Unless congregations are taught to think of outreach to more than young parents with small children, the seeds of decline will be sown. Age and demographics will produce, over time, a dying church without vision.

Finally, a third cause of loss of outreach is that *declining churches are often members of declining denominations.* This was the case with Trinity Church, a member of the Presbyterian Church in the United States of America (PCUSA). As this denomination became more and more unbiblical and less and less faithful to the Gospel, congregations became suspicious of where their evangelistic and mission dollars were invested. Missions monies given by congregations for evangelism and church planting were frequently spent on political lobbying, legal defense funds, World Council of Churches' causes, Marxist activities in the Third World, and social projects contrary to biblical ethics and doctrine. When congregations became aware of these abuses, they channeled missions monies into para-church, independent and non-denominational ministries. While this was certainly a better stewardship of funds, it had a debilitating effect upon a local church's growth in outreach. Let the writer explain the dilemma created.

God has intended the church to reach the lost world for Christ in a cooperative manner; churches are to pool resources with a shared vision and creed in order to maximize investment and concentrate efforts. This investment in and support for denominational ministries and missions have a multiplying effect upon missions giving and involvement. The dollars and time invested in theologically-sympathetic ministries and denominationally-affiliated mission work have the effect of a 'return on investment'. Those impacted and supported by these ministries reinvest in the overall growth of ministry and missions of the denomination. They remain connected to the supporting local churches to fuel even more interest and investment in missions, church planting and outreach. Partnerships between churches and mission stations develop, forming networks of congregations cross-fertilizing growth in missions. In missiological circles, this is known as 'synergism', and it is a powerful inducement to growth in missions.

When the writer came to Trinity Church, its faithful and active missions program had been through exactly this process. Disenchanted with the PCUSA's unreliable use of mission funds, Trinity Church supported mostly independent and para-church ministries. Through direct preaching in the pulpit, by using PCA ministries, missionaries, and denominational leaders as conference speakers, and by setting deliberate goals, Trinity Church developed both trust for and involvement in denominational missions support. The growth of faith-promise giving illustrates how a missiological focus is continuing to grow at Trinity Church. Similar growth trends in giving to local outreach, home missions and mercy ministries are also apparent. The giving for foreign missions is an encouraging sign of growing missiological vision.

The challenge of becoming locally effective and aggressive in evangelism has also been addressed. In 1997 a staff member was added to the ministry team, with the title and responsibilities of 'The Director of Outreach and Missions' (DOM). He has developed an outward face for our congregation. Following the lead of the pulpit and its emphasis on witnessing, mercy ministry and intentional outreach, Trinity Church has seen increased conversion growth, a growing number of people trained in evangelistic techniques and a partnership develop between our congregation and its neighborhood.

We have a growing number of African Americans joining our church – something very difficult to accomplish in the Old South. We have a sports outreach ministry, a tutoring ministry, karate training, contact with the local schools, community groups meeting at our church, a sister-church relationship with an African American congregation and an ongoing Bible-study ministry to the local YMCA. All these ministries serve us well in the context of our urban location.

The joyful aspect of these ministries is that they all came from the DOM and members of the church applying the teaching from the pulpit concerning outreach and mission. We have seen eight couples and two single women head for the mission field through our mission partnerships in Scotland, Uganda, Peru, and inner city New Orleans. Several young men have gone to seminary. All this has happened in the past ten years due to an emphasis on equipping for ministry and sending to missions. The pulpit has led the way in this outward focus, the elders have staffed and funded this priority, the staff has taken the hands-on ministry of outreach and developed it, and the people of Trinity Church, always a missions-minded congregation, have stepped up to a higher level of commitment.

D. James Kennedy has often said that given the opportunity to do anything, the last thing Christians will want to do is to evangelistically reach out to the lost. He is, of course, correct. And for that reason Puritan preachers preached missiological sermons about the state of the unconverted, the plight of the Jews, the evangelistic responsibility of the pulpit and the mercy ministry of the church. Those who would hope to revitalize troubled churches must do the same. Preaching missiologically is not an option; it is the end purpose of the church and thus must constantly be kept before the church as the 'prime mission'.

ENDNOTES

1. Murray, 1971, 135.
2. Parrish, 1995, 1-2.
3. Kehrein, 1996, 14-23.
4. Kennedy, 1983, 2-5.

Chapter 9

Doctrinal Preaching

Puritan preaching was doctrinal preaching. Almost a third (31%) of all their messages were doctrinal in content. The Puritans realized that the primary cause of decline in the churches was what the Scripture sets forth as the disease of all backslidden Christianity: ignorance of God's Word. 'My people are destroyed for lack of knowledge. Because you have rejected knowledge, I also will reject you from being my priest. Since you have forgotten the laws of God, I also will forget your children' (Hosea 4:6) – so said the Lord to His Old Testament Church. Preachers must always remember that they are never responsible to God for what their people do with their knowledge from God's Word, but they are always responsible for what their people know about God's Word. Obedience is the people's responsibility; instruction is the preacher's.

The Puritans realized this and, believing that good living came from good doctrine, they taught their people well. Puritan preaching was theologically both systematic and deep.

Puritan preaching was *doctrinal in its content*. The Puritans received the Bible as a self-contained and self-interpreting revelation of God's mind. This revelation, the 'body of divinity' as they called it, is, they held, a unity, to which every part of 'the best of books' makes its own distinct contribution. It follows that the meaning of single texts cannot be properly discerned till they are seen in relation to the rest of the 'body'; and, conversely, that the better one's grasp of the whole, the more significance one will see in each part. To be a good expositor, therefore, one must first be a good theologian.

Theology — truth about God and man — is what God has put into the texts of Scripture, and theology is what preachers must draw out of them. To the question, 'Should one preach doctrine?', the Puritan answer would have been, 'Why, what else is there to preach?' Puritan preachers were not afraid to bring the profoundest theology into the pulpit if it bore on their hearers' salvation, nor to demand that men and women apply themselves to mastering it, nor to diagnose unwillingness to do so as a sign of insincerity. Doctrinal preaching certainly bores the hypocrites; but it is only doctrinal preaching that will save Christ's sheep. The preacher's job is to proclaim the faith, not to provide entertainment for unbelievers — in other words, to feed the sheep rather than amuse the goats.[1]

Once again, it should come as no surprise to find that the messages to the seven churches of Asia Minor include a message to a church that had doctrinally gone astray. To the angel (messenger = pastor) of the church of Pergamum, Christ gives a warning about false doctrine. The church at Pergamum had given in to the 'teaching of Balaam' (worldliness) and to the 'teaching of the Nicolaitans' (gnosticism).

And to the angel of the church in Pergamum write: The One who has the sharp two-edged sword says this: 'I know where you dwell, where Satan's throne is; and you hold fast My name, and did not deny My faith, even in the days of Antipas, My witness, My faithful one, who was killed among you, where Satan dwells. But I have a few things against you, because you have there some who hold the teaching of Balaam, who kept teaching Balak to put a stumbling block before the sons of Israel, to eat things sacrificed to idols, and to commit acts of immorality. Thus you also have some who in the same way hold the teaching of the Nicolaitans. Repent therefore; or else I am coming to you quickly, and I will make war against them with the sword of My mouth. He who has an ear, let him hear what the Spirit says to the churches. To him who overcomes, to him I will give some of the hidden manna, and I will give him a white stone, and a new name written on the stone which no one knows but he who receives it' (Rev. 2:12-17).

The Pergamum church was not totally apostate: 'I know where you dwell, where Satan's throne is, and you hold fast my name, and did not deny My faith.' Even in the face of bloody persecution, Pergamum was 'officially' a conservative and historic church in its view of doctrine. But false teachers with false teaching had crept in unnoticed (cf. Acts 20:28-30). What happened at Pergamum has happened thousands of times throughout church history. No church ever deliberately forsakes the 'faith once delivered' (Jude 3) for worldly and heretical ideas, and yet it eventually happens to most churches. This is why reform, revival and revitalization are continually the need of the church.

Most churches in decline are living under the same delusion as the church at Pergamum. They believe that they are doctrinally a 'solid church', but in fact they are theologically weak. Error, compromise and cultural ideas have crept in, watering down the apostolic faith.

Declining churches often reflect a sense of satisfaction among more than a few of the long-standing members and officers of the church that they have been and continue to be 'a solid church'. This, however, is not always the case. One conversation the writer had with an elder and his wife exemplifies this point. Unhappy with prophetic and provocative preaching, they came to the writer's office and voiced their disappointment and dismay. They were disappointed that they were not hearing 'more of the gospel, more grace, more about the love of God and less about the law'. The elder also made this statement: 'We are a well-taught church, full of intelligent people, who basically know our doctrine and Bible. What we need from you is not lectures but direction about how to get on with our ministry.' When the writer disagreed with them and informed them that he wanted the church to be better schooled in Scripture, better taught with reference to the Reformed Faith, and evangelistic toward unconverted people, the wife of the elder asked in dismay, 'Do you really think that there are non-Christians in our membership?' She proceeded to scold the writer, informing him that all the members of the church were saved because they had assented to the vows of church membership! Misconceptions about theological depth and 'solidness' need to be corrected from the pulpit by good doctrinal preaching.

These misconceptions develop over time. Churches follow what is a usual route to declining doctrine. Affiliated with a liberal denomination, the church calls as its pastor a man who is not an evangelical. Soon he admits both to the membership and then to the offices of the church, unconverted people. The gospel is seldom preached, the law is virtually ignored, and doctrine is replaced by social concerns. There develops a pattern of sermon after sermon on civil rights, moralistic topics, love and peace among all people, ecumenism and openness to other expressions of faith. The people who grow up under such preaching give testimonies of being saved by good works, church membership and niceness. These pastors of churches in decline are known for being 'very pastoral', for filling the membership roll with names, but for taking few biblical stands on few issues.

The result of such pastoral leadership is predictable: fat membership rolls, poor attendance, unconverted members, unconverted church officers, unbiblical decisions, and a loss of spiritual vitality in the church. Soon many sincere and godly believers begin to leave the church, sensing that something is fundamentally wrong. With their exodus comes a loss of funds, loss of church workers, and loss of biblical vision and vitality. Soon the unconverted or the unschooled leaders are concerned with maintaining the status quo. The theological level of instruction follows the declining level of spiritual life, and the result is that a once solid, biblical church has become doctrinally anemic. This is always a most difficult thing for many members of declining churches to admit. Yet it is a fact. Others outside the leadership and fellowship of the church can clearly see these doctrinal problems. Blame must be placed fully on the shoulders of the leadership of the church, who tolerate this for so many years. This is a predictable pattern for declining churches.

What is called for is 'doctrinal preaching' and that becomes the task of the revitalizing pastor. Following the Puritan pattern, preaching for revitalization necessitates educating people in the full-orbed doctrine of the church. The preacher who wants to see his congregation revitalized must become a doctrinal preacher. He must rediscover the value of preaching with systematic theology interwoven in his sermons. In fact, the writer will go so far as to say that preaching has but three goals: the glory of God, the conversion of sinners and the instruction of the saints in the great truths of the Faith. With these three goals in mind, John R. W. Stott maintains that the primary responsibilities of a pastor are to be a teacher, a theologian and a preacher.[2] In a little book entitled *A Theology of Preaching: The Dynamics of the Gospel*, Richard Lischer writes about 'Preaching as Theology'. His insights are vitally important in addressing the needs of declining churches.

> Today, most assessments of modern theology have found a common point of departure: the brokenness of theology. Everyone decries the fragmentation of theology – its paralyzing over-specialization, its Babel of terminology, its alienation from the life of the church – but until the pain is great enough, no one does anything about it. Nowhere does this fragmentation impact with greater force and nowhere is the pain felt more deeply than in the church's preaching. Although preaching is central to the life of the church, it has had to struggle continually against its exclusion from the church's self-reflection, its theology.... By theology I mean systematic theology. It strides beyond the arrangement of biblical themes and motifs, but stops short of symbolics. Systematic theology includes the church's *dogmata*, but, in its dialectical relationship to the world, surpasses dogmatics. It is the most inclusive and all-encompassing of the categories named, but it never represents a closed system or a monument on which students, like so many mountain climbers or spelunkers, may pick and chip. Systematic theology's openness to the world corresponds with preaching's worldly concerns, yet both arise only from the gospel and both persist only through the sponsorship of the church.... If preaching did nothing more than restate the ideas of sacred texts, theology would have nothing to do, and the text-to-sermon manual would speak the final word to preachers. But preachers are charged with *proclaiming the gospel in texts, by means of texts, and in faithfulness to texts.* Many theologians have recognized theology's function as mediator between exegesis and preaching.... As a reflection on proclamation, theology, as well as the preaching it guides, is judged by a single criterion: its obedience to grace.... Theology requires the preacher to relate all the articles of the broader gospel – creation, fall, providence, sanctification, church, eschatology – and all the texts of Scripture to this constitutive core of the Christian faith. This is 'hard' because other doctrines, not arising from and unrelated to the gospel, have elbowed their way into the company of *the* doctrine. In addition to

these theological options and opinions the preacher is confronted with propaganda, sentiment, and other cultural clutter that all but demand equal time in the pulpit. These theology unceremoniously dumps and prepares the preacher for more serious and constructive work.... We must establish a *theologically* sound conception of the listener's world before we can preach in it, to it, for it, or against it.... Beyond the preacher's pastoral experiences lies systematic theology's perennial dialogue with psychotherapy, anthropology, philosophy, ideology, politics, the arts, science, medicine, cybernetics, and ethics.

Lischer goes on to add that systematic theology adds to preaching four very tangible benefits: substance, coherence, authority and relevance. Looking at preaching from a neo-orthodox position, he reflects what the Puritan preachers knew all along: preaching needs a scaffolding of doctrine on which truth can be hung and by which disjointed issues and problems can be tied together in a world-and-life view. Dogma is drawn from Scripture. Therefore when teaching Scripture to people, dogma helps explain biblical truth. In this anti-intellectual age, people no longer believe that theology is important to faith in God, life in eternity and day-to-day obedience to Christ. They have forgotten that thousands of years of church history have been guided and superintended by the Holy Spirit in order to develop a basic body of divinity designed to guide the saints from here to eternity. They have come to believe the lie that such an academic and classical field of study as Theology could never be of any practical value for daily living. The modern cry to 'make preaching relevant' is just a euphemistic way of telling preachers to 'lay off the doctrine'!

Amazingly, Puritan preachers were masters at applying systematic theology to personal problems facing people in the pew. They referred to this process of applied theology as 'cases of conscience'. Dr. Martyn Lloyd-Jones explains: 'The Puritans are justly famous for their pastoral preaching. They would take up what they called "cases of conscience" and deal with them in their sermons; and as they dealt with these problems they were solving the personal individual problems of those who were listening to them.'[4] As the Puritans did so should modern preachers. Declining churches are filled with 'declining Christians' – people desperately in need of biblical truth to guide their lives. They need definitions, formulas, principles and promises for their lives. This is precisely what doctrine (systematic theology) is meant to do. This is why it is so necessary for preachers to preach doctrinally.[5]

Four rules of thumb will assist the preacher to become a doctrinal preacher. First, preachers should always preach from a 'personal grid' of convictions that guide the entire ministry of the church. These convictions should be written down, plainly and succinctly, communicated to others, and regularly reviewed. When the writer was in seminary, John F. MacArthur Jr. and Gordon MacDonald visited the campus on separate occasions. Both of them spoke about 'non-negotiables' in ministry. The writer wrote down many of their ideas and, in the succeeding years, penned his own non-negotiables (see chart on following pages). These non-negotiables are communicated to new members in the inquirers' class, regularly placed in the newsletter and are referred to often in officer meetings. They form a personal theological framework that becomes the preacher's paradigm for his sermons. They let people know why he preaches as he does, what 'hobby horses' he will ride, and what inflexible convictions guide his overall ministry. True doctrinal preaching flows from the soul of a man who is guided by theological principles in all he does. Every preacher should formulate his own non-negotiables and then live by them.

The second rule of thumb for developing doctrinal preaching is to follow the example of the Reformers and Puritans in preaching through basic catechetical material every few years. The Reformers and Puritans delivered sermon series and wrote books on three great topics basic to Christianity and essential to godly living: the Apostles' Creed, the Lord's Prayer and the Ten Commandments. Such rudimentary material usually comprises the content of the historic evangelical catechisms and is known historically and theologically as 'the Three Formulae'. No minister should ever assume that these three subjects of basic Christian doctrine can ever be known too well or taught too often. The resources and information on each of these topics are absolutely overwhelming. Luther himself preached a series on the Lord's Prayer, preached on it again in his series on Matthew, preached on it a third time in a series on the catechism, wrote two prayer guides using the Lord's Prayer as a model, and wrote hymns for each section of the prayer. The Puritans devoted even more study and developed better resources on the Lord's Prayer than Luther did! The same can be said for the Creed and the Decalogue. John Calvin devotes thorough study to these three topics in his *Institutes of the Christian Religion*. Preachers do their congregations an injustice when they ignore what their forefathers devoted much pulpit time to address. Only the arrogance of post-modernity would assume that people no longer need such basic catechetical teaching and preaching. Michael Horton reminds the church of this very truth:

> Today, most of the cults and sects that have arisen are champions of the 'no creed but Christ' maxim – and with good reason. We have covered this ground before in the controversies of the past: the Mormons are Gnostics; the Jehovah's Witnesses are Arians; and so on. Why should we ignore the successes of the church in the past when facing the same heresies again and again in church history? Beyond the creeds, the church needs to agree on a biblical understanding of the most important matters of faith and life.... Creeds, confessions, and catechisms are not, in the Protestant understanding, in competition with Scripture. They do not violate the principle of *sola Scriptura* but, rather, serve to strengthen it. After all, they are nothing more than the church's carefully thought-out interpretation of the infallible text. My own interpretations may be accurate and even occasionally insightful, but the accumulated wisdom of the church is far richer. We have something to learn about the Bible from those who lived before us, as, Lord willing, those who follow us will have something to learn from our mistakes, controversies, and conclusions. Those who eschew these standards from the past are, in effect, declaring that they are so skilled in the Scriptures that there is nothing they can learn from teachers. One of the first signs of genuine wisdom and education is the recognition that one knows very little. It is this humility that drives one to ask questions, to probe, to read, to examine – in order to learn. But it is a sure sign of ignorance when one dismisses the need to learn from others. Such people are destined to live in a small, dark cell of solitary confinement. What we need desperately right now is greater space, more light, and less

confinement. We need to reconnect ourselves to the communion of the saints and to read the Bible with our spiritual ancestors again. The church must explain the Word of God. Its ministers must proclaim it in preaching, teaching, and pastoral ministry, but to do this responsibly they need to be accountable to the wider body. If creeds, confessions, and catechisms are merely the church's attempt to provide an agreed-upon interpretation of Scripture, we can recover *sola Scriptura* in some fundamental ways.[6]

As a third rule of thumb, the writer suggests that preachers regularly plan for thematic sermon series that devote time to theological subjects. A strong advocate of expository preaching through books, sections and texts of the Scripture, the writer also advocates occasional sermon series on theological subjects. Using Scripture texts and preaching expositorily, preachers should develop from Scripture the great theological themes, essentials and doctrines of the faith. For example, the writer has preached series on 'The Apostles' Creed', 'The Theology of the Cross', 'The Five Pillars of the Reformation,' the Doctrines of Grace (T.U.L.I.P.), 'Baptism,' and the 'Lord's Supper'. These sermon series are designed to help people understand the Reformed Faith, its origins and its basic tenets. They are safeguards against the danger of neo-evangelicalism and its 'mush theology'. Such sermons not only teach basic truths to Christians, but they also communicate that 'theology matters'. Gary L. W. Johnson writes this of theology:

Theology truly mattered for a sixteenth-century monk named Martin Luther. It mattered significantly for all the Reformers. And it mattered for the early Puritans who founded this nation. It also mattered in the struggles with liberalism that our more immediate forefathers engaged in during the earlier decades of our century. But does it matter today? Really? Significantly? Especially among evangelicals who have increasingly become absorbed with the agenda of the popular culture? Theology does matter; indeed, I wish to show that it matters supremely. A healthy Christianity cannot survive without theology, and theology must matter today, especially in our mindless and irrational culture. It should especially matter among evangelicals who confess saving attachment to Jesus Christ. But current challenges to the authority of the biblical gospel often come from within our churches, from practitioners who are increasingly disinterested in serious theology. Efforts to repackage Christian truth into an acceptable 'popular theology' aside, the problem is acute. Yes, theology matters! Whether we are speaking of *how* theology is done according to its various disciplines – exegetical, biblical, systematic, historical, or practical – or how theology speaks to popular culture directly, theology matters! It matters, as a typical Puritan theologian argued, because it is that which enables us to live well unto God. This was once a given in evangelical thought and practice – theology mattered to every true worshiper of the Lord Jesus Christ. William Ames, in a time when theology profoundly mattered, was typical of his era when he contended that theology was for everyone. It was not simply the domain of a small group of academic experts. It was the personal concern of the most humble merchant or homemaker. That was because theology, by its very nature and function, was believed to speak not only to the intellect but also to the common sensus, to human feelings and emotions.[7]

A fourth and final rule of thumb for preaching theologically or doctrinally is that the preacher should often make use of both the Reformed confessions, creeds and catechisms of the church as well as good, reformed systematic theologians. The writer often quotes the *Westminster Standards, Belgic Confession, Heidelberg Catechism, Calvin's Institutes of the Christian Religion* and the systematic theologies of Louis Berkhof, Charles Hodge, Morton Smith, James I. Packer, James Montgomery Boice, R.C. Sproul, David Martyn Lloyd-Jones and others, in addition to works of the Puritans and the Reformers. The assumptions made by preachers that these quotes, references and explanations will be 'over the head' of the man in the pew, smacks of ministerial pride. The writer has preached for fifteen years to common people – some who were actually illiterate and lacked even a high school diploma – and has seen them both understand and appreciate what the fathers and teachers of the faith had to share with them. His suggestion, quite contrary to popular advice for preaching today, is that preachers should worry less about stories, allegories, illustrations, jokes and object lessons and more about insights from the great teachers of the past! The people will thank them for doing so.

One cannot leave the subject of doctrinal preaching without mentioning *evangelistic* preaching. The writer includes this subject under that of doctrine because that is how the Puritans presented the gospel – always in the context of the Dogma of the Church. Or to put it another way, the Puritans preached theology evangelistically! Preachers make a dangerously spurious distinction between doctrine and evangelism, forgetting that the gospel is the first great doctrine that must be grasped and which holds the center of all true biblical theology. 'The Gospel' is that body of theological truth that is found in the Scriptures and that should be applied to sinner and saint alike in a systematic manner. The gospel is more than just 'getting saved'; it is to know God and Christ in every aspect of life (John 17:3).

Preachers often spend too much time trying to sanctify people who have never been justified in the first place. John F. MacArthur has often said that ministers struggle with people's lack of holiness because they approach preaching with misconceptions. Pastors believe it is relatively simple to lead a person to Christ but difficult to sanctify them. In reality, if people were truly converted, sanctification would flow much more naturally from the saving grace in their lives. For this reason, the Puritan preachers preached the gospel 'doctrinally'. That is, they used their preaching and teaching in an evangelistic manner, calling men to Christ as they presented the great truths of the faith. J. I. Packer writes this of Puritan preaching:

> What made Puritan preaching into the reality that it was, however, was less its style than its substance. Puritans preached the Bible systematically and thoroughly, with sustained application to personal life, preaching it as those who believed it, and who sought by their manner to make their matter credible and convincing, convicting and converting.[8]

It can be honestly stated that in all they preached, the Puritans were concerned about the conversion of the lost. Gardiner Spring, one of the last great Puritan preachers of America's Second Great Awakening, once set forth the chief aim of preaching.

> Whatever subordinate ends, therefore, the Christian pulpit may secure in this or the coming world, its legitimate, paramount aim is

the glory of God in the salvation of men. Its great end is one, and only one. If 'the chief end of man is to glorify God, and enjoy him for ever,' the chief end of those who minister his word is to glorify him in that great work with which his manifested glory is most intimately allied. 'Unto me,' says the Apostle, 'who am less than the least of all saints, is this grace given, that I should preach the unsearchable riches of Christ, *to the end* that now unto principalities and powers in heavenly places, might be known, by the church, the manifold wisdom of God.' It is God first, God midst, God last, God everywhere, God exalted in the Gospel of this Son. It is to bring forward, and sustain, and magnify the full claims of the adorable Godhead; so that men who do not know may know him; men who despise may have honourable thoughts of him; men who suspect and slander him may look upon him with a trusting confidence. It is not to make them hypocrites, and induce them to put on the show of friendship, and thus prepare themselves for a greater damnation; it is to prevail upon them truly and honestly to give up their controversy with God, and make peace with him through the blood of his Son.[9]

Puritan pastors realized, more than pastors today do, that their congregations were full of 'wheat and tares', and so they preached to them as such – instructing and evangelizing at the same time. Perkins said this about 'The Use and Application' of preaching:

> Churches with both believers and unbelievers. This is the typical situation in our congregations. Any doctrine may be expounded to them, either from the law or from the gospel, so long as its biblical limitations and circumscriptions are observed (see John 7:37). This was what the prophets did in their sermons, when they announced judgment and destruction on the wicked, and promised deliverance in the Messiah to those who repented. But what if someone in the congregation despairs, when the rest are hardened? What should be done? The answer is: those who are hardened must be made to hear the law circumscribed within the limits of the persons and the sins in view. But the afflicted conscience must be helped to hear the voice of the gospel applied especially to it.[10]

Evangelistic preaching should never be separated from doctrinal preaching, nor should it be trivialized in the least. The writer fears that the preponderance of 'tract evangelism' in this day and age with its four spiritual laws, its steps to peace with God, its keys to fulfillment and its bridge to life tend to conjure up images of a simplistic 'gospel' to which assent is too easily given. The gospel is more than praying a prayer 'to ask Jesus into your heart'. It is a way of life – a conversion process that takes time and leaves in its wake a new creature in Christ (2 Cor. 5:17). Gospel preaching is doctrinal preaching at the most profound and serious level.

Dr. D. Martyn Lloyd-Jones advocated that preachers preach three times a week with three different emphases: evangelistic, experiential and doctrinal instructions:

> But fundamentally I suggest that this man in the pulpit should have that main two-fold division in his mind, and that he must subdivide the second into these two sections – the experimental and the instructional. In other words every preacher should be, as it were, at least three types or kinds of preacher. There is the preaching which is primarily evangelistic. This should take place at least once each week. There is the preaching which is instructional teaching but mainly experimental. That I generally did on a Sunday morning. There is a more purely instructional type of preaching which I personally did on a week night. I would emphasise that these distinctives should not be pressed in too absolute a sense. But for the general guidance of the preacher in his preparation of his message it is good to think of it in that three-fold way – preaching to those who are unbelievers, then preaching to a believer in an experimental manner, and thirdly, in a more directly didactic instructional manner.[11]

Lloyd-Jones is careful to note that both preaching to the unconverted (evangelism) and preaching to the converted (instruction) are theological in content:

> A type of preaching that is sometimes, indeed very frequently today, regarded as non-theological is evangelistic preaching. I well remember how when an evangelistic campaign was being held in London a few years ago, one of the liberal religious weeklies supporting the campaign said, 'Let us have a theological truce while the campaign is on.' It went on to say that after the campaign we must then think

things out and become theological. The idea was that evangelism is non-theological, and to introduce theology at that stage is wrong. You 'bring people to Christ' as they put it; and then you teach them the truth. It is only subsequently that theology comes in. That, to me, is quite wrong, and indeed monstrous. I would be prepared to argue that in many ways evangelistic preaching should be more, rather than less theological, than any other, and for this good reason. Why is it that you call people to repent? Why do you call them to believe the gospel? You cannot deal properly with repentance without dealing with the doctrine of man, the doctrine of the Fall, the doctrine of sin and the wrath of God against sin. Then when you call men to come to Christ and to give themselves to Him, how can you do so without knowing who He is, and on what grounds you invite them to come to Him, and so on. In other words, it is all highly theological. Evangelism which is not theological is not evangelism at all in any true sense. It may be a calling for decisions, it may be a calling on people to come to religion, or to live a better kind of life, or the offering of some psychological benefits; but it cannot by any definition be regarded as Christian evangelism, because there is no true reason for what you are doing apart from these great theological principles. I assert therefore that every type of preaching must be theological, including evangelistic preaching.[12]

In fact, Lloyd-Jones said that he spent more time on preparing evangelistic messages than he did in preparing instructional messages, and confessed that he was, and should be, more diligent in preaching to the lost than in preaching to the saved.

And so, the writer contends, that serious Puritan, doctrinal preaching includes preaching that is evangelistic and theological. He has found that the most fruitful evangelistic preaching occurs, not in special 'evangelistic messages', but rather in the course of the doctrinal preaching from week to week. The writer once witnessed a young woman converted at a Christmas Eve communion service, as he fenced the table and explained the difference between a believer and a nominal Christian. Years ago, in a previous charge, while preaching through Ephesians 5:22-33 on marriage, two couples engaged in a web of adultery began to come to repentance. Over the span of a year, all four adults were converted to Christ and one eventually became a deacon in the church. As the writer preached through First Corinthians at Trinity Church, a young Roman Catholic man was converted when he saw, over the span of several weeks, how the Reformed Faith made such 'good sense' to him. Several years ago, after a sermon in a series on the Apostles' Creed, a seventy-five-year-old man met the writer at the back door, tears streaming down his cheeks, as he exclaimed, 'I have been in church all my life, but I have never understood about Christ until today!' All of these people have seemingly been converted, not through the agency of special evangelistic services or messages 'aimed' at the lost, but rather by means of 'doctrinal preaching', week in and week out.

The writer usually preaches a simpler, more fundamental, and more evangelistic sermon series at the Sunday morning services when he knows there will be more visitors, more nominal Christians, and more unconverted souls. He preaches the series that are more experiential and doctrinal on Sunday evenings when he aims principally at those who he assumes are more committed Christians. Dr. Martyn Lloyd-Jones did the reverse: evangelism on Sunday evening, edification on Sunday morning. In the British culture of his day, visitors came more in the evening than on the Lord's Day morning. The point is simply that the preacher must adjust his evangelistic thrust to that time and place in his context that affords a greater exposure to unconverted and unchurched listeners. But in both instances, he preaches 'doctrinally' and leaves the converting and edifying work to the Holy Spirit.

This discussion of 'doctrinal preaching' is best summarized by listing the six benefits of such preaching set forth by J. A. Howe:

(1) It can be claimed for doctrinal preaching that it brings the characteristic truths of the Gospel to the public mind, and makes clear to it the incomparable system of truth revealed by Christ. (2) As a further reason for doctrinal preaching it may be pleaded that it not only advertises the faith, but also has a direct effect upon the church to make it intelligent in its faith. (3) Doctrinal preaching tends to awaken religious conviction. (4) It may also be pleaded for doctrinal preaching that it works for stability of character in the church. (5) Doctrinal preaching claims to excite interest in the ministrations of the pulpit. (6) The foregoing claims for doctrinal

preaching flow on to another; namely, that doctrinal preaching maintains, as no other class of pulpit themes can do, the influence of the pulpit in society.[13]

ENDNOTES

1. Packer, 1990, 284-85.
2. Stott, 1982, 116-24.
3. Lischer, 1981, 13-22.
4. Lloyd-Jones, 1971, 37.
5. See Spurgeon, 1990, 72-83.
6. Horton, in Armstrong, 1996, 250-51.
7. Johnson in Armstrong, 1996, 57.
8. Packer, 1990, 280.
9. Spring, 1986, 88.
10. Perkins, 1996, 62-63.
11. Lloyd-Jones, 1971, 63; see Sargent, 1994, 250-56.
12. Lloyd-Jones, 1971, 65.
13. Howe, 1900, 181-96.

Chapter 10

Ethical Preaching

One final category of Puritan sermon content that needs to be examined is ethical preaching. The writer has labeled this category in that way following the Apostle Paul's own pattern. Paul often divides his epistles into two parts: the first part being doctrinal instruction and the second part being ethical instruction. A partial survey of Paul's epistles will reveal this subject division:

Book	Doctrinal Instruction	Ethical Instruction
Romans	1–11	12–16
1 Corinthians	1–4, 15	5–14,16
Galatians	1–4	5, 6
Ephesians	1–3	4–6
Colossians	1–2	3–4
2 Thessalonians	1–2	3

These 'ethical instructions' generally include matters of discipleship, Christian ethics, controversial issues, matters of character and conduct, and growth in holiness. Preachers must never forget that the vast majority of the Christian life is spent in the process of sanctification. Preaching must therefore frankly and faithfully deal with the issues and problems facing the people in the pew. This insipid brand of Christianity infecting today's churches in which a person can be 'saved' but never challenged to be sanctified is not only harmful to the soul, but also terribly dishonest – there is serious doubt that the unsanctified soul is a saved soul at all! (Heb. 12:14-16).

The Puritan preachers realized that once a soul was converted ninety-nine percent of the work of preparing that soul for heaven lay before the minister of the gospel. Hence, the Puritan preachers were 'experimental preachers' (i.e. experiential in approach). They were concerned with living the faith one professed. J. I. Packer describes this experiential, ethical, disciple-making preaching in these words:

> Puritan preaching was *experimental in interests*. The preachers' supreme concern was to bring men to know God. Their preaching was avowedly 'practical' and concerned with experience of God. Sin, the cross, Christ's heavenly ministry, the Holy Spirit, faith and hypocrisy, assurance and the lack of it, prayer, meditation, temptation, mortification, growth in grace, death, heaven were their constant themes. Bunyan's *Pilgrim's Progress* serves as a kind of gazetteer to the contents of their sermons. In their treatment of these matters they were deep, thorough, and authoritative. They spoke as holy experienced Christians who knew what they were talking about. Their rule was formulated by David Dickson when he charged a young minister at his ordination to study two books together: the Bible, and his own heart. The Puritans made it a matter of conscience to prove for themselves the saving power of the gospel they urged on others. They knew that, as John Owen put it, 'a man preacheth that sermon only well to others, which preacheth itself in his own soul.... If the word do not dwell with power *in* us, it will not pass with power *from* us.' Robert Bolton was not the only one who 'never taught any godly point, but he first wrought it on his owne heart.'... Their strenuous exercise in meditation and prayer, their sensitiveness to sin, their utter humility, their passion for holiness, and their glowing devotion to Christ equipped them to be master-physicians of the soul. And deep called to deep when they preached, for they spoke of the black depths and high peaks of Christian experience first-hand. An old Christian who heard young Spurgeon, still in his teens, said of him, almost in awe, 'he was as experimental as if he were a hundred years old in faith.' That was a mark of all Puritan preaching.[1]

Pastors of declining churches would do well to follow the Puritan example of ethical, 'experimental' preaching that concerned itself with holiness of both character and conduct. This is necessary because the lesson of the last of the five of the troubled churches of Asia Minor, in the book of Revelation, is a lesson about an immoral, worldly, apostate church whose unholy ways grieved the Lord deeply – the church of Thyatira.

> And to the angel of the church in Thyatira write: The Son of God, who has eyes like a flame of fire, and His feet are like burnished bronze, says this: 'I know your deeds, and your love and faith and service and perseverance, and that your deeds of late are greater than at first. But I have this against you, that you tolerate the woman Jezebel, who calls herself a prophetess, and she teaches and leads My bond-servants astray, so that they commit acts of immorality and eat things sacrificed to idols. And I gave her time to repent; and she does not want to repent of her immorality. Behold, I will cast her upon a bed of sickness, and those who commit adultery with her into great tribulation, unless they repent of her deeds. And I will kill her children with pestilence; and all the churches will know that I am He who searches the minds and hearts; and I will give to each one of you according to your deeds. But I say to you, the rest who are in Thyatira, who do not hold this teaching, who have not known the deep things of Satan, as they call them – I place no other burden on you. Nevertheless what you have, hold fast until I come. And he who overcomes, and he who keeps My deeds until the end, to him I will give authority over the nations; and he shall rule them with a rod of iron, as the vessels of the potter are broken to pieces, as I also have received authority from My Father; and I will give him the morning star. He who has an ear, let him hear what the Spirit says to the churches' (Rev. 2:18-29).

A lack of strong preaching, the loss of gospel purity and the failures of spiritual leadership invariably take their toll on the ethical, moral and spiritual life of a church. All kinds of 'Jezebels' find their way into the church and spread their unholy wares before unprotected sheep. The results are tragic: the lack of church discipline, profanation of the Sabbath day, unbiblical divorces and remarriages, sexual immorality, abortions and a general disregard for oaths, vows and biblical commitments, just to name a few.

As much as preachers may be ridiculed by others as 'puritanical', it is their duty to seek for genuine holiness in the lives of their people and to be about the business of constantly encouraging consistency of holy living. Those who would follow the pattern of Puritan preaching cannot ignore the blatant disobedience, the carnal living, and the low morals of a people who have been neglected by shepherds and have fed for years on ragweed, brambles and poison vines, even acquiring a taste for such rubbish while developing spiritual immunities to their toxic effects.

The church as the 'pillar and support of the truth' (1 Tim. 3:14-16) must devote itself to the 'mystery of godliness' – Christ, the Holy One alive in men to make them holy. Irvonwy Morgan speaks of this mystery of godliness as the great object of all true Puritan preaching:

> So the mystery of godliness is how can a man free himself from the vanity and emptiness and boredom of the world and fit himself to live with the saints and angels in heaven? The answer of the Godly Preacher to this was that faith or conversion was not enough by itself, only faith and a godly life could bring a man to heaven. Conversion was the first sign that a man was one of the elect, one of the saints chosen by God out of a corrupt and damned world. But conversion must be followed by the effort of the convert to make his election sure through daily victory in the constant warfare between the flesh and the spirit in his own nature. The struggle would one day be crowned with glory in the final perseverance of the saints.[2]

With this focus in mind, preaching for revitalization necessitates that sermons on the challenges, struggles, questions and issues of 'Christian living here and now' be regularly preached. Notice that the earlier survey of Puritan preaching revealed that more than a third (34%) of all Puritan sermons were ethical in content and thrust.

Preachers cannot ignore the fact that the ethical and spiritual level of Christianity in the West is in decline. Abortions, homosexuality, feminism, gambling, alcoholism, drug abuse, infidelity, pornography and other abominations are issues believers struggle to face biblically. In addition to these contemporary issues in society, the average Christian struggles also with declining spirituality, neglect of the means of grace, and ignorance of the disciplines of growth that have traditionally strengthened believers.

The writer has deliberately chosen to preach through sermon series that were practical and inspirational, encouraging the flock to press on toward holiness and growth. Some series dealt with the ethical and experiential issues of faith, spirituality, troubles, providence, sexuality and growing in grace. Other series tackled the issues of divorce and remarriage, tongues, church discipline, civil disobedience, persecution, relationships between generations in the church, and so forth.

Two notes of caution are in order when preaching ethical sermons. First, they should address issues – especially controversial issues – in the context of the epistle or book in which they are found in Scripture. Second, they should not be avoided because of cowardice and anxiety. These are biblical issues to be handled in the regular course of biblical preaching. To preach through the New Testament epistles without teaching thoroughly about submission of wives to husbands, discipline of children, tithing, sexual restraint, the ordination of women, working mothers and their priorities, is truly unfaithful and displays a self-centered concern for one's own comfort rather than a pastoral love for the saints and concern for their souls, families and lives.

In the early decades of the twentieth century the evangelical church struggled with doctrinal issues. These were the years of the Modernist vs. Fundamentalist controversies. Liberalism sought to gut the Bible of the miraculous and the revelatory, as Fundamentalism fought back to preserve the belief in the inspiration and authority of Scripture. Evangelicalism won that 'Battle for the Bible'. In the process, however, something greater was lost.

While battling for the integrity of Scripture, the evangelical church lost its integrity of witness. Because they worried over numbers – who had more members – trying to validate their message by their membership, the evangelicals compromised on ethical and discipleship issues in order to gain and hold on to their members. Soon they began to waffle on issues of women's ordination, divorce, abortion, gambling and even homosexuality. Things that would have led to excommunication from any evangelical church in 1920 came to be tolerated among both the laity and clergy in 1970, just a half-century later.

Men who were champions in defending the literal and the intended meaning of Scripture when it states that God 'desires all men to be saved' began to play word games when, eight verses later, the same Pauline epistle said, 'I do not allow a woman to teach or exercise authority over a man.' The Bible was timelessly true on salvation but culturally bound on women's ordination?

In speaking about just such an issue, Wayne Grudem made the following comment:

> The greatest doctrinal controversy is already here: the question of the role of women in the church and of male-female roles in marriage.
>
> The church and the family are really threatened by feminist viewpoints coming into the church. Unless God intervenes, I fear that there will be a large conflict. It could very well become a source of major division among evangelicals.
>
> If evangelicals cannot come to a clear resolution on this issue, where the Bible speaks so clearly, the same principles of interpretation will be applied to other areas. The door will be open to compromise on many issues.
>
> This may be the first time in the history of the church that Christians are engaged in a major controversy over an *ethical* issue, as opposed to a *doctrinal* issue. The moral teachings of Scripture are so clear, Christians haven't been in conflict with each other over them. But now there is a tremendous onslaught of secular culture, combined with evangelicals who are using all their sophisticated exegetical skills to prove the feminist positions.[3]

Agreeing with Grudem is the late James Montgomery Boice. Those of us who had the privilege of speaking with him and hearing him regularly preach in the closing years of his life and ministry can remember his frequent concerns about the worldliness of the twentieth century evangelical church. When he was an associate editor for *Christianity Today*, in the late 1960's, Boice would often comment on the worldliness and corruption of liberal churches. He came to see that some thirty years later he was commenting in his sermons and books about the same worldliness, but this time he was addressing the comments to his own church, his own denomination and to American evangelicals! Here is what he said:

What has hit me like a thunderbolt in recent years is the discovery that what I had been saying about the liberal churches at the end of the 1960s and in the '70s now needs to be said about evangelical churches too.

Can it be that evangelicals, who have always opposed liberalism and its methods, have now also fixed their eyes on a worldly kingdom and have made politics and money their weapons of choice for winning it? I think they have. About ten years ago Martin Marty, always a shrewd observer of the American church, said in a magazine interview that, in his judgment, by the end of the century evangelicals would be 'the most worldly people in America.' He was exactly on target when he said that, except that he was probably a bit too cautious. Evangelicals fulfilled his prophecy before the turn of the millennium.[4]

How does this come to pass? There is no mystery here. God's Word warns us that when we preachers falter in proclaiming and applying any portion of Scripture we cause our people to pay a horrible price. The process goes like this: Ministers become intimidated by the surrounding culture (the world) and what they press and push for. Soon the pulpit becomes silent about an unpopular stand the Scripture takes on a popular position of the world (e.g. feminism, women's ordination, abortion, homosexual unions, etc.). An unspoken but understood contract takes place between preacher and people: If he avoids unpopular stands on ethical issues, they will support and affirm him. If not, then he will pay a price! The preacher then caves in to politically correct pressure. When he graduated from seminary several decades ago he clearly saw that ordaining women, 'no fault' divorce, abortion and issues of gender confusion were sin. But now, due to pressure he invents exegetical escape clauses and uses hermeneutical gymnastics to avoid condemning what God condemns but men condone. He fails to be a true prophet of God.

The people know this – no one is really fooled. The people are not stupid. So they push even harder in the next generation in order to avoid the confinements and censures of Holy Writ. The preachers back up even further. Eventually the people reason this way: 'If the ordination of women is so obvious and we do it anyway; if abortion is murder but no one in the church is disciplined when she gets one;

if divorce is never disallowed under any circumstances; and if the pastors can commit adultery and keep their positions of leadership; then if I want to live in a homosexual relationship who is there to tell me I should not?' A dear price is paid when the pulpit remains silent on ethical issues!

Evangelical preachers think the Gospel is more important than the Law. Reformed preachers believe that dogmatics is more important than ethics. Most pastors assume that 'good doctrine leads to good living'. They are all mistaken. Good living comes from the preaching, teaching and application of Biblical ethics. When we fail to preach on ethical issues – clearly, compellingly, courageously – we rob our congregations of one of the three Biblical hedges God places around his sheep for their protection. We historically refer to these hedges as 'the marks of a true church'. They are (1) the true preaching of God's Word, (2) the proper administration of the sacraments, and (3) the faithful use of church discipline. In other words, the true church is surrounded by Biblical doctrine, Biblical worship and Biblical ethics.

When the evangelical preachers remained silent back in the early 1970s in America, as the debate over legalized abortion heated up, the Church failed the people and guaranteed the legalization of murder in America. Only the Roman Catholic Church spoke out in opposition. When state after state endorsed and instituted state lotteries, and then permitted casino gambling, the evangelical pulpit was silent. Gambling is now America's number one addiction. Only the Catholic bishops wrote pastoral letters of protest and pastoral guidance. In the present debate on same-sex marriages the reformed denominations have said nothing – not a word. How can they? It is but a short distance from ordaining women to a woman's right to abortion; from an adulterous divorce to a lesbian 'marriage'; from a pedophile priest to an adulterous pastor to a homosexual relationship. They are all connected in God's Word and therefore ought to be connected in the preacher's exposition of 'the full counsel of God' (Acts 20:27).

The twentieth century began with a debate about doctrine: the inerrancy of Scripture, the deity of Christ, the miracles of the Bible and the reality of the resurrection. It ended with a concern about ethics: sexuality, life in the womb, gender roles and the future of marriage and family. The twenty-first century has begun with an open forum on the basic issues of human existence: Does God really care if male and female procreate in a bonded-union known as a marriage? Will the evangelical and reformed preaching remain silent for another century? Let us pray that our men in the pulpit will break their cowardly silence.

The Scripture is meant to be applied to lives. Declining churches, however, are used to vague sermons with no more force than 'let's be nice and do good', because tact is prized above truth and propriety above principle. The preacher who seeks for revitalization in his church must remember this truth that burned through the souls of the Puritan preachers into the hearts and minds of their congregations: the cause of truth is always more important than its consequences. Preachers cannot avoid controversy, angry congregants, loss of members and conflict among leadership if they are called to preach ethical, moral and disciplinary truths to people who have never been taught these things. But this very task is set before revitalizing pastors by God as a sacred duty that must not be shirked.

ENDNOTES

1. Packer, 1990, 286.
2. Morgan, 1965, 111-12.
3. Grudem, 1990, 11-12.
4. Boice, 2001, 23-24.

Review of Chapters 5–10

Puritan preaching that revitalized congregation after congregation and brought Revival to the church as well as Awakening to various lands is a balanced preaching comprised of Christological, ecclesiastical, missiological, doctrinal and ethical preaching. This balanced, spiritual diet slowly but surely causes the saints to grow strong in faith. Unpopular as it always is at first, eventually it leaves the saints with an appetite for no other kind of preaching. Revitalizing pastors must remember that this process of renewal in a church does not come easily or quickly. Over time, it is assured by the balanced, biblical and deliberate content of such preaching.

The 'godly preachers' maintained this Biblical balance by preaching systematically through the Bible. Did they consciously realize that they were addressing the issues confronting the churches of the Book of Revelation: Ephesus' loss of a love for Christ, Sardis' need for renewed ecclesiastical vitality, Pergamum's need for doctrinal purity, Thyatira's unethical living and Laodicea's need for zeal in mission? Perhaps they did; after all, these Puritan preachers knew the Word of God from front to back, from Genesis to Revelation. More than likely they addressed the issues set before us in Revelation 2 and 3 because they worked expositorily through books of the Bible, where the Holy Spirit addresses the issue of Christ, the Church, the Great Commission, theology and ethics. Biblical preaching is naturally balanced preaching; its content is full-orbed and comprehensive.

Granted there is more to preaching than just the content of the sermon, but the subject matter of the sermon is the critical mass of the issue. What is preached is more important than anything else in preaching. Attention will now be given to these other elements of preaching, but not without a final reminder that balanced and biblical content in pulpits makes for balanced and biblical saints in the pew.

Part Three

The Characteristics
of Puritan Preaching

Chapter 11

The Puritan Ethos

An ethos to preaching existed in the age of the Reformers and Puritans that has been lost in modern times. Many admit that the life of the sermon, in its present form, may well be on its last leg, gasping for life-sustaining air in these days of mass communication.

> The prophets of doom in today's Church are confidently predicting that the day of preaching is over. It is a dying art, they say, an outmoded form of communication, 'an echo from an abandoned past.' Not only have modern media superseded it, but it is incompatible with the modern mood. Consequently, the sermon no longer enjoys the honour which used to be accorded to it and which was expressed in the quotations collected in Chapter One. Even 'sermon-tasting,' a reprehensible kind of ecclesiastical pub-crawling, which involves erratic churchgoing merely with a view to sampling and subsequently comparing the eminent preachers of the day, has gone out of vogue. Books of sermons, once popular, have become a risky publishing venture. In some churches the sermon is reduced to an apologetic five minutes; in others it has been replaced by either a 'dialogue' or a 'happening.'[1]

Preaching has become undervalued and overlooked in modern ecclesiology for several reasons. Some of these reasons were addressed earlier, in particular the influence of management and marketing approaches of the church growth movement. In fairness to that movement, it must be admitted that long before Donald McGavran, C. Peter Wagner, Win Arn, George Barna, and other church growth specialists published their ideas, the sermon had already lost its preeminent place in worship and its priority in pastoral ministry. As Niebuhr, Williams and Ahlstrom have pointed out, this decline of preaching in the church is rooted in the minister's loss of vision and direction for the ministry. Pastors simply appear unable to discern what expectations should be fulfilled in their ministries.

This common root problem has often been referred to by others in terms of 'preaching without soul', 'hollow men with hollow ministries', or even 'the lack of a divine center in the ministry'. Younger men in the ministry today are more concerned about 'success' than godliness and faithfulness. Preaching requires sustained and tedious effort over many years in order to reap significant and measurable harvests; it often cannot be calculated or observed in its effect because the results occur in the realm of the spirit. Unless the pastors who preach are profoundly spiritual in their orientation, then preaching will continue to be devalued and will eventually be disposed of altogether.

Modern culture mitigates against just such an approach to ministry overall and preaching in particular. This is a fast-paced age of instant information, quick fixes, spontaneous feedback, and direct results. John Stott explains that a number of powerful forces are working against preaching in the modern age. He summarizes these forces in three major categories:

1. *The Anti-Authority Mood* permeates the culture and mitigates against anyone 'telling' anyone else what to do, how to do it and when to do it.

2. *The Cybernetics Revolution* of television, electronics, computers, the mass media and ever-developing advances in communication techniques work against the audio-centered nature of preaching. In short, people are not very good listeners anymore. The age of visual and interactive communication has hindered preaching.

3. *The church's loss of confidence in the gospel* has caused the loss of vision and vitality in the pulpit and led the church to trust in sociological, psychological, managerial and political methods to accomplish an increasingly foggy mission.[2]

Although these three great problems face contemporary Christian ministry, they by no means relegate preaching to the archives of ecclesiastical history, nor do they make modern pulpiteers into dinosaurs. They simply challenge them to counteract these forces with a resurgence of biblical, reformed, Puritan and expository preaching.

> The anti-authority mood makes people unwilling to listen, addiction of television makes them unable to do so, and the contemporary atmosphere of doubt makes many preachers both unwilling and unable to speak. Thus there is paralysis at both ends, in the speaking and in the hearing. A dumb preacher with a deaf congregation presents a fearsome barrier to communication. So completely have these problems undermined the morale of some preachers that they have given up altogether. Others struggle on, but have lost heart. Indeed, all of us have been affected by the negative arguments, even if there are counter-arguments which we have begun to deploy. The best form of defence, however, is attack.... I propose to go over to the offensive and to argue theologically for the indispensable and permanent place of preaching in the purpose of God for his Church.[3]

This study of Reformed and Puritan preaching will yield an answer for what can be done to recapture the soul of preaching and return a sense of power, dignity and purpose to the ethos of the pulpit. The hypothesis is simple: certain characteristics of revitalizing preaching that will positively affect the ethos of one's preaching can be deduced from the study of Reformation and Puritan preaching. The purpose of chapters 12 to 15 is to study just such characteristics.

The Puritan and Reformed Ethos of Preaching

There is a certain personality to the reformed and Puritan pulpit. Or to put it another way, Puritan preaching has a 'flavor' all its own. Puritan preaching, growing out of the preaching of the Reformers,[4] has had 'bad press', and the modern person has been left with visions of a mean-spirited, witch-hunting, shrivel-souled man railing at a beleaguered congregation about insignificant issues, in a lengthy but boring manner that pushes people away from churches in droves.[5] Nothing could be further from the truth. Surely some Puritan preaching was like that. But to characterize all Puritan preaching as such is not only historically inaccurate but intellectually dishonest. It would be like taking any movement of history and judging the entire scope of its life by the final moments of its decline. This tendency toward inaccurate caricature is a most despicable form of revisionistic history. This has been done in blaming Luther and Lutherans for Nazi Germany and the Jewish Holocaust, in characterizing the Southern United States as 'a people who have never outgrown the Civil War', and in stereotyping the African-American people as a race of men possessing a 'slave mentality'. These are most abhorrent stigmatizations that do great injustice to groups of noble people. The same can be said of the modern attitude toward 'Puritanical' preaching.

Puritan preaching indeed had its own ethos, influenced by the Protestant Reformation, shaped by the doctrines of grace, and defined by regulative and theological terms of Presbyterian and Reformed church standards. The historic and definitive *Westminster Directory for the Public Worship of God* and its daughter document *The Book of Church Order of the Presbyterian Church in America* both set forth, in clear and compelling language, the guiding principles of Puritan preaching.

But the Servant of Christ, whatever his Method be, is to perform his whole Ministry, 1. Painfully, not doing the Work of the Lord negligently. 2. Plainly, that the meanest may understand; delivering the Truth, not in the enticing Words of Man's Wisdom, but in Demonstration of the Spirit and of Power, lest the Cross of Christ should be made of none Effect; abstaining also from an unprofitable Use of unknown Tongues, strange Phrases, and Cadences of Sounds and Words, sparingly citing Sentences of Ecclesiastical or other Human Writers, ancient or modern, be they never so elegant. 3. Faithfully, looking at the Honour of Christ, the Conversion, Edification and Salvation of the People, not at his own Gain or Glory; keeping nothing back which may promote those holy Ends, giving to every one his own Portion, and bearing indifferent Respect unto all, without neglecting the Meanest, or sparing the Greatest in their Sins. 4. Wisely, framing all his Doctrines, Exhortations, and especially his Reproofs, in such a Manner as may be most likely to prevail, shewing all due Respect to each Man's Person or Place, and not mixing his own Passion or Bitterness. 5. Gravely, as becometh the Word of God, shunning all such Gesture, Voice and Expressions, as may occasion the Corruptions of Men to despise him and his Ministry. 6. With loving Affection, that the People may see all coming from his godly Zeal, and hearty Desire to do them good, And, 7. As taught of God, and persuaded in his own Heart, that all that he teacheth, is the Truth of Christ; and walking before his Flock, as an Example to them in it; earnestly, both in Private and Publick, recommending his Labours to the Blessing of God, and watchfully looking to himself, and the Flock whereof the Lord hath made him Overseer: So shall the Doctrine of Truth be preserved uncorrupt, many Souls converted and built up, and himself receive manifold Comforts of his Labours even in this Life, and afterward the Crown of Glory laid up for him in the World to come.[6]

The preaching of the Word is an ordinance of God for the salvation of men. Serious attention should be paid to the manner in which it is done. The minister should apply himself to it with diligence and prove himself a 'worker who does not need to be ashamed, rightly dividing the word of truth' (2 Tim. 2:15).... Preaching requires much study, meditation and prayer, and ministers should prepare their sermons with care, and not indulge themselves in loose, extemporary harangues, nor serve God with that which costs them naught. They should, however, keep to the simplicity of the Gospel, and express themselves in language that can be understood by all. They should also by their lives adorn the Gospel which they preach, and be examples to believers in word and deed.[7]

Perhaps no one has set forth the very heartbeat of Puritan preaching so eloquently and yet so plainly as Richard Baxter. The Puritan minister at the Anglican Church in Kidderminster, England, for fourteen years, Baxter professed to have found his congregation ignorant, scandalous and indifferent to religion when he arrived. His combination of personal pastoral ministry and diligent preaching transformed that congregation; a great ministry of revitalization took place. In his classic book *The Reformed Pastor*, Baxter writes to other ministers about ministry. His charge concerning pastoral ministry and preaching captures the heart of the Puritan pulpit:

O brethren! what men should we be in skill, resolution, and unwearied diligence, who have all this to do? Did Paul cry out, 'Who is sufficient for these things?' And shall we be proud, or careless, or lazy, as if we were sufficient? As Peter saith to every Christian, in consideration of our great approaching change, 'What manner of persons ought we to be in all holy conversation and godliness!' so may I say to every minister, 'Seeing all these things lie upon our hands, what manner of persons ought we to be in all holy endeavours and resolutions for our work!' This is not a burden for the shoulders of a child. What skill doth every part of our work require! – and of how much moment is every part! To preach a sermon, I think, is not the hardest part; and yet what skill is necessary to make the truth plain; to convince the hearers, to let irresistible light into their consciences, and to keep it there, and drive all home; to screw the truth into their minds, and work Christ into their affections; to meet every objection and clearly to resolve it; to drive sinners to a stand, and make them see that there is no hope, but that they must unavoidably either be converted or condemned - and to do all this, as regards language and manner, as beseems our work, and yet as is most suitable to the capacities of our hearers. This, and a great deal more that should be done in every sermon, must surely require a great deal of holy skill.[8]

In analyzing the characteristics of Puritan and reformed preaching to gain an appreciation of its ethos, preachers can discover similar characteristics pointed out by various authors as they study the Puritan pulpit. The writer considered several writers of Puritan preaching in order to find the prominent characteristics. In the following four chapters the writer will discuss these various characteristics, devoting a chapter to each: spiritual preaching, romantic preaching, controversial preaching, and camaraderie in preaching. The *content* of Puritan preaching has already been discussed in detail in previous chapters, therefore the writer will not comment here upon such matters as the doctrinal, evangelistic or applicatory aspects of preaching.

ENDNOTES

1. Stott, 1982, 50.
2. Stott, 1982, 50-89.

3. Stott, 1982, 89.

4. Adair, 1986, 55-56.

5. Packer, 1990, 280.

6. *Directory*, 1880, 20-21.

7. *Book of Church Order*, PCA, 53-1, 3.

8. Baxter, 1974, 69-70.

9. Some of these writers were themselves Puritans (Bridges and Perkins) while others are merely students of the Puritans. A total of eight sources were used to develop an assessment of the Puritan pulpit's character. Those resources include the following:

1. William Perkins, *The Art of Prophesying* (originally published in 1592)

2. Charles Bridges, *The Christian Ministry* (first published in 1830)

3. Irvonwy Morgan, *The Godly Preachers of the Elizabethan Church* (1965)

4. D. Martyn Lloyd-Jones, *The Puritans*, "Preaching" (a lecture at the Westminster Ministers Conference, 1972)

5. Peter Lewis, *The Genius of Puritanism* (1979)

6. Leland Ryken, *Worldly Saints: The Puritans as They Really Were* (1986)

7. John Piper, *The Supremacy of God in Preaching*, a study of the preaching of Jonathan Edwards (1990)

8. James I. Packer, *A Quest for Godliness: The Puritan Vision of the Christian Life* (1990).

Chapter 12

Spiritual Preaching

Irvonwy Morgan states that the first general characteristic of Puritan preaching was that it was 'spiritual preaching'.[1] He calls the Puritan preachers 'the Godly Preachers', borrowing that noble title from John Foxe and his classic book *The Acts and Monuments of the Christian Martyrs*.

By 'spiritual preaching', Morgan means that the sermons were evangelistic, scriptural, doctrinal, clear and unpretentious. They were sermons about true religion of the heart rather than mere ceremonial religion. These messages of the 'Godly Preachers' were a stark contrast to the witty, academic, ceremonial and humanistic lectures of the day. Puritan preaching was diametrically opposed to this typical preaching.

The Puritan sermon was spiritual both in content and in delivery. It caused great distress to the Puritan preachers. 'This contrast between ceremonial religion and spiritual religion was one of the chief causes of the quarrel between the Godly Preachers and the Established Church.'[2] The Puritans were ridiculed, expelled from pulpits, imprisoned and eventually martyred. The very nature of this spiritual struggle bears testimony to the Reformed conviction that preaching was a spiritual work to be done in the Spirit.

The ethos of this spiritual preaching is clearly described in another work by Irvonwy Morgan that is entitled *Puritan Spirituality*:

> The Puritan Preachers, on the other hand, thought of religion as confrontation rather than contemplation, the confrontation of sinful man with a righteous God.... the Puritan Preacher was not at home

with humanism which seemed to exalt man above his stature; nor was he terribly interested in Renaissance thinking, since to him, it was mere human knowledge, valuable but not to be intruded into an exposition of the Word. It was the Word that mattered and its spiritual nature had to be spiritually discerned.... The calling, justification, sanctification and glorification of the elect was the work of the Spirit, and the purpose of preaching was not only to expound this methodology of Salvation, but much more to expose the working of the Holy Spirit in the human heart. Election was assured to those who were fighting the battle of the spiritual world and it was to identify this battle in the human soul and to enumerate the helps that the Saint received by Grace that was the aim of the Preacher.... The spiritual man can see the vanity of things so admired by others, he can taste things nature does not relish, he has reasons beyond the reasons of the flesh for his attitude, and if he persevered in holy living he would receive his reward in heaven.... To make you know yourselves better than before, this was the purpose of Puritan preaching, that man should see himself as he really is with his pride stripped from him, his ambitions exposed as selfish egotism, his religion an empty form. When the Puritan preacher had finished with man there was not much left of him to glory in.[3]

The nature of this kind of preaching evolved from sincere and deeply held convictions of the Calvinistic religion. The Puritans saw all of life from a spiritual perspective, and therefore the most important issues of life were always the great doctrines of the Reformed Faith. These were not academic concepts to be bantered about by theologians and then left to gather dust on library bookshelves, but truths to be spiritually preached into the souls of men.

This emphasis on religion as spiritual and not ceremonial was a marked characteristic of godly preaching, and in time the Preachers came to be known as 'spiritual preachers' in contrast to the 'witty' preaching of their opponents. To survive, the Godly Preachers had to impress the multitude upon whom they depended for their personal support and maintenance. They not only had to be understood by the people, but they had to stir their emotions, touch their imaginations, convert them to the Lord, save them from sin and death and hell, help them to discern the striving of the Spirit in their hearts as they struggled to make good their 'election,' and point them to the true end of man which was to glorify God and to enjoy Him forever.... They found in the Bible all they needed of excitement and adventure in soul-searching, and all framed within the great biblical epic of man's fall and his redemption in Christ.... It was the Gospel-preaching aiming at the conversion of men from a life of sin to a life of righteousness set in a framework of a spiritual struggle.... Their spiritual religion was not a passive affair, but a war, a war against Satan, superstition, and the sins of the flesh, for which they were to put on the whole armour of God and 'walk boldly in the light as valiant and faithful soldiers of almighty God.'... It was the conception of religion as spiritual that gave the Puritans their distrust of ceremonial religion for it was impossible to make captive the wind of the Spirit and dispense it through set prayers and sacraments.... Yet a religion cannot be so spiritual that it loses all contact with sinful men, and it was the Calvinist interpretation of the great epic of the fall and redemption of man which anchored this spiritual religion firmly in an intelligible framework. It was a romantic framework, but within it the movements of the Spirit were discernible and even predictable.[4]

This spiritual mindset was the legacy of the great Reformers, found most purely in the heart, life and ministry of the father of the Reformation, Martin Luther, whose spiritual stepchildren were the Puritans.[5] Luther was a profoundly spiritual man, a pristinely 'religious' man – a term most preachers would not want applied to themselves today. And yet, Roland H. Bainton in his definitive biography of Luther, *Here I Stand*, describes the genius and soul of the Reformer, his Reformation and the Protestant movement as a spiritual force in the world:

> Luther's principles in religion and ethics alike must constantly be borne in mind if he is not at times to appear unintelligible and even petty. The primary consideration with him was always the pre-eminence of religion. Into a society where the lesser breed were given to gaming, roistering, and wenching – the Diet of Worms was called a veritable Venusberg - at a time when the choicer sort were glorifying in the accomplishments of man, strode this Luther, entranced by the song of angels, stunned by the wrath of God, speechless before the

wonder of creation, lyrical over the divine mercy, a man aflame with God. For such a person there was no question which mattered much save this: How do I stand before God? Luther would never shirk a mundane task such as exhorting the elector to repair the city wall to keep the peasants' pigs from rooting in the villagers' gardens, but he was never supremely concerned about pigs, gardens, walls, cities, princes, or any and all of the blessings and nuisances of this mortal life. The ultimate problem was always God and man's relationship to God. For this reason political and social forms were to him a matter of comparative indifference. Whatever would foster the understanding, dissemination, and practice of God's Word should be encouraged, and whatever impeded must be opposed. This is why it is futile to inquire whether Luther was a democrat, aristocrat, autocrat, or anything else. Religion was for him the chief end of man, and all else peripheral.[6]

What is most profoundly lacking in modern preaching is this sense of 'the spiritual' or 'the religious' as the all-consuming, driving and life-shaping force of life. It truly cannot be said of the modern evangelical minister that 'the primary consideration with him was always the pre-eminence of religion'. Any minister who regularly has lunch with fellow pastors will testify that the primary conversation centers around building programs, church politics, pastoral moves, and the latest program designed to increase giving and membership. Spiritual preaching has suffered because of a lack of spirituality in today's preachers! No longer is there a sense of the great importance of religion and its timeless truths. Donald Coggan succinctly summarizes the problem:

> Preachers will go to their task as regularly as before – is it not ancient custom that from the pulpit, twice on Sunday, at least a few words should be spoken, probably attached, even if somewhat loosely, to a text? But they will go as men who have lost their battle before they start; the ground of conviction has slipped from under their feet.[7]

By automatically assuming that people are no longer interested in spiritual matters, preachers lack spiritual confidence and focus; 'the ground of conviction has slipped from under their feet.' And here lies the fundamental question: when, may the writer ask, have men ever been interested in spiritual things outside of an awakening work of God? James Montgomery Boice reminded the audience at the 1995 Philadelphia Conference on Reformed Theology that people have never been interested in preaching, good doctrine and the Reformed Faith. Preachers are to preach 'in season and out of season' (2 Tim. 2:2), when preaching is popular and when it is unpopular.

Ministerial concern about 'success' rather than spirituality has had a debilitating influence upon preaching. How many books, studies, surveys and articles have been written about 'Baby Boomers' and what they want in a church? Programs, activities for children, small groups, contemporary music, time efficient (i.e. short) services, and homogeneous fellowship seem to be the concerns of modern ministry. Any mention of preaching is relegated to a reminder to be 'relevant to their needs'. As soon as the preacher becomes convinced of this way of thinking and begins to bend to that philosophy of ministry, the pulpit is lost to worldly ends.

When the decision is made to cater to worldly trends, generational preferences, and cultural values, even in the name of 'contextualizing' the gospel for a post-modern society, an unwritten pact, an unholy covenant, has been drawn with the people. If only they will come in large numbers and make the pastor feel successful, they are given whatever they want, dressed up in religious garb! Intentionally or not, the pastor engages in that very ceremonial religion that the 'Godly Preachers' revolted against, what Paul calls 'a form of godliness without power' (2 Tim. 3:5). People are given the promise of a religious experience at church without possessing the spiritually transforming power that preaching was intended, by God, to bring to His people.

Modern pastors who desire to revitalize churches are facing this very issue, day in and day out. Declining churches are simply churches that have practiced religion for years but have not been transformed by anything spiritual. The lack of 'Godly Preachers' who practice 'spiritual preaching' is the key reason churches need revitalization. To revitalize the church they must not doubt the efficacy of the preached word or the transforming power of the Reformed Faith.

Revitalizing pastors need confidence and conviction about the spiritual issues facing their church and their people. Sin, worldliness, fallen society and spiritual warfare must be addressed with the gospel, the Christian ethics of the New Testament and the means of grace. In fact, it is confidence in these means of grace that is the very key to revitalization. The Word preached, prayer, the Lord's Supper and Christian fellowship are the tools of revitalization in a declining church (Acts 2:37-47). Archie Parrish defines 'Revitalization' in these terms:

> The cure is personal renewal caused by proper use of the spiritual disciplines. This renewal will always be combined with proper involvement in a church that is vital. Vitality of a church is always the result of the leaders properly using the means of grace.... Revitalization is God working in a local church as renewed individuals (especially the official leaders) properly use the means of grace.[8]

'Godly Preachers' see the problems of a local church in decline from spiritual perspectives. They realize that 'nothing physical exists without a spiritual cause'.[9] All problems in a church have spiritual solutions. Spiritual men believe that the conversion of the lost and the sanctification of the saints are the primary goals of the ministry, aim of preaching, and concern of the church. Twelve-step groups, teen clubs, aerobics, social activities for senior members, bowling leagues, softball teams, and dating services for singles are not the major concern of spiritual ministers. These can never deliver a church out of the doldrums of decline. Worldly-minded ministers may think so, but 'spiritual preaching' from the pulpits of 'Godly Preachers' is oriented otherwise. Spiritual men are the men the Lord has historically used to revitalize the church and bring revival and reformation to Christianity.

ENDNOTES

1. Morgan, 1965, 13-14.
2. Morgan, 1965, 15.
3. Morgan, 1973, 20-23.
4. Morgan, 1965, 16-20.
5. Adair, 1986, 284.
6. Bainton, 1950, 167.
7. Coggan, 1958, 13.
8. Parrish, 1995, 3, 5.
9. Evans, 1990, 27.

Chapter 13

Romantic Preaching

There was a great 'romantic' tone to the preaching of both the Reformers and the Puritans.[1] This 'romanticism' was displayed in the preaching of the 'Godly Preachers' in the great themes of spiritual warfare, the Christian pilgrimage, the kingdom of God, the rescue of sinners, and the suffering of Christ and His saints. Their romantic theology, reflected in the pulpits, was one of a fallen race, in bondage to the evil one, and yet rescued by the champion of their souls, Jesus Christ, the Heavenly Prince. Out of this 'romanticism' came such epic works as Milton's *Paradise Lost* and John Bunyan's two classics, *The Holy War* and *Pilgrim's Progress*. John Adair writes, 'They saw human existence as a grimly serious, deeply dramatic conflict between good and evil with heaven and hell as their end.'[2]

Perhaps it can be credited to the preaching of Martin Luther that such a romantic element entered the new evangelical (Protestant) preaching. 'The heart of Luther's theology was that, in Jesus Christ, God has given Himself, utterly and without reserve, for us.'[3] It was not simply that Christ died, or even that He died for sins and sinners, but specifically that He died 'for me', 'for us.' *Christus pro me* – Christ for me; Christ on behalf of me – was the very personal and passionate heartbeat of the gospel of Luther, and therefore of his gospel preaching.

Luther's view of both Scripture and preaching brought to the pulpit this romantic ring. He would speak of the Bible as 'the swaddling clothes of Christ' – in Scripture, one discovered *Christus pro me*:

145

I beg and really caution every pious Christian not to be offended by the simplicity of the language and stories frequently encountered there, but fully realize that, however simple they may seem, these are the very words, works, judgments, and deeds of the majesty, power, and wisdom of the most high God. For these are the Scriptures which make fools of all the wise and understanding, and are open only to the small and simple, as Christ says in Matthew 11 [:25]. Therefore dismiss your own opinions and feelings, and think of the Scriptures as the loftiest and noblest of holy things, as the richest of mines which can never be sufficiently explored, in order that you may find that divine wisdom which God here lays before you in such simple guise as to quench all pride. Here you will find the swaddling cloths and the manger in which Christ lies, and to which the angel points the shepherds [Luke 2:12]. Simple and lowly are these swaddling cloths, but dear is the treasure, Christ, who lies in them.[4]

In his 'Theology of the Cross,' Luther unfolded for the church a number of antithetical statements that both revealed divine truth to simple folks and yet maintained the divine mystery of God and His gracious works: that we are *simul iustus et peccator* (at the same time just and a sinner), that the Hidden God reveals His glory in the shame of the Cross, that God must first make a man a sinner in order to make him a saint, that reason is the 'devil's whore,' and other delightfully surprising, yet wonderful truths.

Luther's genius lay in his ability to take profound theological truth and preach it powerfully yet plainly to theologians, burgomeisters, college boys and milkmaids. For him faith in Christ was both an adventure in God's kingdom and an unfolding love affair with Jesus Christ. He captured the minds and imaginations, the hopes and fears, and the hearts and affections of all Germany. Theology and experience, biblical text and daily life, and the common and the sacred converged in Luther's preaching.

His view of God's Word and its purpose was the fountainhead of such romantic preaching. Henry Steward Wilson summarizes Luther's view of preaching:

For Luther, God's Word, as it is found in the Scripture, comes alive to people in preaching. The aim of this live message is human salvation. Since sin is a rebellion against God, forgiveness must come from God Himself. God forgives and accepts sinners as His children, for Christ's sake. That means that human salvation is dependent on what Christ has done on the cross. People are justified by putting their faith in what God has done for their salvation in Christ. But, how do people come to know Christ? Through the Word, of course – the preached Word. People have to be told where to turn for hope. They have to be told by none other than God Himself. Luther, with St. Paul, strongly held to the notion that faith is an 'acoustical affair.' Since faith comes by hearing, justification by faith and preaching are related, even dependent on each other in Luther's theology. What one hears through preaching becomes a message of new life and hope through the internal ministry of the Holy Spirit. The doctrine of the Holy Spirit holds an important place in Luther's overall theology, as well as in his theology of preaching.[5]

This living nature of God's Word compels the preacher to make the truth of the Scripture 'come alive' by the use of 'imaginative participation' in the biblical story being preached. Luther is not reluctant to see the antichrist in the Pope, an evil Pharaoh in the Holy Roman Emperor, and the small band of disciples in the fledgling Reformed church. The Word of God demands such marriage of timeless truth, historical fact and the *Sitz im Leben* of one's times.

This living character of the Word is seen in the way Luther contemporized the biblical text. Just as God is not merely 'there' (*da*) but 'there for thee' (*dir da*), so, too, the stories in the Bible are not simply historical acts, back there and then, but living events, here and now. Luther called for imaginative participation in the biblical stories, as we see in his treatment of Gideon: 'How difficult it was for [Gideon] to fight the enemy at those odds. If I had been there, I'd have befouled my breeches for fright.' The distance between the ancient people of God and the contemporary believer collapses before the timeless Word of God. This is not to lessen the historical reality of the biblical event – remember Luther's insistence on the grammatical-historical sense – but to confront every reader with the existential demand and promise of Scripture which requires a present response.[6]

This romantic approach to preaching does indeed 'make Scripture come alive'. Those who are fiery and passionate preachers with a romantic vision of God and His kingdom attract listeners. When once asked by young preachers how he managed to draw such crowds, John Wesley replied, 'When a man is on fire for God in the pulpit, people will come to see him burn.' The writer contends that this fiery, zealous, passionate and romantic preaching is sorely lacking today for several reasons.

First, far too much concern is placed on both intellectual credibility and respectability with the world. Contemporary authors often chide evangelicals for being intellectually lazy and irrelevant to the modern world.[7] As a result, modern preachers are so concerned with respectable presentations of theological truth that is both defensible and academically cogent that they have lost the fire and romance that allow them to tell the biblical story with existential zeal so that the sermon 'lives.' J. W. Alexander explains it this way:

The complaint is becoming common, respecting young men entering the ministry, in every part of the Church, that many of them lack that devotion to their work, which was frequently manifested twenty or thirty years ago. It is vain to attribute the alleged change to any particular mode of education. In this there has been no such alteration as will account for the loss of zeal. The cause must be sought in something more widely operative. The effect, if really existing, is visible beyond the circle of candidates and probationers. Nor need we go further for an explanation, than to the almost universal declension of vital piety in our Churches, which will abide under every form of training, until the Spirit be poured out from on high. The fact, however remains. Here and there are young ministers, visiting among vacancies, and ready to be employed in any promising place, who are often well educated persons, of good manners, and irreproachable character: but what a want of fire! There can be no remedy for this evil, but a spiritual one; yet it is of high importance that the young man should know what it is he needs. He has perhaps come lately from his studies, in the solitude of a country parish, or from some school in the mountains; or from some sound but frigid preceptor, who, amidst parochial cares, has afforded him few means of stimulation. His thoughts are more about the heads of divinity, the

148

partitions of a discourse, the polish of style, the newest publications, or even the gathering of a library, than about the great, unspeakable, impending work of saving souls. He has no consuming zeal with regard to the conversion of men, as an immediate business. Let us not be too severe in our judgments. It cannot well be otherwise. None but a visionary would expect the enthusiasm of the battle in the soldier who, as yet, has seen nothing but the drill. Yet this enthusiasm there must be, in order to any greatness of ministerial character, and any success; and he is most likely to attain it, who is earliest persuaded that he is nothing without it. It is encouraging to observe, that some of the most useful and energetic preachers are the very men whose youthful zeal was chiefly for learning, but who, under providential guidance, were brought at once into positions where they were called upon to grapple with difficulties, and exert all their strength in the main work.[8]

Secondly, in an age where the office of the pastor is less and less respected, preachers often suffer from very subtle forms of inferiority complex. They are convinced that no one is interested in what they have to say. Jeremiah's 'fire in the bones' has been quenched in both discouragement and self-doubt.

Thirdly, preachers of today know just how far they can challenge their congregations. Academic, calm and rationally predictable sermons are 'safe'. No one is ever aroused or convicted by such 'lectures in living well'. But the man who preaches with romantic love for God in his heart, his voice and his message will make the nominal Christian quite uncomfortable. The writer would venture to say that the more professional, wealthy and socially prominent the congregation, the less the minister feels free to preach with imagination, romance and zeal. He might 'shout too much', be 'too common', or just flat 'make a spectacle of himself.' This fear of men will stifle the romance of preaching.

Finally, the low level of genuine spirituality in the ministry, referenced earlier, that causes preachers to be more concerned about success than godliness, is a damper to zealous preaching. Paul's exhortation to be 'fools for Christ's sake' (1 Cor. 4:10) is simply not compatible with worldly success. Doctor of ministry programs may devote more time to 'dressing for success' than preaching with reckless abandon. As a result, this professionalization of the ministry mitigates against expressions of romance with God.[9]

Men with the same genuine convictions, commitments and calling of Luther, Calvin and Zwingli are desperately needed today. Romantic preaching is never a matter of one's temperament, intellect or even style. John A. Broadus notes the vast differences of personality but the shared romance of preaching among these three principal Reformers.

> It would be difficult to find so marked a contrast between any two celebrated contemporaries in all the history of preaching as that between Luther and Calvin. Luther (1483–1546) was a broad-shouldered, broad-faced, burly German, overflowing with physical strength; Calvin (1509–64) a feeble-looking little Frenchman, with shrunken cheeks and slender frame, and bowed with study and weakness. Luther had a powerful intellect, but was also rich in sensibility, imagination and swelling passion – a man juicy with humor, delighting in music, in children, in the inferior animals, in poetic sympathy with nature. In the disputation at Leipzig he stood up to speak with a bouquet in his hand. Every constituent of his character was rich to overflowing, and yet it was always a manly vigor, without sentimental gush.... Calvin, on the other hand, was practically destitute of imagination and humor, seeming in his public life and works to have been all intellect and will, though his letters show that he was not only a good hater, but also a warm friend. And yet, while so widely different, both of these men were *great preachers*. What had they in common to make them great preachers? I answer, along with intellect they had force of character, an energetic nature, will.
>
> Luther is a notable example of intense *personality* in preaching. His was indeed an imperial personality, of rich endowments, varied sympathies and manifold expressions. They who heard him were not only listening to truth, but they *felt the man*. Those who merely read his writings, in foreign lands and languages, felt the man, were drawn to him, and thus drawn to his gospel.
>
> Zwingle (*sic*) (1484–1531) was a bold and energetic preacher, a thoroughly energetic man, and a most laborious student. Like

Luther he was very fond of music, and would set his own Christian songs to music, and accompany them on the lyre.... Zwingle was not merely energetic and ardent but tenderly emotional, as shown by his sorrowing tears during the great Conference with Luther at Marburg.[10]

The writer is not speaking just from theory or from mere historical perspective but from actual experience. For years, he has purposefully endeavored not to hold back but to let the fire and freedom of his love affair with Christ spill over into the pulpit. Many are the dear saints who have testified to the Scripture 'coming alive' for them. But, in addition, he pays the price of being considered by many as too crude, too common and too 'rough cut' to be invited to preach in certain places. The writer is not considered theologically profound or socially acceptable. These opinions of others have been both painful and humbling to him. Such is the price one pays to be a 'fool for Christ's sake' in an age and generation caught up with being culturally correct! The Reformers and Puritans feared no man, held on to reputation lightly and preached with the heat of those consumed with a great love affair with Christ and a glorious vision of the greatness of their calling. The writer has sought for the same romance in his preaching.

Declining churches become negative, defeated, discouraged and cynical about the great venture of faith in Christ. The only thing they 'romanticize' about is the era known as the 'good old days'.[11] They desperately need spiritual men, 'Godly Preachers,' to reintroduce them to the joy and excitement of an adventure with Christ and the 'romance' of His calling on the lives of all His chosen ones. The writer's homiletics professor in seminary, Paul Ferris, used to remind students that 'it was a sin to bore people with the Word of God'. And preaching professor, Harold Burchett, emphasized that preaching, heaven, hell, the Cross and the Christ should be as real as the preacher who spoke of them. Both of these men were advocating 'romantic preaching'. The writer thanks God for them.

This great romance with God and His Christ must naturally spill over into a romance with His bride, the Church. Cyprian of Carthage has told the church that honoring God the Father also necessitates

honoring His bride, the Church, the mother of all believers.[12]
Likewise, today's preachers must believe that a love for Christ brings
with it a love for the local church. Luther did. He referred to the
church as 'The Worthy Maid' and wrote a hymn in her honor.

> To me she's dear, the worthy maid,
> And I cannot forget her;
> Praise, honor, virtue of her are said;
> Then all I love her better.
>> I seek her good,
>> And if I should
>> right evil fare,
>> I do not care,
> She'll make up for it to me,
> With love and truth that will not tire,
> Which she will ever show me;
> And do all my desire.
>
> She wears of purest gold a crown
> Twelve star their rays are twining;
> Her raiment, glorious as the sun,
> And bright from far is shining.
>> Her feet the moon
>> Are set upon.
>> She is the bride
>> With the Lord to bide.
> Sore travail is upon her;
> She bringeth forth a noble Son
> Whom all the world must honor,
> Their king, the only one.
>
> That makes the dragon rage and roar,
> He will the child upswallow;
> His raging comes to nothing more;
> No jot of gain will follow.
>> The infant high
>> Up to the sky
>> Away is heft,
>> And he is left

On earth, all mad with murder.
The mother now alone is she,
But God will watchful guard her,
And the right Father be.[13]

Men who would revitalize a discouraged church must bring to that church a sense of romance with Christ and the local congregation. Their love affair with God and His godly ones can well be contagious. Without 'romantic preaching', little will happen from the pulpit to revitalize an unloved and uncared for church. Churches fall into decline because preachers lose their passion for both their ministry and their people. Revitalizing pastors rekindle these romantic fires with their sermons.

Martin Luther was the father of Puritanism – even more so than John Calvin. He was an earthy man and a spiritual man. Luther was what Leland Ryken called the Puritans, 'a worldly saint.' He was a Christian who loved life in the world but whose joy was in the City of God. He would thank God for three 'real blessings', as he called them: salvation in Christ, a good and godly wife, and rich German beer! For him there was a seamless garment of common grace and saving grace that wrapped the redeemed man in the love and grace of God. Luther celebrated life – every day. And therefore he celebrated eternal life – forever. His joy in Christ, his infectious enthusiasm for gifts of God, and his spellbinding interest in the affairs of men with God gave his life the essence of the German motto: 'Arbeit macht das leben suss' (Work adds zest to life!). The work of man in the context of the work of God was an adventure, enough to fill a whole lifetime with sacred romance.

Where are the men in the pulpit 'lyrical over the divine mercy'? God so loved the world that he sent his only begotten Son into this life to rescue the damsel in distress, the Church! The warfare, the drama, the epochal nature of the Gospel story is a romantic tale, waiting to be told again, and again, and again. Who could ever tire of hearing this story? Who could ever tire of telling such a tale? Woe to us who live in an age where the romance has gone from the pulpit!

ENDNOTES

1. Morgan, 1965, 20-25.
2. Adair, 1982, 281.
3. George, 1988, 59.
4. Luther, 1960, 35:236.
5. Wilson, 1980, 2-3.
6. George, 1988, 85.
7. McGrath, 1994, 143.
8. Alexander, 1988, 101-02.
9. Guiness and Seel 1992, 183-84.
10. Broadus, 1889, 118-27.
11. Reeder, 1986, 167.
12. Roberts and Donaldson, 1990, 384.
13. Luther, 1965, 53:293-94.

Chapter 14

Controversial Preaching

Another characteristic of the 'Godly Preachers', which is even less popular or 'acceptable' today than either spiritual preaching or romantic preaching, is 'Controversial Preaching'. There can be little doubt that the great Reformers[1] and the Puritans were prophetic men who preached 'controversially'.

> The Reformation involved a revival of *controversial* preaching. Religious controversy is unpopular in our day, being regarded as showing a lack of charity, of broad culture, and in the estimation of some, a lack even of social refinement and courtesy. It is possible that a few preachers, even some of our Baptist brethren, are too fond of controversy, and do perhaps exhibit some of the deficiencies mentioned. But it must not be forgotten that religious controversy is inevitable where living faith in definite truth is dwelling side by side with ruinous error and practical evils. And preachers may remember that controversial preaching, properly managed, is full of interest and full of power.[2]

Although written over a century ago, these words from the famous Southern Baptist preacher and professor, John A. Broadus, ring true. Puritan preachers followed their Reformer fathers in the art of controversial preaching. They did not look for issues and incidents in which to engage in controversy; they were not pugnacious by nature. Yet they knew that such genuine biblical controversy was inevitable for three reasons.

First, the very nature of the Christian life and message brings the saints into controversy with the world. Paul warned Timothy, 'And indeed all who desire to live godly in Christ Jesus will be persecuted'

(2 Tim. 3:12). The preacher's message will be prophetic if it is true to both the text and the tone of Scripture. Countless passages about spiritual warfare and Christ's great cause confirm this fact.

Preachers who seek for frictionless ways to preach 'Thus saith the Lord' are indeed destined to compromise the Scripture in some manner. Whoever is a friend to this world must indeed be an enemy to God (Jas. 4:4). Therefore, it is quite impossible for a faithful preacher to please the unconverted world and his God. Controversial preachers make up their minds to please God at the risk of offending men (Gal. 5:11; 6:14-17).

Secondly, controversial preaching often must confront false theology and apostate religion. The great controversy between the Evangelical Church and the Roman Catholic Church is not over. Recent proselytizing of the evangelical ranks by a resurgent Catholicism has sent shock waves through Protestant circles. Those who truly read the small print will realize that present 'ecumenical' efforts under the label of 'Evangelicals and Catholics Together' are merely a cloaking device for Rome's ageless intention to bring all spiritual and temporal institutions under the See of Rome. This age of benign attitudes toward unchanged Roman heresy must be confronted with truth. Those who would model Reformed and Puritan preaching cannot deceive themselves into believing that Catholics and Protestants possess 'the same religion but different theologies'.[3] The same could be said of other efforts to join godless ideologies with the true Christian faith. The psychologizing of religion, the politicizing of faith, and the professionalizing of ministry all make for controversy in the preaching ministry of those men who desire to preach 'the faith once delivered' (Jude 3).

Controversial preaching is almost taboo in this genteel culture of pluralistic tolerance. But the Word of God warns preachers that if they fail to sound the alarm where spiritual danger threatens the flock, the blood of the saints is on their hands (Ezek. 33). Those spiritual heresies, apostate movements and pagan religions that threaten the true faith and the gospel church must be openly expressed by preachers who would protect the saints (Acts 20:27-32). The New Age movement, Evangelical and Catholic Ecumenism, the rising tide of cults, the occult, and an insipid, permeating and eclectic neo-evangelicalism are the enemies and competitors of the Reformed Faith today. Preachers cannot be afraid to engage in controversial preaching at these points of tension. Martin Luther once said:

> If I profess with the loudest voice and clearest exposition every portion of the truth of God except precisely that little point which the world and the devil are attacking at that moment, I am not confessing Christ, however boldly I may be professing Christ. Where the battle rages, there the loyalty of the soldier is proved, and to be steady on all battlefields besides, is mere flight and disgrace if he flinches at that point.[4]

Thirdly, there is a form of controversy that God enters into with His beloved elect ones. This assertion may sound strange to modern ears, but in fact is a well known spiritual truth. 'For those whom the Lord loves He disciplines and He scourges every son whom He receives' (Heb. 12:6; cf. Prov. 3:12 and Ps. 119:75). The old Puritan preachers knew this well. They would often enter into 'controversy' with God's people who were in a backslidden and carnal condition because they saw themselves as God's spokesmen, His watchmen, modern day prophets to the 'Israel of God' (Gal. 6:16). And indeed they were.

A famous Puritan poem, written in 1662 by Michael Wigglesworth, entitled 'God's Controversy with New England,' expresses something the 'Godly Preachers' accepted as a fact of spiritual life with God, but that many modern preachers refuse to acknowledge. These excerpts from the thirty-one stanzas of calamities which their stubborn sinfulness induced 'give testimony to God's controversies' with His people.

God's Controversy With New England

Our healthful days are at an end
    and sicknesses come on
From year to year, because our hearts
    away from God are gone.
New England, where for many years
    you scarcely heard a cough.

And where physicians had no work,
    now finds them work enough.
Our fruitful seasons have been turned
    of late to barrenness,
Sometimes through great and parching drought,
    sometimes through rain's excess.
Yea now the pastures and corn fields
    for want of rain do languish;
The cattle mourn and hearts of men
    are filled with fear and anguish.
The clouds are often gathered
    as if we should have rain;
But for our great unworthiness
    are scattered again.
We pray and fast, and make fair shows,
    as if we meant to turn;
But whilst we turn not, God goes on
    our fields and fruits to burn. [5]

The 'Godly Preachers' were of a prophetic spirit and heart and saw things from a prophetic mindset. They believed that when God's hand was heavy on a people, His smile was not upon them because of unrepentant sinfulness. When they saw droughts, disease, and difficulties, they rose up and preached with compassion and controversy to the dear saints whom they shepherded. They loved their people enough to argue with them and anger them, considering their spiritual welfare as more important than their own ease and comfort in ministry.

> This type of sermon was preached so often that it would eventually become known as a jeremiad, in honor of the Old Testament prophet who had thundered at a complacent Israel, and from whose writings the Puritan ministers frequently took their inspiration. Sunday after Sunday, they inveighed from their pulpits, and all across New England, meetinghouse rafters rang with the likes of Jeremiah 8:5,6: 'Why then has this people turned away in perpetual backsliding? They hold fast to deceit; they refuse to return. I have given heed and listened, but they have not spoken aright; no man repents of his wickedness, saying, "What have I done?"' [6]

A typical 'jeremiad' sermon delivered in the spirit of loving controversy was one preached by Puritan preacher Thomas Foxcraft (1696–1769), pastor of the First Congregational Church of Boston for over forty-nine years. On July 30, 1724, he expounded Jeremiah 44:10-11 in a message entitled, 'God's Face Set Against an Incorrigible People.'[7] The sermon had four points:

1. God expects a people under His corrective hand to humble themselves, fear, and turn their feet unto His testimonies and to walk in His Law.
2. It is sometimes the sad case of a people under divine rebukes that they continue, notwithstanding all, unhumbled and unreformed.
3. God observes a people's conduct under His judgments and marks against them all their obstinacy and impenitence.
4. When a people are finally irreclaimable, God will set His face against them for evil.

The prophetic boldness and controversial tone of the message can be deduced from these excerpts:

Sometimes they are stupid under the tokens of God's displeasure and remain insensible under all the means used to awaken them out of their spiritual slumber.... God pours on them the fury of His anger and the strength of battle; and it sets them on fire round about, yet they know it not; and it burns them, yet they lay it not to heart (Isa. 42:25). His hand is lifted up but they will not see. They are a foolish people and without understanding. They have eyes and see not and ears which hear not. A revolting and rebellious heart have they, even a heart of stone that will not relent. They harden their faces as a rock. Are they ashamed when they commit abominations? No, they are not at all ashamed, neither can they blush (Jer. 6:15). They are like brass and iron, as hard as an adamant stone, harder than flint. If they are not altogether insensible, they are unsubdued and inflexible, being very resolute and madly in love with their lusts. They are as the untamed horse or unbroken mule that has no understanding. They reject the council of God against themselves and say in the pride of their hearts, like those in our context said to Jeremiah, 'As for the word that thou hast spoken unto us in the name of the Lord, we will not hearken unto thee. But we will certainly do whatsoever thing goeth forth out of our own mouth' (Jer. 44:16,17).... Many times they proudly assert their own innocence in the face of all the convictions offered them. They will not see and own their iniquity. They call evil good and good evil. They put darkness for light and light for darkness. They deny the charge of guilt and stand upon their own vindication.... All too commonly it is the unhappy case of a people that every individual shifts the blame off from himself, imputing the cause of divine judgments to the sins of others, so looking on himself as unconcerned in the calls to repentance. Many times the most needy will scoff at God's messengers, laugh at their solemn rebukes and warnings and turn all into banter and ridicule.[8]

Such controversial preaching would be a refreshing and effective change from typical sermons. Despite many textbook exhortations to 'be positive',[9] preach 'winsomely,' and act 'pastorally' – are these not euphemistic ways of telling modern preachers to be nice? – there is a genuine place and time for controversial preaching.

People who are in spiritual declension usually have a low view of God and of their sin. They have lived in a backslidden, spiritual lethargy for a long time. Being 'nice' or being 'positive' will not shake them loose from imprisoning sins. These people must be addressed in a prophetic voice; the minister must enter into controversy with them on behalf of God and for their sake. He must show them 'the wages of sin' and awaken them to feel the heavy hand of God's discipline upon them. Therefore, 'Godly Preachers' must set forth the spiritual relationship of sin and its dire consequences: AIDS as a judgment of God upon sexual immorality, the national debt as God's discipline for gross covetousness, the crumbling of the family as the fruit of adultery and unbiblical divorce, and the spiritual causes of a host of other 'natural' problems. This kind of preaching is neither well received nor intellectually acceptable in today's post-modern age, but it is what controversial preaching demands in desperate times.

There is, of course, a danger here, one the writer has frequently fallen into. The preacher must be careful to ensure that the offense taken is the offense of the cross and not the offensiveness of either his manner of speaking or his personality. Some preachers cause controversy not because of what they say but because of how they say it. Rather than facilitate revitalization in the church, such offensive mannerisms hinder it. Preachers ought to be careful to avoid engaging in controversy just for the sake of controversy. When God enters into controversy with His people, it is for a spiritual purpose. There is a specific end in His mind as He confronts His people. God is not a quarrelsome God, nor does He delight to use quarrelsome ministers (2 Tim. 2:24-26).

Preaching controversially involves great risk. It will cause more than a few to become irritated, angry or even retaliatory. It will drive some away. But without such preaching, revitalization will not take place.[10] Churches in need of revitalization are in decline because of an unholy and unspoken, yet very real, covenant made between preacher and people. That unholy covenant is this: the preacher agrees never to make the people too uncomfortable by pointing out entrenched sin problems, and in return, the people promise to come to church, give some money and be friendly to the preacher. Because of such unspoken agreements, churches decline, the Spirit is both quenched and grieved, and sin continues to spread like leaven, producing a sick church in need of revitalization. There is only one way to address these problems, and that is by means of controversial preaching. Without it, revitalization will not take place. Spiritual courage is needed to engage in controversial preaching. Pastoral love is needed to ensure that such preaching is prophetic rather than merely pugnacious. Only the Holy Spirit can give this balance.

ENDNOTES

1. George, 1988, 85-86.
2. Broadus, 1889, 116-17.
3. Kreeft, 1996, 125.
4. Colson, 1985, 11.
5. Love, 1895, 190-91.
6. Marshall and Manuel, 1977, 215.
7. Roberts, 1994, 163-81.
8. Roberts, 1994, 177-79.
9. Wiersbe and Wiersbe, 1986, 65.
10. Seaver, 1970, 31-33.

Chapter 15

Comaraderie in Preaching

Unlike the promotion and planning of sermons, preaching with Puritan ethos cannot be deliberately orchestrated. Unlike the *content* of Puritan preaching, the *ethos* of reformation and revival preaching cannot be arrived at through some deliberate mix. This Puritan character in preaching can only grow out of a man's life. Charles H. Spurgeon, in lecturing to ministerial students about 'The Preacher's Power, and the Conditions of Obtaining It,' spoke of the great need for the internal life of the preacher to reflect such a Puritan passion:

> We now purpose to consider the way in which we are to obtain the power we so much desire. We need to feel it within ourselves when we are receiving our message. In order to have power in public, we must receive power in private. I trust that no brother here would venture to address his people without getting a message fresh from his Lord. If you deliver a stale story of your own concocting, or if you speak without a fresh anointing from the Holy One, your ministry will come to nothing. Words spoken on your own account, without reference to your Lord, will fall to the ground. When the footman goes to the door to answer a caller, he asks his master what he has to say, and he repeats what his master tells him. You and I are waiting-servants in the house of God, and we are to report what our God would have us speak. The Lord gives the soul-saving message, and clothes it with power; He gives it to a certain order of people, and under certain conditions.[1]

Notice Spurgeon's last sentence: 'The Lord gives the soul-saving message, and clothes it with power; *He gives it to a certain order of people,* and under certain conditions' (emphasis added). Spurgeon went on to say that there are found in such men six 'conditions' of heart and life that enable them to preach like the Puritans:

1. a simplicity of heart that has been emptied of self
2. a great humility of mind to receive God's Word in faith
3. a singleness of eye to the glory of God and understanding of His will
4. a complete subordination to Christ in the fear of the Lord
5. a deep seriousness of heart and labors
6. a sympathy with God resulting in an enthusiasm for His kingdom.

These men, this 'certain order of people,' are one of the keys to developing the Puritan ethos in one's preaching. There are always two contending groups of preachers in the church: the popular preachers and the Puritan preachers. They approach the Word of God with differing methods and handle it with differing motives. This was so in the Apostle Paul's day, as it is today, something that one addresses in writing on the subject of 'Why Be a Preacher?':

There were preachers who, in Paul's judgment, did seek converts through 'deception' and by 'distorting the word of God.' Though the exact nature of this rival faction is the subject of interminable academic debate, I have argued that one of their characteristics was that they disapproved of the openness with which Paul preached in public.... They preached, of course. But it was most likely 'sales patter,' the kind of empty rhetoric that was so fashionable and admired in that society. 'We can offer you secret *gnosis* that will lift you up to a higher level of consciousness; knowledge that will send you on a trip like no other trip you have ever experienced and will take you into the mysteries of God himself.' Appealing, no doubt to first-century Greeks, but it was rather short on Christian doctrine. There was nothing about sin; nothing about judgment; nothing about the cross; not even, I suspect, very much about Jesus. No doubt if you had quizzed them they would have admitted they did believe in all these things; Paul does not call them heretics. So presumably they were, at least nominally, orthodox in their creed. It was their methodology Paul objected to. It was all too crafty, too devious, too shaped by the artful marketing techniques of the world, and for Paul that would not do. He had repudiated that kind of strategy of enticement the day he received his calling to be a preacher. The ministry God had called him to simply was not like that. We renounced, he says, all that disgraceful secrecy non-sense, all that subterfuge and adulteration of the gospel message. No, his method – if you could call it a method at all – was to tell people the straightforward, unvarnished facts.[2]

Preachers today must soberly admit that there exist two schools of thought on preaching. One school of thought warns the preacher to be careful lest he 'upset' anyone. The preacher's task is to keep the people happy, meet their needs and maintain the status quo. The other school of thought exhorts preachers to open-heartedly preach for change without concern for how popular or acceptable such preaching may be. Affiliation with one group or the other will indeed impact a man's preaching.

For this reason, those who desire to preach with a Puritan ethos should associate with men who have or seek the same in their own preaching. History gives testimony of the fact that like-minded men often shared and exchanged pulpits and formed informal 'ministerial fraternals' to encourage each other in preaching like the Puritans. John Armstrong of Reformation and Revival Ministries in Carol Stream, Illinois, has formed just such associations to encourage men of a similar mind concerning reformation and revival. On a regular basis these fraternals meet to pray together, to discuss Puritan books, and to preach to one another. Their sole purpose is to encourage others in ministry toward reformation and revival.

There are few men in the ministry engaged in revitalizing efforts, although many churches need that kind of ministry. Plenty of men can be found to encourage church growth principles and techniques. There is no shortage of men who will bend to the whims and fancies of the local culture and pressure from the pew to present a 'Christianity Lite' brand of faith to the congregation. But what revitalizing pastors need are fraternals of other ministers who will encourage, model and reinforce a Puritan passion for preaching.

Sermon planning and promotion can be learned from books and marketing techniques. Balanced content in preaching can be deliberately measured and mixed. But Puritan ethos in preaching must be caught rather than taught. Fellowship with other men of the heart and mind of the Puritans is the key to acquiring this spirit in preaching.

Annually, the writer attends the Philadelphia Conference on Reformed Theology, and other similar conferences by such ministries as The Banner of Truth, Reformation and Revival Ministries, and the North American Convocation on Revival (NACOR), to be refreshed, challenged and reinforced in his desire and work toward reformation, revival and revitalization. What these conferences do on an annual basis, ministerial fraternals could do on a regular, ongoing basis.

What has been interesting in the study for this book is that, in all the hundreds of works reviewed and the dozens cited, not one that the writer has examined has explicitly devoted any attention to this genuine need for ministerial fraternals. Yet history confirms that in times past these fraternals were a God-sent source of encouragement and cross-fertilization in the ministry. During the opening years of the Protestant Reformation, Ulrich Zwingli developed just such a fraternal. On Thursday afternoons Zwingli and the other reforming pastors in the vicinity of Zurich, Switzerland met in the choir loft of the Gross Munster (Great Church), Zwingli's church in the heart of Zurich. They exegeted a book of the Bible together, and thereby taught each other the Biblical languages. They took turns preaching a text and then discussed and critiqued the messages. In so doing they came together in both theology and in philosophy of ministry. This fraternal gave cohesion and camaraderie to the Reformation in German-speaking Switzerland. This idea of a fraternal of preachers would be duplicated again, this time 400 years later and in London, England.

In 1941, Dr. D. Martyn Lloyd-Jones began the Westminster Fraternal that regularly met for decades, encouraging men in the pulpit to pastor and preach like the Reformers and Puritans. Iain H. Murray, in his biography of Lloyd-Jones, describes the membership and format of their fraternal.

The second new agency which came into existence in the early years of the war was the group of ministers who were later to be known as 'The Westminster Fellowship.' This seems to have begun in 1941 as a quarterly Tuesday morning meeting at Westminster Chapel intended for pastors and men in positions of Christian leadership. It was a private meeting, with attendance only by invitation. The inspiration for it came from ministerial contacts made through Inter-Varsity, aided by the usual encouragement from Douglas Johnson who knew of the similar gatherings which ML-J had led at Aberavon.... In form the meetings differed from what they became in later years. The afternoon was divided into two, with a fifteen-minute break in between. In the first session opportunity was given for everyone present (upwards of a dozen men) to speak from personal experience of recent blessings or difficulties in their work – a procedure which led someone to dub the fraternal 'The Confession' (a name which stuck for a few years). The smallness of the numbers attending required a room rather than a hall for the venue and the only one suitable on the premises of Westminster Chapel was the downstairs 'parlour' where the light of the sun soon grew heavy. ML-J was not in agreement with Spurgeon's dictum that the next most important thing to grace is oxygen and remained unperturbed when 'The black hole of Calcutta' became another nickname for the fraternal. It is clear from the form which the first session took that Dr. Lloyd-Jones did not envisage the gatherings as a place for listening to addresses. He wanted it to be a 'fellowship.' The experimental and practical issues were to be prominent, and at the same time he sought that men should learn, through discussion, how basic biblical theology points to the solution of almost all problems in the life of the church... . The time of meeting certainly curtailed the number of laymen in positions of Christian leadership who could attend but in ML-J's view this was not a handicap to the meeting. Other gatherings existed for them, whereas pastors had experiences which they needed to discuss together. In later years it was stipulated that membership in the 'Fellowship' was for those in the work of the ministry. Students did not attend.[3]

What a blessing to the 'Godly Preachers' such fraternals would be. If the work of revitalization is to be truly accomplished in today's churches, it will be because many pastors will realize that their own churches need revitalization. They will seek the friendship and support of other like-minded ministers in search of the Puritan spirit in preaching and overall ministry. They will support and encourage one another and each other's congregations toward this revitalization ministry.[4] In this way, the Puritan ethos of preaching – spiritual, romantic and controversial preaching – can be confirmed by kindred spirits with a heart for reformation, revival and revitalization.

ENDNOTES

1. Spurgeon, 1986, 329.
2. Clements, 1996, 67-68.
3. Murray, 1990, 86-89.
4. Sargent, 1994, 36.

Review of Chapters 11–15

Sometimes the intangibles of life are the true essentials of life. So it is with preaching. The intangibles of spirituality, romance, controversy and camaraderie in preaching are essential to a prophetic spirit in the pulpit. This age of quantifiable measurements may be frustrated with concepts that cannot be programmed, but the Lord introduces these variables into formulas of ministry to force preachers to acknowledge their absolute dependence on Him.

The writer is convinced that Puritan preaching can only rise up in the church again as a result of prayer. Congregations and ministers need to importunately seek God's blessings on the pulpit once again, a blessing that will result in the Puritan ethos in preaching. John Stott shares this conviction with the writer. His prayer for the renewal of powerful preaching can serve as a pattern for all:

> I pray earnestly that God will raise up today a new generation of Christian apologists or Christian communicators, who will combine an absolute loyalty to the biblical gospel and an unwavering confidence in the power of the Spirit with a deep and sensitive understanding of the contemporary alternatives to the gospel; who will relate the one to the other with freshness, pungency, and authority and relevance; and who will use *their* minds to reach *other* minds for Christ.... I myself have a growing burden that God will call out more men for this teaching ministry today; that he will call men with alert minds, biblical convictions and an aptitude for teaching; that he will set them in the great capital cities and university cities of the world; that there, like Paul in Tyrannus's hall in Ephesus, they will exercise a thoughtful, systematic teaching ministry, expounding the ancient Scriptures and relating them to the modern world; and that such a faithful ministry under the good hand of God will not only lead their own congregation up to Christian maturity but will also through the visitors who come briefly under its influence spread its blessing far and wide.[1]

ENDNOTES

1. Stott, 1972, 52, 55.

Part Four

The Expository Style
of Puritan Preaching

Chapter 16

Expository Preaching Defined

Three of my four hypotheses have been set forth and explained in the previous chapters. Now the fourth will be examined: there is a certain style of revitalizing preaching that will positively affect the impact of one's preaching. This hypothesis simply states that the Reformers and Puritans preached in a certain manner, with a certain style, that affected their listeners in a profound way. They differed in style from all those who had preached before them, and the impact of their style permanently changed the nature of preaching. Among conservative evangelical preachers, the Reformed and Puritan style commands tremendous respect and has to this day inspired many imitations in modern pulpits.

Expository Preaching
The expository method of preaching was the standard style of homiletics practiced by the Puritans. It is not true, as many presume, that the Puritans invented expository preaching. Such preaching was already entrenched in reformed churches a century before the Puritans rose to ascendancy in England and America. The expository method of preaching was indeed a direct result of the Reformation. That is not to say that expository preaching was never practiced prior to the Reformation, but only that during the Reformation it became the predominant genre of preaching. It can, in fact, be stated that during the Reformation 'preaching' became synonymous with 'expository' methods of homiletics; in other words, expository preaching became the preaching of God's Word.

Before the history of expository preaching is reviewed in the next chapter, there is a need to define exactly what expository preaching is. Preaching, by its very nature, is difficult to define.

Defining becomes sticky business because what we define we sometimes destroy. The small boy dissected a frog to find out what made it jump, but in learning something about the parts he destroyed its life. Preaching is a living process involving God, the preacher, and the congregation, and no definition can pretend to capture that dynamic. But we must attempt a working definition anyway.[1]

A 'working definition' of expository preaching arrived at by Haddon Robinson is today a much referenced, standard explanation of expository preaching: 'Expository preaching is the communication of a biblical concept, derived from and transmitted through a historical, grammatical, and literary study of a passage in its context, which the Holy Spirit first applies to the personality and experience of the preacher, then through him to his hearers.'[2] Expository preaching therefore is biblical preaching rather than topical or textual preaching. These three types of preaching are compared and explained by Richard L. Mayhue:

> Discussions about preaching divide it into three types: topical, textual and expository. Topical messages usually combine a series of Bible verses that loosely connect with a theme. Textual preaching uses a short text or passage that generally serves as a gateway into whatever subject the preacher chooses to address. Neither the topical nor the textual method represents a serious effort to interpret, understand, explain, or apply God's truth in the context of the Scripture(s) used. By contrast, expository preaching focuses predominantly on the text(s) under consideration along with its (their) context(s). Exposition normally concentrates on a single text of Scripture, but it is sometimes possible for a thematic/theological message or a historical/biographical discourse to be expository in nature. An exposition may treat any length of passage.[3]

It is important to know that much of what passes for biblical exposition today is indeed far from the historic and biblical pattern that deserves the label 'expository'. Here is what expository preaching is not:

1. It is not a commentary running from word to word and verse to verse without unity, outline, and pervasive drive.
2. It is not rambling comments and offhand remarks about a passage without a background of thorough exegesis and logical order.
3. It is not a mass of disconnected suggestions and inferences based on the surface meaning of a passage but not sustained by a depth-and-breadth study of the text.
4. It is not pure exegesis, no matter how scholarly, if it lacks a theme, thesis, outline, and development.
5. It is not a mere structural outline of a passage with a few supporting comments but without other rhetorical and sermonic elements.
6. It is not a topical homily using scattered parts of the passage but omitting discussion of other equally important parts.
7. It is not a chopped-up collection of grammatical findings and quotations from commentaries without a fusing of these elements into a smooth, flowing, interesting, and compelling message.
8. It is not a Sunday-school-lesson type of discussion that has an outline of the contents, informality, and fervency but lacks sermonic structure and rhetorical ingredients.
9. It is not a Bible reading that links a number of scattered passages treating a common theme but fails to handle any of them in a thorough, grammatical, and contextual manner.
10. It is not the ordinary devotional or prayer-meeting talk that combines running commentary, rambling remarks, disconnected suggestions, and personal reactions into a semi-inspirational discussion but lacks the benefit of the basic exegetical-contextual study and persuasive elements.[4]

Expository preaching is not so much defined by the actual structure of the message, or even by the style of delivery, as it is by the source of the message, the formation of the sermon, and the intent of the delivery. Each of these distinguishing marks of an expository sermon is definitively important:

1. The source of the message is the actual passage of Scripture and not the ideas of the preacher or other human source. Whether it is a survey of a Bible book, a chapter of an epistle, a paragraph, a verse or even a single Greek or Hebrew word, the text defines *what* is to be preached.
2. The formation of the sermon is also derived from the text. This simply means that the number of main points and sub-points is gleaned from the passage of study with biblical cross-references used to explain the text's points of information.
3. The intent of delivery should be to make clear, understandable and applicable the doctrinal truths that are 'exposed' (hence: exposition or 'expository') in the text. The goal of the sermon is to make God's Word easily understood so that it can be obeyed. The preacher is not to be as concerned with his ideas as much as he is with promoting God's ideas for application and compliance.

Mayhue, MacArthur, *et al* give a good summary definition of expository preaching in five identifying elements:

1. The message finds its sole source in Scripture.
2. The message is extracted from Scripture through careful exegesis.
3. The message preparation correctly interprets Scripture in its normal sense and its context.
4. The message clearly explains the original God-intended meaning of Scripture.
5. The message applies the Scriptural meaning for today.[5]

When the reformed and Puritan style of preaching is called expository, once again, Haddon Robinson's definition is brought to mind: 'Expository preaching is the communication of a biblical concept, derived from and transmitted through a historical, grammatical, and literary study of a passage in its context, which the Holy Spirit first applies to the personality and experience of the preacher, then through him to his hearers.'[6] This style of preaching was uniquely dominant during the fifteenth through nineteenth centuries, having been revived and refined by the Reformers and their children, the Puritans.

ENDNOTES

1. Robinson, 1980, 19.
2. Robinson,1980, 20.
3. Mayhue, 1992, 9.
4. Mayhue 1992, 10.
5. Mayhue, 1990, 12-13.
6. Robinson 1980, 20.

Chapter 17

A Brief History of Expository Preaching

It is not presumptuous to state that expository preaching is biblical preaching because it is the style of preaching exemplified by Jesus Christ and the Prophets and the Apostles of the Scripture. Ezra preached expositorily in the time of the restoration of Israel:

> And all the people gathered as one man at the square which was in front of the Water Gate, and they asked Ezra the scribe to bring the book of the law of Moses which the LORD had given to Israel. Then Ezra the priest brought the law before the assembly of men, women, and all who could listen with understanding, on the first day of the seventh month. And he read from it before the square which was in front of the Water Gate from early morning until midday, in the presence of men and women, those who could understand; and all the people were attentive to the book of the law. And Ezra the scribe stood at a wooden podium which they had made for the purpose. And beside him stood Mattithiah, Shema, Anaiah, Uriah, Hilkiah, and Maaseiah on his right hand; and Pedaiah, Mishael, Malchijah, Hashum, Hashbaddanah, Zechariah, and Meshullam on his left hand. And Ezra opened the book in the sight of all the people for he was standing above all the people; and when he opened it, all the people stood up. Then Ezra blessed the LORD the great God. And all the people answered, 'Amen, Amen!' while lifting up their hands; then they bowed low and worshiped the LORD with their faces to the ground. Also Jeshua, Bani, Sherebiah, Jamin, Akkub, Shabbethai, Hodiah, Maaseiah, Kelita, Azariah, Jozabad, Hanan, Pelaiah, and the Levites, explained the law to the people while the people remained in their place. And they read from the book, from the law of God,

translating to give the sense so that they understood the reading (Neh. 8:1-8).

Jesus Christ used the prophet Isaiah to expositorily describe His own ministry:

> And He came to Nazareth, where He had been brought up; and as was His custom, He entered the synagogue on the Sabbath, and stood up to read. And the book of the prophet Isaiah was handed to Him. And He opened the book, and found the place where it was written, 'The Spirit of the Lord is upon me, because He anointed me to preach the gospel to the poor. He has sent me to proclaim release to the captives, and recovery of sight to the blind, to set free those who are downtrodden, to proclaim the favorable year of the Lord.' And He closed the book, and gave it back to the attendant, and sat down; and the eyes of all in the synagogue were fixed upon Him. And He began to say to them, 'Today this Scripture has been fulfilled in your hearing.' And all were speaking well of Him, and wondering at the gracious words which were falling from His lips; and they were saying, 'Is this not Joseph's son?' And He said to them, 'No doubt you will quote this proverb to Me, "Physician, heal yourself! Whatever we heard was done at Capernaum, do here in your home town as well." ' And He said, 'Truly I say to you, no prophet is welcome in his home town. But I say to you in truth, there were many widows in Israel in the days of Elijah, when the sky was shut up for three years and six months, when a great famine came over all the land; and yet Elijah was sent to none of them, but only to Zarephath, in the land of Sidon, to a woman who was a widow. And there were many lepers in Israel in the time of Elisha the prophet; and none of them was cleansed, but only Naaman the Syrian' (Luke 4:16-27).

Paul exhorted the elders of Ephesus to be faithful to the Word and, in so doing, described his own preaching ministry with these words:

> Therefore I testify to you this day, that I am innocent of the blood of all men. For I did not shrink from declaring to you the whole purpose of God (Acts 20:26-27).

Paul instructed Timothy to be faithful in fulfilling his own ministry and told him to 'preach the Word':

> I solemnly charge you in the presence of God and of Christ Jesus, who is to judge the living and the dead, and by His appearing and His kingdom: preach the word; be ready in season and out of season; reprove, rebuke, exhort, with great patience and instruction (2 Tim. 4:1-2).

When the sermons of the Book of Acts are analyzed, each of them clearly gives evidence of being expository in nature and style. Peter's Pentecost Sunday sermon of Acts 2 is an exposition of Joel 2:28-32, Psalm 16:8-11 and Psalm 110:1. Stephen's martyrdom sermon of Acts 7 is an exposition of Old Testament history, interpreted and applied, from sixteen passages in Genesis, as well as passages from Exodus, Kings, Deuteronomy, Isaiah, and other Old Testament books. Philip's sermon to the Ethiopian eunuch in Acts 8 is an exposition of Isaiah 57:7-8. Paul preaches from 1 Samuel during his first missionary journey in Pisidian Antioch (Acts 13). Even in his famous discourse on Mars Hill in Athens (Acts 17), Paul preaches biblical ideas from Deuteronomy, Job, Daniel, Isaiah, and the apostles. Therefore, it is not inaccurate to state that the style of preaching modeled in the Scripture is expository.

In the post-apostolic age, there was 'great decline in the power of preaching after the death of the apostles'.[1] This was due to the growing tendency toward formalism, liturgy and sacramentalism that soon turned the sermon into a 'homily' – a short message more like a devotional talk than biblical exposition. These homilies were structureless, rambling exhortations focusing upon Apostolic tradition, Scripture and the personal ideas of the preacher. Each of these three elements varied in its import and prominence in these homilies.[2] With the exception of St. John Chrysostom (347–407), the early church was not known for expository preaching.

During the Middle Ages, the classical style and tone of Greek and Roman oratory became the popular form of preaching. Rhetorical refinement, allegorical devices, and philosophical polemics became the characteristics of such medieval preaching.

Between the structureless homily or exhortation of the early times, and the closely articulated, minutely analyzed sermon of the Scholastics and the Puritans of later ages, we find the fourth century discourse. Retaining the Scriptural motive and tone, and in large degree the familiarity, of the homily, and avoiding the tedious division and sub-division of the scholastic sermon, the *logos*, or oration, of this age is more assimilated to the classic models of oratory. It has form indeed, but its bony structure is not obtrusive. The delivery was extemporaneous. Some of the extant sermons were written by the preacher before or after delivery – more commonly perhaps the latter, – but many of them were reported by shorthand writers, with or without revision by the author. Thus Gaudenitus, bishop of Brescia, a contemporary and friend of Chrysostom, in one of his letters, speaks of certain sermons as not acknowledged by him as his own because they were hastily taken down by reporters and had not been submitted to him for correction; but others he had looked over and put into shape. Of course the spirit and motive of these fourth century sermons varied with the individual preachers, as is ever the case. But even among the best preachers of the time there is too often apparent the effort to strike and please by rhetorical display and to win applause by popular utterances. The taste of the age called for more oratorical exuberance than is fitting for the themes of sacred discourse, and the preachers did not rise far above their hearers in this respect. But with these drawbacks frankly noted, we cannot fail to see in many of these homilies the mastering desire of the preacher to glorify his Lord and to win the souls of his fellow men.[3]

During this period there arose the order of 'preaching friars' – monks whose main duty was to plainly and simply set forth and apply God's Word to common folk. Their style of preaching was the opposite of that of the Scholastics. The followers of Francis of Assisi (the Franciscans) and Dominic (the Dominicans) revolutionized preaching by giving Scripture priority over tradition, oration and rhetoric.[4] One of these great preaching friars, Antony of Padua, a Franciscan monk from Portugal, became a tremendously popular preacher who was an earnest reformer and prophetic voice in the thirteenth century.[5] He was among the first to logically and progressively divide his sermons into careful divisions or topical headings (i.e. preaching points).[6]

Antony's sermons were full of common illustrations, but he still followed the popular method of allegory in his exegesis. Broadus states that 'his allegorizing is utterly wild and baseless',[7] a thing not uncommon for his times.

Thomas Aquinas, the greatest of the Scholastics, or Schoolmen, and father of Roman Catholic Theology, was also given to an expository method of preaching.[8] His sermons were the exception to the rule of Scholastic preaching. Overall, his preaching was homely, lively and highly imaginative. Still, he retained the Scholastic bent toward Aristotelian thought in his exegesis and exposition. Generally, the Middle Ages was a time when preaching hit a low-water mark in terms of content and style.

Theoretically the Bible was recognized as the source and foundation of preaching. But the following great errors show that in reality it had less influence than in appearance: (1) The use of extra-biblical material as biblical, that is, the Fathers of the church and legends; (2) Gross and willful errors of interpretation and application; (3) Extreme use of allegory, even to the point of teaching things contrary to Scripture; (4) Frequent lack of any text at all. In general the doctrinal and moral teachings of the twelfth century preachers were, from the Catholic standpoint, Christian and sound; and with much of the teaching Protestants find themselves gladly in accord. But, on the other hand, there is, of course, much, both in principle and detail, which from a true biblical standpoint must be regarded as erroneous and hurtful. We have just seen that ostensibly the Bible was accepted as the source of teaching, but that in many ways it was departed from or misapplied. Also the great central Christian doctrines were proclaimed and urged, but in many points they were misunderstood, obscured, perverted.[9]

On the eve of the Reformation, preaching had settled into one of three styles: scholastic, popular or mystic. The scholastic was philosophical, the popular was practical, and the mystic was esoteric.[10] All of these styles were highly allegorical in approach.

The stage was set for the revival of biblical and expository preaching. Broadus states, 'Scholasticism had run its course, the Papacy became frightfully corrupt, and the better spirits were either

183

absorbed in Mysticism, or engaged in unsuccessful attempts to *reform* the Church. With the general corruption, the great preaching orders rapidly degenerated.'[11] With this decline in medieval preaching, a vacuum in the pulpit was formed. That void was filled by the great Reformers and their expository method of preaching. Broadus gives this summary of the reformation of preaching:

> We come now to the preaching of the great Reformers. In devoting to them the mere fraction of a lecture, we have at least the advantage that here the leading persons and main facts are well known. Let us notice certain things which hold true of the Reformation preaching in general. It was a *revival of preaching*. We have seen that in the Middle Ages there was by no means such an utter dearth of preaching as many Protestant writers have represented. Yet the preachers we have referred to were, even when most numerous, rather exceptions to a rule.... It was a revival of *Biblical* preaching. Instead of long and often fabulous stories about saints and martyrs, and accounts of miracles, instead of passages from Aristotle and Seneca, and fine-spun subtleties of the Schoolmen, these men preached the Bible. The question was not what the Pope said; and even the Fathers, however highly esteemed, were not decisive authority – it was the Bible. The preacher's one great task was to set forth the doctrinal and moral teachings of the Word of God. And the greater part of their preaching was *expository*. Once more, after long centuries, people were reading the Scriptures in their own tongue, and preachers, studying the original Greek and Hebrew, were carefully explaining to the people the connected teachings of passage after passage and book after book.... The expository sermons of the Reformers, while in general free, are yet much more *orderly* than those of the Fathers. They have themselves studied the great scholastic works, and been trained in analysis and arrangement, and the minds of all their cultivated hearers have received a similar bent. And so they easily, and almost spontaneously, give their discourses something of a plan. Accordingly they are in many respects models of this species of preaching. In general, it may be said that the best specimens of expository preaching are to be found in Chrysostom, in the Reformers, especially Luther and Calvin, and in the Scottish pulpit of our own time.[12]

'Expository ... orderly ... planned ...', these are accurate words to describe the reformation of the pulpit that led to the Reformation of the church. The three principal Reformers on the continent were all known for their expository preaching. Edwin Charles Dargan succinctly but accurately describes the expository power and thrust of Reformation preaching:

> Luther cannot be said to have had a rigid and unvarying homiletical method. In his earlier work the traces of his Catholic training appear in the stiffer scholastic form than is to be found in his later sermons.... But in the larger number of his discourses, as reported by Cruciger and others, we have his most characteristic method of verse by verse comment on the Gospel or Epistle for the day, or on some extended passage of his own selection. Luther's views of preaching, as being properly an exposition of the Word of God, are unfolded in many places in his sermons and his *Table Talk*.
>
> Calvin began his career as an expository preacher while yet a young law student at Bruges, when, in an informal way, at the earnest request of the people, he taught the Scriptures to small gatherings. It became the delight and the established method of his life. His preaching differed from Luther's as the men themselves differed. It has less of fancy, less of warmth, less of popular appeal, but more of steadiness, of logical connection, of severely exact interpretation. While he also commonly employed the verse by verse comment, both unity of theme and logical connection of thought are much in evidence.
>
> Of the Zurich reformers Zwingli was also prevailingly expository in method, but, strictly speaking, no specimens of his sermons survive.[13]

Although no extracts of Zwingli's sermons survive, he remains the father of expository preaching for the Reformation. On January 1, 1519, this young Catholic priest set aside the lectionary readings and homily-style of preaching and announced to his congregation at the Grossmünster Church in Zurich that he would preach, verse by verse, through the New Testament, beginning with the Gospel of Matthew. He did, and so began the Reformation in Switzerland.

Zwingli's evolution from humanist to Protestant is a matter of debate among Reformation historians. He himself placed the pivotal transition in 1516 when 'led by the Word and Spirit of God I saw the need to set aside all these [human teachings] and to learn the doctrine of God direct from his own Word.' Another decisive event was the call to serve as 'people's priest' at the famous Great Minster church in Zurich. Over the portal of this church today one reads the following inscription: 'The Reformation of Huldrych Zwingli began here on January 1, 1519.' On this date the new pastor shocked his congregation by announcing his intention to dispense with the traditional lectionary. Instead of 'canned' sermons, Zwingli would preach straight through the Gospel of Matthew, beginning with the genealogy in chapter 1. Matthew was followed by Acts, then the Epistles to Timothy, then Galatians, 1 and 2 Peter, and so on until by 1525 he had worked his way through the New Testament and then turned to the Old. This was certainly an important move, one which prepared the citizens of Zurich for the complete acceptance of the Reformation several years later.[14]

The Puritans came by expository preaching honestly. They formed their English Reformation and 'purifying' of the church out of the ideas of the Great Reformation of the fifteenth century. The Puritans naturally led their reforming movement by the clear exposition of Scripture. They were a 'race of preachers' given totally to expository preaching like that of their fathers in the faith – Luther, Calvin, Zwingli.

> The ancestry of the Puritan sermon goes back at least to the day in 1519 when Huldreich Zwingli started to preach his way verse by verse through Matthew's Gospel in Zurich Minster; but Cambridge was its proper birthplace. The Puritan tradition in preaching was created there at the turn of the sixteenth and seventeenth centuries by the leaders of the first great evangelical movement in that university – William Perkins, Paul Baynes, Richard Sibbes, John Cotton, John Preston, Thomas Goodwin and their fellows.... Their Puritanism was rather the deep Calvinistic piety and urgent concern for vital religion that our previous chapters have described. Their principles in preaching, first formulated by Perkins in his *Arte of Prophecying*,

found their best balanced expression in the Westminster Assembly's *Directory for the Publick Worship of God*, and reached perhaps their highest point of development in the pastoral and evangelistic sermons of Richard Baxter.[15]

Their method of preaching was almost exclusively expository. As such, they have left behind a rich and useful repository of expositional writings taken from their sermons. In describing Puritan sermons, J. I. Packer accurately reflects their style of preaching.

> It was *expository in its method*. The Puritan preacher regarded himself as the mouthpiece of God and the servant of his word. He must speak 'as the oracles of God.' His task, therefore, was not imposition, fastening on to Scripture texts meanings they do not bear; nor was it juxtaposition, using his text as a peg on which to hang some homily unrelated to it ('take it in the writer's meaning,' said Simeon, 'not as a motto'); the preacher's task was, precisely, exposition, extracting from his texts what God had encased within them.... The Puritan method of 'opening' a text (their regular word, and a good one) was first to explain it in its context (they would have agreed with J. H. Jowett that a 'text without a context is a pretext'); next, to extract from the text one or more doctrinal observations embodying its substance; to amplify, illustrate and confirm from other scriptures the truths thus derived; and, finally, to draw out their practical implications for the hearers. The Puritans were devotees of continuous exposition, and have left behind them magnificent sets of expository sermons on complete chapters and books of the Bible as well as on single texts.[16]

Puritan William Perkins wrote about expository preaching in the Elizabethan age of England. Perkins sets forth a simple method of exposition in four summary steps:

1. Read the text clearly from canonical Scriptures.
2. Explain the meaning of this Scripture reading.
3. Gather a few profitable points of doctrine from the passage.
4. Apply the doctrines to the life and practice of the congregation in straightforward and plain speech.[17]

Read. Explain. Gather doctrine. Apply the truth. With these four rules, the effectiveness and simplicity of expository preaching are set forth 'in straightforward and plain speech'. Such was the 'genius of Puritanism'.[18]

During the nineteenth century in America, topical and textual sermons eclipsed the expository method of preaching. Verse by verse exposition gave way to the 'classical' method – a text, a story, a poem, and a powerful closing. The emphasis in the nineteenth century was again on oratorical skill rather than biblical exposition. In an effort to recover Puritan preaching, a series of lectures were delivered before the Maine Minister's Institute at Cobb Divinity School, in Lewiston, Maine, in 1899. John S. Sewall of the Bangor Theological Seminary delivered two lectures on expository preaching. In the first of those addresses, Sewall said:

> Expository preaching, as its name denotes, is based on interpretation. That is the fundamental idea. It is not the evolution of a topic, it is the elucidation of scripture. The main purpose is to get at the real meaning of God's truth – to illuminate, clarify, explain; and when the truth is thus made clear, to illustrate and enforce. And this is true preaching. In the topical method a theme opens itself by natural evolution of thought, somewhat as a bud opens into a blossom. In the textual sermon, the text supplies not only the topic, but the details of thought which will develop it, and even the forms of statement which will make the beams and timbers of its frame. These are both natural and legitimate kinds of preaching. The expository method also, when we consider its special purpose, is just as natural, and just as legitimate. It is worthy of our study. For a method which was sometimes employed by our Lord himself, and by his apostles, a method which prevailed for centuries in the early church, a method to which preachers and churches instinctively returned when the Reformation lifted them out of darkness into light – such a mode of biblical presentation must have a *raison d'être*; it cannot be all a delusion. And all the more does it demand our attention when we find that in our most spiritual churches now the current is setting in the same direction.[19]

Sewall's final statement – 'when we find that in our most spiritual churches now the current is setting in the same direction' – warrants attention. In other words, in those churches that were spiritually growing and prospering the most, expository preaching pointed the way and led the charge. Sewall goes on in his second lecture to set forth several rules for expository preaching:

1. Get thorough possession of the passage chosen, together with its context and relations. Master it.
2. Illuminate the text with the best results of reading and culture. Do not allow the sermon to degenerate into mere comment.
3. Compare the sermon on rhetorical principles.
4. Make the exegetical part of the sermon brief and hasten on to the practical use.
5. In interpretation make use of development, illustration and enforcement.
6. Do not slight the application of the truths expounded.[20]

These simple rules are amazingly similar to the four rules propounded by William Perkins four centuries earlier. Even today, the process of expository preaching is seen as essentially the same as it has always been. John Koessler of Moody Bible Institute sets forth three rules for his students as he teaches them expository preaching:

1. State your principle that you derive purely from Scripture.
2. Paint a picture to both explain and illustrate your principle.
3. Show them what it looks like by both implications and applications.[21]

During the twentieth century, there was a flourishing of expository preaching under the ministries of Martyn Lloyd-Jones, John R. W. Stott, Eric J. Alexander and others in Great Britain and Donald Gray Barnhouse, John F. MacArthur Jr., James Montgomery Boice, Charles Swindoll and others in the United States. During the 1950s through the 1970s, expository preaching was the dominant form of preaching among the young evangelical ministers of the age. Their convictions about that style of preaching could well be summarized in John Stott's own comments about preaching:

There are topical sermons and textual sermons, they say. Some are evangelistic or apologetic or prophetic, others doctrinal or devotional or ethical or hortatory, while somewhere down the line 'exegetical' or 'expository' sermons are included. I cannot myself acquiesce in this relegation (sometimes even grudging) of expository preaching to one alternative among many. It is my contention that all true Christian preaching is expository preaching. Of course if by an 'expository' sermon is meant a verse-by-verse explanation of a lengthy passage of Scripture, then indeed it is only one possible way of preaching, but this would be a misuse of the word. Properly speaking, 'exposition' has a much broader meaning. It refers to the content of the sermon (biblical truth) rather than its style (a running commentary). To expound Scripture is to bring out of the text what is there and expose it to view. The expositor prizes open what appears to be closed, makes plain what is obscure, unravels what is knotted and unfolds what is tightly packed. The opposite of exposition is 'imposition,' which is to impose on the text what is not there. But the 'text' in question could be a verse, or a sentence, or even a single word. It could equally be a paragraph, or a chapter, or a whole book. The size of the text is immaterial, so long as it is biblical. What matters is what we do with it. Whether it is long or short, our responsibility as expositors is to open it up in such a way that it speaks its message clearly, plainly, accurately, relevantly, without addition, subtraction or falsification. In expository preaching the biblical text is neither a conventional introduction to a sermon on a largely different theme, nor a convenient peg on which to hang a ragbag of miscellaneous thoughts, but a master which dictates and controls what is said.[22]

During this period of church growth principles and marketing techniques, it is fashionable to focus on one main point, major on illustrations and stories, and devote attention to avoiding all theological and biblical terms and concepts, while seeking to communicate in 'relevant' terms. In response to this erroneous way of thinking, D. A. Carson gives six reasons why one should 'accept no substitutes' to expository preaching:

1. It is the method least likely to stray from Scripture. It focuses on the 'main things'.

2. It teaches people how to read their Bibles. People follow the preacher's example of thinking through a passage, understanding the text and applying its truth to their lives.

3. It gives confidence to the preacher and authorizes the sermon. Faithfulness to the text yields both liberty and prophetic authority to the preacher.

4. It meets the need for relevance without letting the clamor for relevance dictate the message. It keeps the eternal central and applicatory to the discussion.

5. It forces the preacher to handle the tough questions.

6. It enables the preacher to expound systematically the whole counsel of God. As men preach through the Bible they cover all the genres, messages and theology covered in the Holy Writ.[23]

These six reasons are rationale enough to reinforce the need for expository preaching today. Even this cursory review of the history of preaching gives one an appreciation for the recovery of expositional preaching by the Reformers and Puritans. In the following pages, as a workable method for thorough exposition is looked at, it must be remembered that this method is fully in line with the great preachers of the Reformation and the Revivals of the past. James F. Stitzinger has the final statement on the history of expository preaching:

A study of the history of expository preaching makes it clear that such preaching is deeply rooted in the soil of Scripture. Thus, it is the only kind of preaching that perpetuates biblical preaching in the church. Throughout history, a few well-known men in each generation representative of a larger body of faithful expositors have committed themselves to this ministry of biblical exposition. Their voices from the past should both encourage the contemporary expositor and challenge him to align his preaching with the biblical standard. Scripture demands nothing less than God-enabled exposition as demonstrated by those worthy saints who have dedicated their lives to this noble task.[24]

Endnotes

1. Dargan, 1968, 35.
2. Dargan, 1968, 39.

3. Dargan, 1968, 70-71.

4. Stott, 1982, 21-22.

5. Broadus, 1889, 101-02.

6. 'Antony of Padua was the first preacher so far as I can learn, who made a careful division of his sermons into several heads — which his extant sermons show that he commonly did, though not universally.... These formal divisions, a new thing in the history of preaching, came from applying to practical discourse the methods then pursued in the Universities. Most of the great schoolmen were predecessors or contemporaries of Antony, and all the most vigorous thought of the time adopted their method.... Thus logical division, formally stated, became the passion of the age. And while then and often afterwards carried to a great extreme, and though there have been many reactions, in preaching as in other departments of literature, yet this scholastic passion for analysis has powerfully affected the thought and the expression of all subsequent centuries. (Broadus, 1889, 103-05).

7. Broadus, 1889, 105.

8. Broadus 1889, 107.

9. Dargan, 1968, 190-91.

10. Dargan, 1968, 196, 230; Broadus, 1876, 110-13.

11. Broadus, 1889, 110.

12. Broadus, 1889, 113-18.

13. Dargan, 1968, 380-82.

14. George, 1988, 113.

15. Packer, 1990, 280.

16. Packer, 1990, 284.

17. Perkins, 1996, 79.

18. Lewis, 1979, 19.

19. Sewall, 1900, 103-04.

20. Sewall, 1900, 142-63.

21. Koessler, 1996, 20-22.

22. Stott, 1982, 125-26.

23. Carson, 1996, 87-88.

24. Stitzinger, 1992, 60.

Chapter 18

A Workable Method for Expository Preaching

The writer will now set forth the method of preparation for expository preaching that he has developed over the past twenty years. This method is tailored to his own unique style of both study and preaching. Yet it is, in all honesty, dependent upon several sources of influence.

First of all, this method follows the five basic rules of expository preaching highlighted by Haddon W. Robinson in his seminal work *Biblical Preaching: The Development and Delivery of Expository Messages*, that was for the writer, as well as for thousands of other seminarians, a basic textbook in homiletics:

1. The passage governs the sermon by giving to it the substance of the message.
2. The expositor communicates the concept that was intended by the original biblical author.
3. The concept comes from the text itself by means of historical, grammatical and literary study of the passage.
4. The concept is applied first to the expositor as it flows through the personality and experience of the preacher.
5. The concept is applied to the hearers. This gives the expositor purpose and practical power. Inept application is as destructive as poor exegesis or shoddy delivery.[1]

Secondly, the writer's method is an adaptation of the 'Perry Method' set forth by Lloyd Perry in his textbook entitled *A Manual for Biblical*

Preaching. This helpful workbook was the homiletical guide in the sermon preparation and delivery class taught by Dr. Harold Burchett at the Columbia Biblical Seminary in 1982. The writer has modified Perry's method to simplify it but maintain the bulk of his approach in the writer's sermon preparation. This disciplined and effective method of writing sermons can be mastered with a little practice by any preacher. It streamlines and systematizes the process of sermon preparation.

Thirdly, the exegetical methods the writer uses were taught to him by his Greek and exegesis professor, William J. Larkin, and his Hebrew and exegesis professor, Paul W. Ferris. Both of these able expositors taught methods for sermon planning and preparation that have served the writer well to this day. The practical insights gleaned from the preaching and teaching ministry of these two men have truly enriched and enabled the process of exegesis the writer follows each week.

Fourthly, the writer has listened to hundreds and hundreds of hours of the preaching of John F. MacArthur Jr. of the Grace Community Church in Panorama City, California. In addition, the Shepherd's Conference at Grace Church, other ministerial seminars taught by MacArthur, and dozens of his publications comprised of his preaching have influenced the writer tremendously. Additionally, the writings of Dr. D. Martyn Lloyd-Jones have benefited the writer tremendously, especially in the area of sermon delivery. The preacher under whose pulpit the writer was converted, James M. Latimer, of the Central Church in Memphis, has also modeled expository preaching for him.

Finally, the writings of Luther, Calvin and the Puritans have aided in preaching theologically as well as biblically in an expository manner. The rich legacy of their tracts, sermons, commentaries and dissertations helps to give depth and historical insight in the writer's exposition of Scripture.

Any preacher will be able to point to his textbooks, professors, manuals and models for the genesis of his own preparation and delivery style. But each preacher must hone his own style into a comfortable and convenient method over years of preaching. There are seven basic steps the writer follows in preparing to preach expositorily. These seven steps will be explained in the following seven sub-headings:

1. Selection of the Preaching Text
2. Development of Supporting Resources
3. Outline of the Sermon Series
4. Devotion to Introductory Matters
5. Sermon Preparation: Exegesis
6. Sermon Construction: The Preaching Outline
7. Codification and Filing

Step One: Selection of the Preaching Text

The first step in expository preaching is to select that portion of Scripture to be exegeted and expounded upon. There is more involved in this than appears to most. One contemporary preacher has said that he merely preaches on that which interests him, but this method of selecting a preaching text lacks purpose. As a Dispensationalist this preacher spends all his time in the New Testament. In his thirty-five years of expository ministry he has preached through only two Old Testament books: Daniel and Zechariah (because in them he finds support for his view of eschatology). In that same time period he has expounded upon Romans three times. There is a definite loss of balance in his preaching due to the fact that he preaches only what interests him, and apparently he has no interest in God's Old Testament Church because of his Dispensational views. The pastor must balance the needs of his congregation with the biblical mandate to preach 'the whole counsel of God'. What preachers must realize is that not only are the particular texts of various biblical books inspired, but also the various genres of the actual sixty-six books of the Bible. To preach biblically, the minister must also preach through various kinds of biblical literature.

Churches that need revitalization are usually churches where the choice of preaching texts has been plagued by haphazardness and even laziness. Since these pulpits lack both emphasis and direction, the sermons often tend to be topical in style and random in purpose. In addition, many preachers lack the work ethic and energy to invest time and thought in their selection of sermon series. Most churches in decline are not the beneficiaries of expository preaching in biblical book series. Many ministers are too lazy to engage in fresh exegesis and new exposition in order to ensure a good diet of the Word for their people. These preachers have a set stack of sermons they recycle every five or six years.[2]

Revitalized churches are churches where the sermon series are new, fresh, relevant and well-prepared. The enthusiasm and investment the preacher puts into his selections and preparation show. These series produce an atmosphere where the preaching is appreciated for its obvious attention to study, preparation and timely topics.

The writer recommends a balance, maintained in three ways. First, there must be a balance of both Old and New Testament studies. Over the years he has generally sought to alternate between Old Testament and New Testament sermon series. While preaching a New Testament series in the morning, he will usually preach an Old Testament series in the evening, and vice versa. Again, a Covenant View of Scripture demands such – all Scripture is inspired by God, Old and New Testaments (2 Tim. 3:16).

A second measure of balance in selecting preaching texts has to do with their length. It is possible, the writer believes, to completely exhaust a congregation by remaining in a sermon series too long or by allowing one lengthy series to follow another. He is aware that James Boice preached for eight years through the Psalms and almost as long through Romans, and that John MacArthur took eight years to go through the Gospel of Matthew. However, these congregations have been trained, over decades, to engage in and respond to such intense preaching. Until a congregation develops to that point of maturity in listening, the preacher will need to 'pace his preaching'.

People need to see the preacher and themselves 'cover ground' in Scripture, i.e. to work their way through portions of Scripture, completing such studies successfully. One of the most harmful things a preacher can do is to announce a sermon series, begin it, and then get side-tracked into another series without finishing what he started. Likewise, it can be discouraging to prolong a sermon series that never seems to end. Immature congregations must be led gradually into longer, extended series, spacing longer series by placing shorter series in between them.

It is helpful to break larger books (e.g. Isaiah, Romans, Matthew or Genesis) into their major parts and in between those major divisions of the book place shorter series that give the congregation a break without losing the continuity of the larger book's sections. For example, Genesis can be divided into five sections: The Introduction – 'The Parameters of Life' (Gen. 1–11); the Life of Abraham (Gen. 12–25); the Life of Isaac (Gen. 25–27); the Life of Jacob (Gen. 28–36); and the Life of Joseph (Gen. 37–50). The writer has preached through the first three sections over a twelve-year span. He intends to finish the last two sections over the coming years.

It is healthy for congregations to see and hear expounded three kinds of material: books, sections and short texts. 'Book studies' are self explanatory – begin at the start of a biblical book or epistle and preach through until the end. 'Sections' of Scripture are those texts that form their own blocks of instruction within a book (e.g. the Ten Commandments, the Sermon on the Mount, Paul's resurrection teaching in 1 Cor. 15). 'Texts' are simply short portions of Scripture expounded in detail: a psalm, a sermon in Acts, or a parable.

A third measure of balance is also helpful to preaching: balance of genre. Congregations should be exposed to a variety of biblical genres. The Bible is God's library, and in it are a dozen or so different genres of literature. Care must be taken to ensure that God's people receive more than just Gospels and Epistles in their spiritual diet.

Selection of the Scripture portions to preach must be more deliberate than merely preaching through what the preacher wants to learn. Why expound upon Romans for a second or third time when the Psalms, the Megilloth, and the Prophets remain untapped? The goal is to strive to give the congregation a good mixture of Old and New Testament; books, sections, and texts; long, intermediate, and short series; and the full complement of biblical genres.

Step Two: Development of Support Resources
Once a section of Scripture has been selected, the preacher must master the purpose, theme and flow of thought, long before he actually begins to prepare sermons week by week. Here is where many preachers make fatal mistakes. They wait until a week or two before the new sermon series is scheduled to begin before they commence preparatory study on that series. They are barely a week or two ahead of their congregations and may be well into the series before they know where the series is headed!

The writer always begins to prepare six months before a series is scheduled to begin. The first step in such preparation is to begin a 'sermon file'. This file, kept in his desk drawer, is compiled for several months prior to launching a new series. Into the file go articles, illustrations, essays, and the book titles that form the bibliography for study.

During these preceding months, the preacher should look through his library to see what resources he already has available. Then he should survey academic bookstores, seminary libraries, and book catalogs to become familiar with the new and useful resources available for his sermon series. During this process, annotated bibliographies should be consulted. Purchasable for little expense, these are highly valuable and practically useful.[3]

Ministers must learn to use their book allowances wisely. Popular books written for public consumption are not good investments. These publications can be borrowed, checked out of libraries, or copied for specific parts and purposes. The writer limits his book spending on popular books to a small fraction of his book allowance. The vast majority of book money should be spent on good commentaries, reference books, sets of books by the Puritans, Reformers and church fathers, theological works, and exegetical aids and manuals. The aim is to build a good, well-stocked reference library for study and research. Therefore, it is not unusual for the writer to purchase a dozen or more commentaries on a single book series. Once they are used, they remain a permanent part of his pastoral library for future study and cross-reference or for help to others.

If popular books are to be purchased, care must be taken to limit their acquisition if they cannot be used again and again for reference, quotes, statistics, and illustrations. The writer has selected several authors whose books he purchases because of the theological position and the scholarly approach reflected in their books.[4]

Finally, the writer recommends that two types of Reformed theological books be purchased. First, good Reformed systematic theologies are hard to obtain but are useful as commentaries. The works of Berkhof, Hodge, Murray, Thornwell, Dabney, Warfield, and other Reformed theological sets ought to be procured for use. Second only to biblical commentaries, good theological works will be referred to by earnest expositors. Secondly, good individual works on specific theological subjects need to be purchased when they supplement understanding of a Bible book's theology and theme. For example, when preaching in Ruth, pastors should acquire books on Providence; while in Revelation, books on Eschatology; and while in Romans, works on Soteriology; and so forth.

To begin to acquire the necessary commentaries, theological books, reference works, popular publications, articles and miscellaneous materials needed to support exegesis and exposition for a sermon series, the preacher must initiate his preliminary studies months in advance of his actual first sermon in the new series. This preliminary study and the subsequent development of support readings, resources, and sermon files will both enrich sermon series and build a good pastoral library for use in years to come. Expository preaching begins, in earnest, long before chapter one, verse one is ever exegeted by the preacher. This fact leads to a third vital step.

Step Three: Outline of the Sermon Series
A preacher once told the members of a seminar, in which the writer was a participant, that he read through the book of the Bible he was about to preach once every day for thirty days prior to beginning the sermon series. When he preached through longer books, he divided the book into its key sections and read each section, once per day, for thirty days prior to preaching through it. In this way, he became familiar with the overall flow of thought in the book. The writer has practiced this approach for years, and as a result, when he begins a sermon series, he feels as if he has a command of the process of thought expressed by the biblical author.

The sermon series should be outlined, in some detail, prior to the beginning of the actual sermon deliveries. These 'scratch outlines' will form a skeleton upon which the particular sermon outlines will be hung. Preachers need to be aware that no in-depth exegesis has been done at this point, and thus scratch outlines may be revised to more accurately reflect the flow of thought in the book. Nevertheless, outlining the book, section, or text is of great value in putting each particular sermon in its biblical context.

The combination of repeated reading and preliminary study of resources and references allowed the preacher to see the nature of the biblical book and its flow of thought and to adjust the preaching plan to reflect the uniqueness of its specific genre. This example points to the value of step four. As week to week exegesis and detailed study unfolded new insights, the series' outline was revised, but it was not substantially changed from this original, preliminary skeleton outline.

Step Four: Devotion to Introductory Matters
Preachers often fail at this particular step in the process. Their eagerness to get into the meat of the issues and the flow of the sermon series causes them to either ignore important introductory matters or to cover such matters in a cursory manner. Caution and patience are called for at this step.

Having gathered a number of good commentaries, the expositor must patiently and persistently plod through all those preliminary pages in the commentaries devoted to the 'introduction' of the biblical book. Perseverance in studying commentaries, survey books, and introductions to the Testaments will yield tremendous insights into the series about to be developed and preached. Examples that prove the value of this process are not difficult to find, even in the writer's own preaching. Introductory study in Ruth yielded tremendous insight into the unique genre called 'short story' and caused the writer to revise his entire approach to the series. When he studied through Lamentations in preparation for preaching, the introductory studies caused him to exegete the laments differently than other poetic passages (like psalms) and to revise the way he constructed the actual expositional outlines from which he preached. The Song of Solomon has absolutely critical issues of an introductory nature that must be grappled with to properly preach through its content, with an accurate reflection of the author's intent.

The fewer the resources available for a specific biblical book, the more critical is the introductory matter for a sermon series. The fewer the resources, the less a pastor has to draw upon to put the book in historical context and provide application for the congregation. The study of Ruth was limited by the fact that Ruth is traditionally tacked onto the end of commentaries on Judges. Few individual commentaries on Ruth exist. Of the nine major resources at the writer's disposal, only three devoted adequate attention to Ruth as a separate work from Judges. And only one developed the study out of the understanding of Ruth as a short story. The fewer the resources, the better a pastor must be at 'detective' work – digging, exploring, investigating for the unique aspects of his sermon series subject.

Five principal questions must be addressed in introductory studies to facilitate the congregation's understanding of the book. These five introductory aspects must be communicated clearly to the congregation to increase their comprehension of the sermon series over the weeks and months to follow:

1. What is the unique place in the Canon of Scripture that this book (or text) holds? History, date, authorship, purpose and theme(s) must be introduced here and applied to the congregation's life.

2. What is unique about the genre of this book or text? This question will aid in interpreting, preaching and understanding the Scripture being studied.

3. What major doctrines does this book or text unfold for the church? What is received from it that cannot be found elsewhere in Scripture? What does this book or text add to the richness of this Holy Library called the Bible?

4. How has this book been used in the life of the church throughout church history? The congregation should understand how Old Testament Israel, Jesus Christ and the Apostolic church, the early church, the Reformers, and the Puritans understood, applied and benefited from this book or text.

5. Why does the congregation need to study this particular book or text? The reason for the sermon series, the need of the times, and the overall application to the local church should be forcefully made clear to those who will hear the sermon series.

Preachers need to realize that, although they may grasp all this introductory material and understand the answers to these five questions, deliberate effort must be devoted to helping the congregation understand these things as well. Preachers must not forget that by the time they mount the steps to the pulpit for the first sermon in a series, they have been immersed in study for weeks. The congregation, however, knows none of this background information and will be asking these five questions in their own ways, in their own minds. The people will glean immeasurably more from the sermon series if they are well-informed by the preacher, at the start of a series, by means of essential introductory information clearly and simply communicated. These introductory matters can surprisingly make for some very interesting and practical sermons that 'connect' with the people, bringing the past and the present together and making the Scripture come alive. One or two introductory sermons will help the congregation assimilate the sermon series more than most preachers ever imagine. The writer maintains that such introductory sermons are essential to truly preach expositorily through the Bible. Wiersbe makes the same point:

> It has well been said that nobody goes to church to find out what happened to the Jebusites. A sermon that lingers in the past tense is not really a sermon at all: it is either a Bible story or a lecture. We *live* in the present tense and we need to hear what God has to say to us *today*. All Scripture is inspired and all Scripture is profitable. This means that there is a present-day message and application for each portion of the Word of God. It is the preacher's job to discover the timeless truths and principles that are in the Word, clothe them in understandable language, and apply them to the needs of a waiting congregation.... The main points of your message must focus on life today and not on Moses, David, or Paul. What God did for the men and women of old, the heroes of faith, is meaningful to us today by way of warning (1 Cor. 10:1-12) and encouragement (Rom. 15:4). This includes the Old Testament, for, after all, that was the only Bible Jesus and the early church possessed. In their ministries, the apostles were able to give a modern, relevant message from the ancient Scriptures, and God blessed their words.[5]

It is true that people do not go to church 'to find out what happened to the Jebusites' unless they see the Jebusites living next door to them. They must be helped to meet the challenge of facing these twenty-first century Jebusites with biblical ammunition! The writer's task is to relate the Jebusites to Jacksonians. The introductory matters of a book help him to do just that.

Step Five: Sermon Preparation (exegesis)
When the time comes for studying the actual texts of Scripture selected, researched and undergirded by resources, the writer follows a simple procedure in developing each sermon. This process of exegesis, which can be used by anyone, involves five stages that make preparation a manageable task within a limited time frame. Dr. William J. Larkin of Columbia Biblical Seminary used to tell his students to 'fit the task to the time'. This five-step process allows a minister to do just that, and produces what the writer calls the 'master outline'.

Before these five steps are looked at in more detail, three preliminary rules of thumb are in order. The first rule is simply to slow down the process of preaching through books of the Bible. This process should not be hurried. Time needs to be taken, over the number of weeks necessary, to move through a book at a comfortable pace. When the writer first began to preach, he felt the pressure from within to move quickly through books of the Bible, so he lived on a treadmill of feeling that he had to finish sermon series by certain arbitrary dates. This forced him to slide through the last two chapters of an epistle before Christmas arrived, or to try to preach 'chunks' of Scripture to finish a series before a two-week vacation, and so forth. Such arbitrary deadlines should be forgotten, and the appropriate amount of time to preach through a series – not too long, but not too short – should be taken.

A second rule involves selecting a manageable section of Scripture to be preached in each sermon. Usually, especially in epistles, the writer works paragraph by paragraph (or idea by idea) through the epistle. In other literature, the psalm, the parable, the story or event, the scene, the stage of thought or other such progressive element of the biblical book needs to be determined. Each is then preached, one at a time. The common exhortation to younger preachers to preach through larger sections of Scripture, to gain expertise in exegesis and exposition and to allow them to preach shorter sections in the future, is unwarranted. The more they choose to preach on each Sunday, the more they have to exegete and the longer their outline will need to be to do justice to the text.

The book of Ruth is logically divided by changes of place (scene), and for preaching purposes, these scenes establish the divisions of the book. The Gospels break down into pericopes; the epistles into paragraphs, doctrines or ethical instructions; the historical books into events; and apocalyptic literature into visions or dreams. The preacher must find the preachable section then exegete, and expound, only that section.

A third rule is surprisingly at odds with what is taught in most seminary exegesis courses: a preacher should work primarily from the English text. Because the writer uses the *New American Standard Bible* as both his exegesis text and preaching text, he is able to work from the English text as his primary source. Because it is a literal translation, its accuracy is far superior to that of the dynamic equivalency versions so popular today.[6] The writer recommends that the expositor use the NASB version and his Greek or Hebrew text and key the one to the other. He does this for one reason: the people in the pew will not be looking at *The United Bible Societies Greek New Testament* or at the *Biblia Hebraica* when he is preaching. His exegesis is not hindered by working primarily from the literal English text, and his exposition is certainly aided. He could not follow this procedure as effectively by using a dynamic equivalency text like the *New International Version*. By using the NASB text, he is not slowed by rusty Greek and Hebrew (a fact most preachers must deal with two or three years out of seminary), but he is keyed into the original texts. The writer is able to use the English and original texts side by side, thanks to the literal translation of the NASB. This method allows him to develop sermon outlines out of the Bible version the people will be using each Sunday, while remaining faithful to the original text.

With these three rules of thumb in mind, the preacher is now ready to exegete the preaching text and develop the master outline. This actual exegesis takes place in five *stages*. The first stage has already been discussed in some length above, namely that the logical section of Scripture is selected for exegesis and exposition. Once the writer has selected the preachable section of Scripture, he asks the questions: "Why is this section in the book and what does it communicate to the reader?"

In the preliminary examination of this first preaching text the writer develops initial ideas that will lead to stage two: the exegetical outline. This exegetical outline does not worry about form, or symmetry, or even communicability. The purpose of the exegetical outline is to set forth, in detailed outline, what the text actually communicates.

To truly preach biblically (expositorily) the expositor must draw his preaching points directly from the text, without the aid of commentaries, other preacher's outlines, or his own preconceived notions about the text. This basic, even crude, exegetical outline is essential to fresh and pure expositional preaching. But the process does not linger long at this stage. The next stage in the process is the expositional outline. This the writer calls stage three.

This expositional outline, derived purely from the exegetical outline, adds points to be preached in an effort to 'fill in the holes' in the outline.

The exegetical outline leads, point by point, to the expositional outline except where balance is needed and where material is rearranged for ease in preaching. Preachers should not impose an outline on the text (eisogesis) but rather pull the outline from the text (exegesis). This expositional outline becomes the 'master outline' that the expositor will actually preach.

In stage four of the exegesis, the expositor asks three key exegetical questions:

1. What are the key words and phrases that need to be pointed out to the congregation?
2. What are the historical facts and background that need to be told to the congregation?
3. What are the textual difficulties and problems that need to be explained to the congregation?

These three questions deal respectively with the grammatical, historical and literary issues present in the original text. Conservative, evangelical and reformed expositors need not shy away from these higher critical questions. They shed light upon the text and force honest engagement with the biblical material. It is for this very reason that the writer always purchases a couple of higher critical commentaries. Although he usually rejects their interpretations of theology, he does benefit from the grammatical and historical issues they wrestle with in their exegesis.

The fifth and final stage of exegesis is introducing related literature and cross-references into the exegetical process. For Ruth 1:1-5, the biblical accounts of similar events in Judges, encyclopedia articles on famine, atlas information on Judah (Bethlehem) and Moab, and research on both the religious life and cultural setting of Israel in the twelfth century before Christ were invaluable in making the sketchy details of five verses take on 'more life' for the congregation. It is at this stage that the detailed study of resources begins to yield its fruit.

These five stages of exegesis, in step five of the sermon development process, are the heart of the entire process. The lion's share of study occurs in these five stages of step five. Only after such detailed study is the expositor ready to move forward in sermon development.

Step Six: Sermon Construction (the preaching outline)

In step six, the expositional outline is developed. The expositor begins to fill in the 'master outline' derived from his exegesis. In this step the preacher constructs the sermon notes he will use in the pulpit. This step involves eight stages of development:

1. Writing the outline of the main points and sub-points: 'the body' of the sermon. The preacher rewrites and refines the expositional outline as described in step five above.
2. Filling in the expositional outline with definitions and explanations of both theological and historical key points.
3. Selecting key quotes from resources: These may be read to the congregation or used only for the preacher's use in his delivery.
4. Finding and positioning appropriate SAIs – stories, analogies and illustrations – that will enlighten the text.
5. Developing applications; placing them throughout the sermon, and using key, summary applications in the conclusion.
6. Writing the conclusion to the sermon next to last.
7. Writing the introduction to the sermon last, thus setting the stage for what will follow in the body of the sermon.

8. Supplementing the sermon and worship service with related hymns, creeds and catechism readings, and related biblical passages for (responsive) reading.

Once this process is finished, the preaching outline will be ready for review, memory and delivery.

Step Seven: Codification and Filing
The last step in the expository process involves preparation for use of the sermon outline in the pulpit and preservation of sermon notes for future occasions. Preachers should treat with care this valuable asset developed after hours and hours of preparation, study and writing. The writer advises the preacher to do three things with his outline.

First, the preacher should color code the outline. This color coding obviously cannot be duplicated here, but an explanation of how it works can nonetheless be given. The writer uses four colors, purchased in the typical highlighter set in any store: yellow, orange, pink and blue. Each point and all key words or phrases in the actual preaching outline are highlighted with a specific color. Each color communicates something to the writer as he preaches. Here is his color-coding system.

1. *Yellow*: All main points (Roman numerals) and major sub-points (A, B, C...), as well as statements that communicate the main ideas of the sermon, are in yellow. This information is the 'meat' of the sermon and the most important thing said in the pulpit.
2. *Orange*: All the explanatory, background, historical, and clarifying points are in orange. The orange information clarifies, explains and reinforces the 'yellow points.'
3. *Pink*: All cross references, Greek and Hebrew words and other foreign or key English words and phrases are in pink. The pink information is purely exegetical information.
4. *Blue*: Quotes by others, illustrations, examples, book titles and references, and related information are in blue. The blue highlighting stands out, enabling this information to be seen at a glance.

There is a 'method to this madness'. The writer always prepares more than he can preach. Although his sermons last from forty to forty-five minutes, he consistently has from fifty to sixty minutes' worth of information prepared. As he preaches, he begins to edit. By color coding the outline, he is alerted to the relative value and the intended purpose of each point of the outline, permitting him to leave pertinent information out of his delivery and still adequately and logically cover the text set before the congregation. On rare occasions, when a service left the writer only twenty minutes or so to preach, he was able to cover the yellow and orange material and still do some justice to the exposition of the text. Other preachers have different ways of coding their messages.[7] The writer finds this color-coded method most helpful and recommends it to others.

Sermons also need to be referenced and filed for future use. The writer numbers each sermon with a six-digit number. For example, the sermon number for the Ruth 1:1-5 message is RU9402. These six digits communicate precise information:

1. RU ... The Book of Ruth (A two-letter abbreviation for the book or series title. First Corinthians is 1C; Genesis is GN; the Apostles' Creed is AP; and the Lord's Prayer is LP, etc.)
2. 94 ... These next two numbers are the year that the sermon series began. (The sermon series in Ruth began on October 23, 1994.)
3. 02 ... These two numbers are the sermon number in the sequence of the series. (RU9402 was the second of ten messages in this series on Ruth.)

These numbers are used in three ways. First, they enable the sermon notes to be filed in sequence. Second, they are used in the radio ministry at Trinity to file the original tape recordings. Third, they serve as the order numbers for those sitting in the congregation or listening to the radio program who would like to order a specific sermon on cassette tape or compact disk.

The filing of the sermon notes is quite simple. The writer's sermon notes are typed on to 8 ½" by 5 ½" sheets of paper and placed in chronological order in three-ring binders. Three sets of these notes are then reproduced: one for a master file, one for the church library, and one for the homiletics department of Reformed Theological Seminary for their use. These sermon series are filed, by volume and binder sets, in the writer's office.

ENDNOTES

1. Robinson, 1980, 20-26.

2. There is absolutely no excuse for such laziness and negligence in the pulpit. Saints need to be fed a fresh diet of biblical exposition. In the ten years the writer preached at Surfside PCA Church, he repeated no sermon series and not one sermon. In preaching at Trinity Church over these last twelve years, he has prepared new material each week. He has preached six sermon series at Trinity Church that he preached at Surfside (First Corinthians, Acts, Song of Solomon, Genesis 1-11, Titus and the Songs of Ascents). But, in each case, the sermons were studied for and prepared afresh without dependence upon or duplication of previous notes. Each sermon series was different — always longer — than before. In these twelve years only one sermon series (Acts) has been repeated because the Book of Acts is such a foundational book to church life and mission. The first series in Acts was in 1992 when the writer first arrived at Trinity Presbyterian Church. The second series in Acts was in 2003, and was significantly different than the 1992 series. The notes of 1992 were never referred to in 2003. Fresh exegesis cannot come from old outlines.

3. The writer refers to the Dallas Theological Seminary publications, the Banner of Truth bibliography of C. H. Spurgeon, and a bibliography by Derek Thomas published by Reformed Academic Press. Others are available, especially from seminaries. He also recommends that seminary professors who teach Old Testament and New Testament studies be asked for their course bibliographies for specific biblical books or texts.

4. J. I. Packer, Alister E. McGrath, James M. Boice, Michael S. Horton, John H. Armstrong, R. C. Sproul, John F. MacArthur Jr., David F. Wells, D. Martyn Lloyd-Jones, Iain H. Murray, Francis Schaeffer, R. O. Roberts, and John R. W. Stott are men whose works he trusts and finds beneficial. He also purchases expensive sets of historical works that will enrich his library for years to come: Calvin's Commentaries, The Works of Martin Luther, The Church Fathers, The Works of John Owen, and other classic sets of the Puritans, Reformers and Church Fathers and Theologians.

5. Wiersbe and Wiersbe, 1986, 66-67.

6. Price, 1987, 9.

7. Mayhue, 1992, appendix.

Chapter 19

The Expositional Process

The expository method of preaching was the method of the Reformers and Puritans. It maximized the amount of biblical content communicated to congregations and minimized the influence of extra-biblical ideas upon the listeners. This expository style of preaching requires an exegetical method of sermon preparation. The exegetical method the writer uses to prepare for expository preaching is neither original nor copied. It is a distillation of concepts taught to him by others over the years, as well as his own unique adjustments learned by experience. Those wanting to develop their own method for expository preaching will be greatly benefited by the book *Rediscovering Expository Preaching: Balancing the Science and Art of Biblical Exposition* by John MacArthur Jr. and the faculty of the Master's Seminary (edited by Richard L. Mayhue). Each preacher should deliberately develop his own method of exegesis and exposition.

James Montgomery Boice, one of America's ablest reformed expositors, has touched a tender nerve concerning the need for scholarly exegesis and faithful exposition:

Over the years I have developed a number of concerns for which I am nearly always ready to go on a crusade. One is the place of scholarship in preaching. We have a pernicious doctrine in contemporary evangelicalism – I do not hesitate to call it that – which says that if a minister is average in his skills and intelligence, he should take an average church. If he is above average, he should take a larger church. If he is really exceptional – if he is keen about books and simply revels in the background, content, and application of the Word of God – he should teach in a seminary. Ugh! I am convinced that those with the very best minds and training belong in the pulpit, and that the pulpit will never have the power it once had (and ought to have) until this happens. When I say this I do not suggest that the pulpit should become a seminary lectern, though it would be better that than the sad stage prop it has become for many minister-entertainers. Obviously a sermon is not a lecture. It is exposition of a text of Scripture in terms of contemporary culture with the specific goal of helping people to understand and obey the truth of God. But to do that well the preacher must be well studied. To do it exceptionally well he must have exceptional understanding of (1) the Scripture he is expounding, (2) the culture into which he is expounding it, and (3) the spirituality and psychology of the people he is helping to obey God's Word. These understandings do not come merely from native abilities or mere observance of life. They come from hard study as the preacher explores the wisdom of both the past and the present to assist him in his task.[1]

The principal time of the preacher's work week must be spent on the exegesis of Sunday's passage of Scripture to be expositorily expounded. The writer uses two days each week to prepare his two Sunday messages: Tuesday (the morning message) and Wednesday (the evening message). Often his exegesis begins on Monday evenings and spills over into Thursday mornings. Including the study time in the office and at home and the hours (weeks) of preliminary study, the writer usually devotes twelve to fifteen hours to each sermon. This time is greatly reduced by the extensive preliminary work that is done.

Pastors must struggle to carve out this time for sermon preparation, and congregations must be taught to appreciate the pastor's study time, guard it, and not criticize it. Those going into revitalizing pastorates will be criticized by people for being too much of a 'book worm', not enough of a 'people person', and unfaithful in 'pastoral duties' (i.e. visitations, phone calls, luncheons, and so forth). Revitalizing pastors will inevitably follow men who were either negligent or incompetent (or both) in the study and in the pulpit. The people of the parish must be taught that 'pastoring' is pre-eminently feeding the flock. A good pastor is not one who spends all of his time with undernourished and soul-sick sheep! A good pastor is one who feeds his flock well: solid, biblical content, an abundance of truth, and a steady, balanced diet of spiritual nourishment. Pastors must not shy away from detailed and diligent exegesis and exposition. It is far better to have their congregations grumble about 'too much' and 'too long' than 'not enough'. Healthier is the overfed lamb than the emaciated goat! The one thing a faithful expositor will never hear is this, 'I left the church because I wasn't being fed!' The writer has seen many people leave the congregations he has served, and they did so for a variety of reasons. In the decades he has preached, few have ever said that they were 'not being fed' spiritual truth from his sermons.

Pastors must develop congregations that facilitate expository preaching at every level of parish life and ministry. They must engender support for this exegetical process in five different ways. First, they must develop the discipline of thorough study in their own libraries. Secondly, they must teach staff to complement their study schedules by taking up slack in other pastoral duties left by the preacher. Thirdly, they must train their secretaries and administrative personnel to aggressively protect their sermon preparation time. Fourthly, they must ensure that their families understand and accept that the preacher must complete his exegesis and expository preparations before any other priority in the weekly schedule is addressed. Finally, they must help the congregation grow to the point where they both expect and even demand solid exposition rooted in diligent study.

The Old Puritan preacher, Richard Rogers, once said, 'I serve a precise God.'[2] And so it must be that this God's preachers expound the word 'precisely'. The faithful pastor who wants to see revitalization take place in his local church must heed Paul's exhortation to 'study to show thyself approved unto God, a workman that needeth not be ashamed, rightly dividing the Word of truth' (2 Tim. 2:15, KJV). Paul considers preaching expositorily of such great importance that the destiny of the souls of men depend upon it:

Until I come, give attention to the public reading of Scripture, to exhortation and teaching. Do not neglect the spiritual gift within you, which was bestowed upon you through prophetic utterance with the laying on of hands by the presbytery. Take pains with these things; be absorbed in them, so that your progress may be evident to all. Pay close attention to yourself and to your teaching; persevere in these things; for as you do this you will insure salvation both for yourself and for those who hear you (1 Tim. 4:13-16).

Revitalization of a local congregation rests upon diligent exegesis and faithful exposition. The Reformers and Puritans used the Word of God with such power, precision, and persistence that the church blossomed under their exposition. Luther will have the final word of exhortation to preach expositorily God's Word:

In short, I will preach it, teach it, write it, but I will constrain no man by force, for faith must come freely without compulsion. Take myself as an example. I opposed indulgences and all the papists, but never with force. I simply taught, preached, and wrote God's Word; otherwise I did nothing. And while I slept [cf. Mark 4:26-29], or drank Wittenberg beer with my friends Philip and Amsdorf, the Word so greatly weakened the papacy that no prince or emperor ever inflicted such losses upon it. I did nothing; the Word did everything. Had I desired to foment trouble, I could have brought great bloodshed upon Germany; indeed, I could have started such a game that even the emperor would not have been safe. But what would it have been? Mere fool's play. I did nothing; I let the Word do its work. What do you suppose is Satan's thought when one tries to do the thing by kicking up a row? He sits back in hell and thinks: Oh, what a fine game the poor fools are up to now! But when we spread the Word alone and let it alone do the work, that distresses him. For it is almighty and takes captive the hearts, and when the hearts are captured the work will fall of itself.[3]

ENDNOTES

1. Boice, 1986, 91-92.
2. Ryken, 1986, 1.
3. Luther, 1959, 51:77-78.

Epilogue

Chapter 20

'A Charge to Keep I Have'

'I solemnly charge you in the presence of God and of Christ Jesus, who is to judge the living and the dead, and by His appearing and His kingdom: preach the word; be ready in season and out of season; reprove, rebuke, exhort, with great patience and instruction. For the time will come when they will not endure sound doctrine; but wanting to have their ears tickled, they will accumulate for themselves teachers in accordance to their own desires; and will turn away their ears from the truth, and will turn aside to myths' (2 Tim. 4:1-5).

The revitalization of a local church is indeed a multifaceted undertaking. Preaching for revitalization takes place within the scope of a deliberate pursuit of church health. It is the minister's task to pursue, with the assistance of church officers and pastoral staff, church health. It is God's prerogative and purpose to give the increase. The Biblical assumption is that healthy churches, like healthy bodies, will grow.

When the writer first came to Trinity Church he set before the elders, then the staff and finally the congregation a set of 'Fifteen Factors': a list of church characteristics that must be pursued at all costs in order for the congregation to become what the New Testament presents as a healthy church. That list of fifteen church-health factors can be found on Page 229.

Care must be taken to communicate again that the writer does not believe preaching alone can bring about revitalization to a church. God uses many instruments to revive and restore his work. Prayer, faithful pastoring, godly leadership, Biblical vision, church discipline, involved laity and proper priorities are all necessary to bring about revitalization. In fact, these fifteen factors must be 'in place' and functioning well in order for a troubled church to be revitalized. The writer has arrived at these fifteen factors that constitute a healthy church through his own experience in the pastorate and the study of several key books by John MacArthur Jr., Michael Griffiths, Donald MacNair and Gene Getz.[1] If compared to a building project with a foundation, a frame and furnishings, then preaching that revitalizes is a vital part of the foundation (see Fifteen Factors, page 229).

These fifteen factors, led by Biblical preaching and teaching, are so vital to the life of a congregation that in 1993 the staff of Trinity Presbyterian Church preached a sermon series on these fifteen elements of a dynamic church. Ligon Duncan, Chris Shelt, Glenn Durham and the writer expositorily presented each of these fifteen factors and called the church to focus on them. This sermon series was entitled 'Building Together God's Way: 15 Essential Commitments of a Dynamic Church.' Here again, the pulpit led the way.

The church will go where the pulpit leads it. All other aspects of congregational life – the remaining fourteen key factors – will be affected, for better or worse, by the preaching of the pastors of the church. For this reason the writer maintains that preaching is the key to the revitalization of the church.

No single action of pastors attracts or repels people so directly as the pulpit ministry. Visitors come to church hoping for spiritual nourishment and will not return if the sermon is boring, irrelevant, or wearisome. Established members with deep ties to the church may stick through the ministries of poor pulpiteers, but growth – both spiritual and numerical – is unlikely without good preaching.... Never underestimate the cumulative effect of good preaching. Many of today's sizable churches can attribute their growth mainly to good preaching. The late psychologist George Crane shocked many preachers by saying: 'many clergyman couldn't rate even a D in any high school public-speaking class! You are an ally of Satan if you drive parishioners away from church by your stodgy public-speaking methods.' The torrential outpouring of words week after week simply makes no difference in thousands of churches. Mediocrity in the pulpit stunts church growth, wastes thousands of hours, and injures the spiritual lives of millions of Americans.[2]

In turn, there should flow from these characteristics a set of 'non-negotiables' that are expected of the congregation in order to promote church health and then church growth.

These non-negotiables of Christian living are published in and promoted by our Inquirer's Class. They can be found on Pages 227-228. A careful examination will find that Biblical Preaching and Teaching and the Absolute Authority of Scripture head the lists. Once again, the church will go where the pulpit leads. Therefore the pulpit must be preeminent, planned, purposeful and proactive in leading the church toward reaching the characteristics of church health and in helping church members flesh out the non-negotiables of holy living. Help is needed in preaching with such direction.

The Help the Preacher Needs

Revitalizing preaching cannot be accomplished by the preacher alone. He will need the assistance and unflagging support of the officers of the church and the church's staff. He will need a 'job description' (ministry description) that will direct him and allow him to devote significant time to all the facets of expository preaching: prayer, planning, study, promotion, preparation and refinement. His first and foremost duty must be the pulpit, not just 'on paper' but in reality. The senior minister (or solo pastor) must be treated as a preacher – not as a CEO, a manager of a small business, a therapist or a social club director.

The officers of the church must assume administrative and pastoral duties that will free the pastor to become the preacher. Once again the pastor's office must become the pastor's study. This is more easily said than done in an age addicted to pragmatism, visible activity and immediate results. The officers must train the congregation to allow the preacher the time needed to prepare to preach the Word.

The pastoral staff must rise to the challenge of becoming, in reality, assistant or associate ministers. They must take up the bulk of pastoral duties – counseling, visitations, classes and programs

– in order to free the senior minister's time. They must also adopt, without reservation, the fifteen factors of church health, the non-negotiables and the overall philosophy of ministry so that the pastoral ministry is truly following and implementing the vision coming from the pulpit.

A danger exists when even one staff member is 'not on board'. His independence can build a church within a church and cause friction, jealousy and competition in the church that can lead to division. Staff members who are not primarily preachers often have a genuinely difficult time in believing the pulpit must be preeminent. Music, outreach, youth work, administration, foreign missions, Christian education or counseling can be pitted against the pulpit for prime time and influence. The officers must ensure that people are brought onto the pastoral team who believe the pulpit must be preeminent.

Finally, the congregation must be taught to appreciate and respond to such reformed and Puritan preaching. This may be the most difficult and painful dimension of preaching for revitalization. Short, anemic and harmless sermons pepper the ecclesiastical landscape in America, England and the Western world. Convincing a congregation that long, substantial and pointed sermons are what the church needs for church health and growth is very costly and quite difficult. In fact, such preaching may initially shrink the church rolls before any revitalization begins to take place. There are real hazards to preaching for revitalization.

The Hazards the Preacher Encounters

Stephen F. Olford, in advising the pulpit committee that called the writer to Trinity Church, warned of the consequences of expository preaching aimed at revitalization. He told the committee that such preaching would likely empty the church before it filled it! For obvious reasons, the writer has prayed that this not be so. But much of Olford's warning has come to pass. Trinity Church has grown and shrunk at the same time. What the writer means is this: Over the first four and one-half years, many members were added and attendance increased. But many members also moved elsewhere. All of these losses cannot be attributed to the writer's preaching, although he ventures to say great portions of them are. He believes, as do the elders of the church, that this has been, overall, a positive development for three reasons.

First, many inactive members have either been removed from the rolls or have joined other churches. Thus on-roll membership is smaller than its peak in 1968, but active membership is larger. The writer attributes this shift to the emphasis in the pulpit on genuine conversion, active participation in the life of the church, Sabbath observance, and commitment to both discipleship and ministry. People who want to drop into church a half dozen times per year are no longer comfortable at Trinity Church when they come to 'hear the preacher'.

Secondly, the elders and the writer believe that more than a few spurious believers have been 'run off' because of the doctrines of grace and the clear, compelling call to gospel faith. When the Word of God is truly preached it *is* a two-edged sword (Heb. 4:12). The man who has crowds coming to hear him preach and few who ever leave disturbed or 'offended' over the gospel is a man who is in trouble in his preaching. Jesus, the Prophets, the Apostles, the Reformers, and the Puritans ran many off as they drew many more. Unconverted people usually cannot remain long under Puritan preaching before they are either convicted and converted or convicted and driven away. The minister of revitalization cannot be discouraged by these dropouts.

The serious problem of our age is that Christian men and women are sinning against the Holy Spirit. The Puritan, John Calvin, was right when he pointed out that the sin of Old Testament times was the rejection of Jehovah God, the sin of New Testament times was the rejection of the Son of God, and the sin of the Church age is the rejection of the Holy Spirit. There are so-called believers all over Christendom today who refuse to acknowledge the sovereignty of the Holy Spirit in individual and congregational life. These people are not living in the fullness and freedom and fellowship of the Spirit. This is why we do not know a contagious revival. But let us not be pessimistic; revival *can* come and *will* come, carrying in its wake all the blessings which are promised to us in Christ, if we are prepared to discover the secret, discern the signs and determine the scope of a heaven-sent revival.[3]

Thirdly, those who came to the church because it was 'the place to be' soon left. Every 'new preacher on the block' has an initial flurry of interest that surrounds his ministry. He has not been around long enough to offend anyone. During those initial days of his ministry, he will draw the 'church gypsies' who go from congregation to congregation, those who come because their friends come, and those who are upset at some other church or minister. Under Reformed and Puritan preaching, these folks will quite often move on to other pastures.

Those who remain, however, grow in their faith. They slowly but surely adapt to the preacher's style and then adopt the preacher's priorities. Some may be offended at such a comment: 'Is it the goal of preaching for the congregation to adopt the pastor's agenda?' The answer is, quite honestly and frankly, yes. Leadership leads by an agenda. This is always the case. If the pastor-preacher is weak, lazy or directionless then the "agenda" will be a hodge-podge of the mob. Committees, ministries, staff and programs will all take on a disjointed and uncoordinated life of their own. If the preacher and officers set the 'agenda', and pursue it with a vengeance, then unity and cooperation will result. What is hoped for and prayed for is that the people will catch the vision from the pulpit and run with it.

The Hope the Preacher Has

Such 'moral earnestness', as the Puritans used to call it, is contagious. Show the writer a congregation zealous for the Lord and he will show you the pastor(s) who helped them to feel and live in such a manner.

'And so it will be, like people like priest...' (Hos. 4:9).

'And the people will be like the priest...' (Isa. 24:2).

Some things are taught and some things are modeled. In the case of the ethos of preaching, the latter is true. People can 'catch' the heart of their pastor as he preaches just as surely as they can grasp the content of his words. The people of Trinity Church are growing in their desire to live for the Lord and serve others in love because of the passion of Puritan preaching they sense in the sermons. Often people weep during the sermons. Some have lingered long after the services in a spirit of prayer. And still others have been moved to confession of sin and to seek counseling for help in troubled areas of their lives. The writer has often told the people that 'Puritan preaching' will not eliminate the need for counseling but will actually increase it because the Spirit of God will probe deeply as preachers speak to the conscience. Such has been the case. People have come to Trinity's pastors seeking help with sexual addictions, adulterous relationships, crumbling marriages, assurance of salvation, financial troubles, depression due to sin, and help in becoming a Christian – all of these confessions due to the heart-stirrings caused by preaching.

The writer would be untruthful if he gave the impression that this spiritual, romantic and controversial preaching is popular with all and well received by everyone. He has received anonymous notes about poor English used in the pulpit. He has been rebuked for inappropriate humor and unnecessary shouting. He has been lectured to 'preach only the Word and keep his own opinions to himself.' He has been taken to task for exaggerations, overstatements and incorrect assessments. He has been accused of not being true to the Reformed Faith, speaking against his Puritan tradition, and twisting the Word of God to suit himself. In the balance, most of the negative comments have some truth to them. Passionate preaching can easily step over the line and become fleshly preaching, unbridled by the Spirit. But these actual failures and false accusations are few. The benefits of preaching with a Puritan ethos are certainly worth the risks.

Preaching expository, well-exegeted sermons will powerfully impact the congregation. The proof of this statement could rest solely in the fact that this exegetical-expositional process has served the writer well for over two decades. In the normal course of preaching verse by verse on a variety of topics in Biblical texts, the writer has seen scores converted, people called into the ministry, families restored, and lives changed. While at Surfside PCA Church in Myrtle Beach, South Carolina, the writer preached in this manner for a decade (1982–1992). In that time, he saw converted forty percent (40%) of the five hundred and fifty (550) people who at one time or another joined that church in those ten years. Fifteen men and women were sent into pastoral ministry or mission work. A congregation of fifty-five charismatics and ex-Methodists became a leading church in the presbytery. Preachers can confidently anticipate that after an extended time they will witness similar responses to such expository preaching.

People do notice, do respond to, and do hunger for solid study that undergirds rich exposition. People know when they are being fed meat and potatoes and when they are being fed cotton candy! It is the Word of God that changes people's lives – not illustrations, not stories, not jokes, not even poetry and song. 'The Word of God is living and active...' (Heb. 4:12), and for that reason expository preaching that increases exposure to and understanding of the Word will have the greatest impact on people's lives.

Conclusion

James E. Means in writing about true, lasting and full-orbed growth in a church spoke candidly about the place of preaching. In his comments about the kind of preaching needed today – thematic, inspirational, passionate and truthful – he touched upon the same four aspects of preaching examined in these four hypotheses:

> Effective preaching features major biblical themes and identifies, illuminates, underscores, and applies one of God's profound revelations. Bad preaching is pedantic, marked by fractured thinking and trifling concerns.... The temptation to substitute catchy contemporary topics for dominant scriptural themes seduces many modern preachers. Some pastors have capitulated to superficial sermonic fads in the name of relevance. Growth produced by superficial or sensational preaching will be characterized by nothing more than spiritually anemic crowds. Effective preaching inspires.... Every good sermon helps the listener to understand the Bible better, but the real business of preaching is to bring about change in human lives. For that to happen, the springs of human motives must be touched. A good sermon animates, quickens, persuades, elevates, and impels. Only truth made alive in the preacher and empowered by the Spirit transforms people.... Hardly anything engenders revulsion so much as dispassionate objectivity.... Listeners hunger for evidence that preachers believe their own message. Perhaps our greatest pulpit need is for the warmth of spiritual fire. Carefully crafted sermons help, but spiritual preachers aflame with truth make the real difference in people's lives. Preachers sometimes compromise truth with

expediency by taking texts out of context, twisting interpretation to fit prejudice, and citing authorities to buttress fallacy. No dividends achieved by such tactics justify the contamination or dilution of truth. Most listeners cannot be deceived by oratory for long. Deluded people become disillusioned people, and then absent people. Preachers cannot escape the necessity of a rigorous integrity in the handling of Scripture…. Sometimes pastors preach what they do not believe, but wish they did. Some things sound great in sermons and make profound impressions, but simply are not rue. Some sermons are attractive, even elegant, but play fast and loose with reality. After listening to one eloquent presentation, an unmoved listener responded: 'That's a bunch of sentimental slop.' Unfortunately, he was right. Much of our religion, hymnody, and preaching is sentimentally magnificent, but theologically weak. Rhetoric and passion that conflict with spiritual truth is contemptible and self-defeating.[4]

One fact is certain: Revitalization can take place. It is the will of the Lord that His churches grow in every way possible – qualitatively, quantitatively, and organically. Generally speaking, He desires to revitalize those churches that are dying (Matt. 16:18). This revitalization will entail radical change for the majority of weakening churches. And such radical change will require preachers who preach like the Reformers and Puritans. Preaching that revitalizes is possible. It remains for preachers in the majority of American pulpits to wake up to the challenge before them and rise up to preach for revitalization. In the hope of such renewal, this book is offered for the good of Christ's Church and the glory of God.

A charge to keep I have, a God to glorify,
A never dying soul to save, and fit it for the sky.

To serve the present age, my calling to fulfill;
O may it all my pow'rs engage to do my Master's will!

Arm me with watchful care as in Thy sight to live,
And now Thy servant, Lord, prepare a strict account to give!

Help me to watch and pray, and still on Thee rely,
O let me not my trust betray, but press to realms on high.

Charles Wesley

ENDNOTES

1. MacArthur, 1996; Griffiths, 1978; McNair, 1980; Getz, 1974.
2. Means, 1995, 189.
3. Olford, 198, 106.
4. Means, 1993, 190-92.

TEN NON-NEGOTIABLES

A HIGH VIEW OF GOD

A reverent and sober-minded relationship to the sovereign God that causes us to worship Him in spirit and truth, serve Him diligently and obey Him in fear and love.

THE ABSOLUTE AUTHORITY OF SCRIPTURE

A belief in the inerrant, infallible, inspired and authoritative Word of God that shapes our whole life and ministry around the relevant, absolute and life-changing truth revealed to us and communicated by preaching and teaching.

SOUND DOCTRINE AND A PURE GOSPEL

The conviction that good living flows from good doctrine; doctrine found in the Reformed and Biblical Faith and rooted in the true Gospel of repentance from sin and dead works and faith toward God in Christ, who is both Savior and Lord to all true Christians.

BIBLICAL AUTHORITY

A commitment to obey the channels of God's delegated authority in marriage and family, church and government, in such a way that we are blessed by spiritual and godly leaders who direct us in the ways of God.

MUTUAL ACCOUNTABILITY

A lifestyle of reciprocal living whereby we follow the reciprocal commands of the New Testament to live for one another in such a way that we bring glory to Christ, fulfill our duties to one another and enrich the life of the church.

HOLINESS OF LIFESTYLE

A call from God to be separate from the world and set aside for Him in such a way that we work out our salvation with fear and trembling in order to become like Jesus Christ and giving testimony to the world of what a true Christian looks like in character and conduct.

THE PRIMACY OF PRAYER

The realization that the source of spiritual power in the Christian life is found in Spirit-driven prayer and the responsibility as a Christian to be part of a praying people at worship, work, witness and warfare.

COMMITMENT TO EXCELLENCE

An effort to do whatever we do to the glory of God and to give Him our very best in service, stewardship, study and steadfastness for His Heavenly Kingdom so that our lives become living and holy sacrifices acceptable to God in Christ.

LOVING FOCUS ON PEOPLE

A decision to place the interests of others before that of our own in order to meet their spiritual needs if at all possible: salvation for the unconverted, sanctification for the saints, support for the Kingdom of God and sympathy for those in need.

REVIVAL AND REFORMATION

The great need of the Twenty-first Century Church whereby God baptizes, awakens and empowers us with His Holy Spirit as He renews the saint, revitalizes the congregation, revives the church, reforms religion and restores our fortunes in Jesus Christ our Lord.

FIFTEEN FACTORS OF A DYNAMIC CHURCH

BUILDING TOGETHER GOD'S WAY

Theme Verse: ' ... You also, as living stones, are being built up as a spiritual house for a holy priesthood, to offer up spiritual sacrifices acceptable to God through Jesus Christ' (1 Peter 2:5).

THE FOUNDATION
A BIBLICAL PURPOSE AND PHILOSOPHY
BIBLICAL PREACHING AND TEACHING
THE PRIMACY OF PRAYER
A PLURALITY OF GODLY LEADERS
AN ACTIVELY INVOLVED LAITY

THE FRAME
DEVOTION TO THE FAMILY
LIVING BY FAITH
SACRIFICIAL LIVING
HOLINESS OF LIFESTYLE
A WILLINGNESS TO CHANGE

THE FINISHINGS
DISCIPLESHIP AND DUTY
RECIPROCITY IN FELLOWSHIP
WORSHIP: THE ULTIMATE PRIORITY
CULTURAL PENETRATION
THE MISSIONS MANDATE

Bibliography

Adair, John. 1986. *Founding Fathers.* Grand Rapids: Baker Book House.

Adams, Jay. 1982. *Truth Apparent: Essays on Biblical Preaching.* Phillipsburg, NJ: Presbyterian and Reformed Publishing Company.

Adams, Thomas. 1861. *The Works of Thomas Adams: Being the Sum of His Sermons, Meditations and Other Divine and Moral Discoveries.* Edited by James Nichols. Edinburgh: James Nichols.

Alexander, J. W. 1988. *Thoughts on Preaching.* Edinburgh: Banner of Truth Trust.

Alexander, Robert and Donaldson, James eds. *Ante Nicene Fathers: translations of the writings of the fathers down to 325 A.D.* Eerdmans 1990

Altham, Elizabeth. 1996. Protestant pastors return to Rome. *Sursum Corda: The Catholic Revival,* Special Edition, 2-13.

Bainton, Roland. *Here I Stand: A life of Martin Luther.* Meridian, New York, 1977

Barker, Kenneth L., Bruce K. Walke and Roy B. Zuck, Comp. 1979. *Bibliography for Old Testament Exegesis and Exposition.* 4th ed. Dallas, TX: Dallas Theological Seminary.

Baxter, Richard. 1974. *The Reformed Pastor.* Edinburgh: Banner of Truth Trust.

Beates, Michael. 1996. The evangelical shuffle. *Tabletalk,* September, 12-13.

Bezilla, Robert, ed. 1993. *Religion in America: Princeton Research Center (1992–1993) 25th Anniversary Edition.* Princeton: Princeton Research Center.

Boice, James Montgomery. 1986. The Preacher and Scholarship. In *The Preacher and Preaching,* ed. Samuel T. Logan, 91-104. Phillipsburg, NJ: Presbyterian Reformed Publishing Company.

Boice, James Montgomery and Eric Alexander. *What Ever Happened to the Doctrines of Grace: recovering the Doctrines that shook the world.* Crossway Books, Wheaton 2001

The Book of Church Order of the Presbyterian Church in America. n.d. Decatur, GA: Presbyterian Church in America.

Booth, John Nicholls. 1943. *The Quest for Preaching Power.* New York: Macmillan Company.

Bridges, Charles. 1967. *The Christian Ministry with an Inquiry into the Causes of Its Insufficiency.* Edinburgh: Banner of Truth Trust.

Broadus, John A. 1889. *The History of Preaching.* New York: A. C. Armstrong.

Brown, Colin, ed. 1978. *The New International Dictionary of New Testament Theology.* Vol. 5. Grand Rapids: Zondervan Publishing House.

Brown, H. C., Jr., Gordon Clinard and Jesse J. Northcutt. 1963. *Steps to the Sermon: A Plan for Sermon Preparation.* Nashville: Broadman Press.

Brown, H. C., Jr. 1968. *A Quest for Reformation in Preaching.* Waco, TX: Word Books.

Bugg, Charles B. 1992. *Preaching from the Inside Out.* Nashville: Broadman Press.

Burns, James. 1960. *Revivals: Their Laws and Leaders.* Grand Rapids: Baker Book House.

Burns, William C. 1980. *Revival Sermons: Notes of Addresses by William C. Burns.* Edinburgh: Banner of Truth Trust.

Burroughs, Jeremiah. 1990. *Gospel Worship or the Right Means of Sanctifying the Name of God in General: Sermons by Jeremiah Burroughs.* Edited by Don Kistler. Ligonier, PA: Soli Deo Gloria Publications.

Butterick, David. 1987. *Homiletic: Moves and Structure.* Philadelphia: Fortress Press.

Carson, Donald. 1996. Accept no substitutes: Six reasons, not to abandon expository preaching. *Leadership,* Summer, 82-88.

Carpenter, Joel A. *Revive us Again: the Reawakening of American Fundamentalism.* Oxford University Press, 1997

Cartier, Myron R. 1981. *Preaching As Communication: An Interpersonal Perspective.* Nashville: Abingdon.

Chapell, Bryan. 1992. *Using Illustrations to Preach with Power.* Grand Rapids: Zondervan Publishing House.

Clarkson, David. 1988. *The Works of David Clarkson.* Edinburgh: Banner of Truth Trust.

Clements, Roy. 1996. *The Strength of Weakness: How God Can Use Your Flaws to Achieve His Goals.* Grand Rapids: Baker Book House.

Coggan, Donald. 1958. *Stewards of Grace.* London: Hodder and Stoughton.

Colquhoun, Frank. 1965. *Christ's Ambassadors: The Priority of Preaching.* Philadelphia: Westminster Press.

Colson, Charles. 1985. *Who Speaks for God?* Westchester, IL: Crossway Books.

Conn, Harvie M. 1976. *Theological Perspectives on Church Growth*. Nutely, NJ: Presbyterian Reformed Publishing Company.

Cyprian. 1990. Epistle LXXII: To Jubaianus, concerning the baptism of heretics. In *The Ante-Nicene Fathers*, Vol. 5, ed. Alexander Roberts and James Donaldson. 379-386. Grand Rapids: Wm. B. Eerdmans Publishing Company.

Dargan, Edwin Charles. 1968. *A History of Preaching*. Vols. 1 and 2. New York: B. Franklin.

deWitt, John R. 1981. *What Is the Reformed Faith?* Edinburgh: Banner of Truth Trust.

Evans, Tony. 1990. *America's Only Hope*. Chicago: Moody Press.

Fant, Clyde E. 1987. *Preaching for Today*. San Francisco: Harper and Row Publishers.

Gallup, George Jr., and Jim Costelli. 1989. *The People's Religion: American Faith in the 90's*. Princeton: Princeton Research Center.

George, Timothy. 1988. *The Theology of the Reformers*. Nashville: Broadman Press.

Getz, Gene A. 1974. *Sharpening the Focus of the Church*. Chicago: Moody Press.

Goring, Jeremy. 1983. *Godly Exercises or the Devil's Dance? Puritanism and Popular Culture in Pre-Civil War England*. London: Dr. William's Trust.

Greenway, Roger S. 1986. Forward. In *The Pastor-Evangelist: Preacher, Model, and Mobilizer for Church Growth*, ed. Roger S. Greenway, v-viii. Phillipsburg, NJ: Presbyterian Reformed Publishing Company.

Griffiths, Michael. 1978. *God's Forgetful Pilgrims: Recalling the Church to Its Reason for Being*. Grand Rapids: Wm. B. Eerdmans Publishing Company.

Grudem, Wayne A. Interview. "Evangelicalism." *Faith and Renewal*, Vol. 15, No. 1 (July - August, 1990), pp. 10-12.

Guiness, Os and John Seel, ed. 1992. *No God but God: Breaking with the Idols of Our Age*. Chicago: Moody Press.

Guthrie, Donald. 1987. *The Relevance of John's Apocalypse*. Grand Rapids: Wm. B. Eerdmans Publishing Company.

Hall, Thor. 1971. *The Future Shape of Preaching*. Philadelphia: Fortress Press.

Harding, Joe A. 1982. *Have I Told You Lately ...? Preaching to Help People and Grow Churches*. Pasadena, CA: Church Growth Press.

Harrington, Frank. 1992. A preaching interview with Frank Harrington. Interviewed by R. Albert Mohler, Jr., *Preaching* (July–August): 8-13.

Horne, Chevis F. 1975. *Crisis in the Pulpit*. Grand Rapids: Baker Book House.

Horton, Michael Scott. 1992. ed. *Power Religion: The Selling Out of the Evangelical Church*. Chicago: Moody Press.

Horton, Michael Scott. 1996. Recovering the plumb line. In *The Coming Evangelical Crisis*, ed. John H. Armstrong, 245-64. Chicago: Moody Press.

Howe, J. A. 1900. Doctrinal preaching. In *Preachers and Preaching: Lectures Delivered Before the Maine Ministers' Institute at Cobb Divinity School, Lewiston, Maine, September 4-12, 1899*, 179-209. New York: Silver, Burdette and Company.

Hybels, Bill. 1992. A preaching interview with Bill Hybels. Interviewed by R. Albert Mohler, Jr., *Preaching* (January–February): 2-10.

Jensen, Ron, and Jim Stevens. 1981. *Dynamics of Church Growth*. Grand Rapids: Baker Book House.

Johnson, Gary L.W. 1996. Does theology matter? In *The Coming Evangelical Crisis*, ed. John H. Armstrong, 57-76. Chicago: Moody Press.

Kehrein, Glen. 1996. Isolated Christianity. *Urban Mission*, June, 14-23.

Kennedy, D. James. 1983. *Evangelism Explosion: The Coral Ridge Program for Lay Witness*, 3rd ed. Wheaton: Tyndale House Publishers.

Kistler, Don, ed. 1990. *The Puritans on Conversion: Three Sermons by Samuel Bolton, Nathaniel Vincent, and Thomas Watson*. Ligonier, PA: Soli Deo Gloria Publications.

Kittel, Gerhard, ed. 1976. *Theological Dictionary of the New Testament*. Vol. 3. Grand Rapids: Wm. B. Eerdmans.

Koessler, John. 1996. A view from the pew: Lessons about preaching from the other side of the pulpit. *Preaching*, July-August, 20-22.

Kreeft, Peter J. 1996. *Ecumenical Jihad*. San Francisco: Ignatius Press.

Lehman, Louis Paul. 1975. *Put a Door on It! The 'How' and 'Why' of Sermon Illustration*. Grand Rapids: Kregel Publications.

Lewis, Peter. 1977. *The Genius of Puritanism*. Sussex, England: Carey Publications.

Licher, Richard. 1981. *A Theology of Preaching: The Dynamics of the Gospel*. Nashville: Abingdon.

Lloyd-Jones, D. Martyn. 1971. *Preaching and Preachers*. Grand Rapids: Zondervan Publishing House.

Lloyd-Jones, D. Martyn. 1983. *Evangelistic Sermons at Aberavon*. Edinburgh: Banner of Truth Trust.

Lloyd-Jones, D. Martyn. 1987. *The Puritans: Their Origins and Successors*. Edinburgh: Banner of Truth Trust.

Lloyd-Jones, D. Martyn. 1987. *Revival*. Westchester, IL: Crossway Books.

Love, William DeLoss. *The Fasts and Feasts of Thanksgiving Days of New England*. Pp 190-191, Houghton, Mifflin, and Co. Boston 1895

Luther, Martin. 1959. *The Works of Martin Luther*. Edited by Helmut T. Lehmann. Vol. 51, *Sermons, I*. Edited by John W. Doberstein. Philadelphia: Fortress Press.

Luther, Martin. 1960. *The Works of Martin Luther*. Edited by Helmut T. Lehmann. Vol. 35, *Word and Sacrament, I*. Edited by E. Theodore Bachmann. Philadelphia: Fortress Press.

Luther, Martin. 1962. *The Works of Martin Luther*. Edited by Helmut T. Lehmann. Vol. 54, *Tabletalk*. Edited by Theodore G. Tappert. Philadelphia: Fortress Press.

Luther, Martin. 1965. *The Works of Martin Luther*. Edited by Helmut T. Lehmann. Vol. 53, *Liturgy and Hymns*. Edited by Ulrich S. Leupold. Philadelphia: Fortress Press.

Luther, Martin. 1995. *Sermons of Martin Luther*. Edited and Translated by John Nicholas Lenker. Grand Rapids: Baker Book House.

MacArthur, John F., Jr. 1991. Faithfully proclaiming the truth: An interview with John MacArthur. Interviewed by R. Albert Mohler, Jr., *Preaching* (November–December): 2-10.

MacArthur, John F., Jr. 1991. *The Master's Plan for the Church*. Chicago: Moody Press.

MacLeod, Donald. 1987. *The Problem of Preaching*. Philadelphia: Fortress Press.

Markquart, Edward F. 1985. *Quest for Better Preaching: Resources for Renewal in the Pulpit*. Minneapolis: Augsburg Publishing House.

Marshall, Peter, Jr. and David Manuel. 1977. *The Light and the Glory*. Old Tappan, NJ: Revell.

Mayhue, Richard L. 1992. Rediscovering expository preaching. In *Rediscovering Expository Preaching: Balancing the Science and Art of Biblical Exposition*, ed. Richard L. Mayhue, 3-21. Dallas, TX: Word Publishing.

McDow, Malcolm and Alvin L. Reid. *Firefall: How God Shaped History Through Revivals*. Broadman and Holman, Nashville 1997

McGavran, Donald A. 1970. *Understanding Church Growth*. Grand Rapids: Wm. B. Eerdmans Publishing Company.

McGrath, Alister E. 1990. *Understanding Doctrine*. Grand Rapids: Zondervan Publishing House.

McGrath, Alister E. 1993. *Reformation Thought*, 2nd ed. Oxford: Blackwell.

McGrath, Alister E. 1994. *Evangelicalism and the Future of Christianity*. London: Hodder and Stoughton.

McGrath, Alister E. 1996. *A Passion for Truth*. Downers Grove, IL: InterVarsity Press.

McNair, Donald J. 1980. *The Living Church: A Guide for Revitalization*. Philadelphia: Great Commission Publications.

McNicol, Bruce. 1991. Churches die with dignity. In *Christianity Today*, 4 January, 68-70.

Mead, Matthew. 1991. *The Sermons of Matthew Mead: Original Sermons on the Jews and on Falling into the Hand of the Living God*. Edited by E. Bickersteth. Ligonier, PA: Soli Deo Gloria Publications.

Means, James F. 1993. *Effective Pastors for a New Century*. Grand Rapids: Baker Book House.

Mitchell, Henry M. 1977. *The Recovery of Preaching*. San Francisco: Harper and Row.

Morgan, Irvonwy. 1965. *The Godly Preachers of the Elizabethan Church*. London: Epworth Press.

Morgan, Irvonwy. 1973. *Puritan Spirituality*. London: Epworth Press.

Murray, Iain H. 1971. *The Puritan Hope: Revival and the Interpretation of Prophecy*. Edinburgh: Banner of Truth Trust.

Murray, Iain H. 1982. *David Martyn Lloyd-Jones: The First Forty Years, 1899–1939*. Edinburgh: Banner of Truth Trust.

Murray, Iain H. 1990. *David Martyn Lloyd-Jones: The Fight of Faith*. Edinburgh: Banner of Truth Trust.

Murray, Iain H. 1994. *Revival and Revivalism: The Making and Marring of American Evangelicalism: 1750–1858*. Edinburgh: Banner of Truth Trust.

Nettleton, Asahel. 1995. *Asahel Nettleton: Sermons from the Second Great Awakening (taken from the original hand-written manuscripts: 1783–1844)*. Ames, IA: International Outreach, Inc.

Niebuhr, H.R., D.D. Williams, and S.F. Ahlstrom. 1983. *The Ministry in Historical Perspective*. San Francisco: Harper and Row.

Olford, Stephen F. 1980. *Heart Cry for Revival*. Memphis: EMI Books.

Owen, John. 1967. *The Works of John Owen*. Edited by William H. Goold. Vol. 8 and 9. Edinburgh: Banner of Truth Trust.

Packer, James I. 1990. *A Quest for Godliness: The Puritan Vision of the Christian Life*. Wheaton: Crossway Books.

Parker, Ken. 1979. Seven characteristics of a growing church. In *The Pastor's Church Growth Handbook (Volume One)*, ed. Win Arn, 61-68. Pasadena, CA: Church Growth Press.

Parrish, Archie. 1995. *Do It Again Lord! Personal and Church Preparation for the Coming Great Awakening*. Decatur, GA: Presbyterian Church in America.

Patterson, Ben. 1986. Five temptations in the pulpit. In *Preaching to Convince*, ed. James D. Berkley, 147-156. Waco, TX: Word Books Publishers.

Pearce, J. Winston. 1967. *Planning Your Preaching*. Nashville: Broadman Press.

Perkins, William. 1996. *The Art of Prophesying*. Edinburgh: Banner of Truth Trust.

Perry, Lloyd M. 1965. *A Manual for Biblical Preaching*. Grand Rapids: Baker Book House.

Piper, John. 1990. *The Supremacy of God in Preaching*. Grand Rapids: Baker Book House.

Pitt-Watson, Ian. 1986. *A Primer for Preachers*. Grand Rapids: Baker Book House.

Pleuthner, Willard A. 1951. *Building Up Your Congregation: Help from Tested Business Methods*. New York: Wilcox and Follett Company.

Poe, Harry L. 1994. Improving creativity in preaching. *Preaching*, March—April, 4-13.

Price, James D. 1987. *Complete Equivalency in Bible Translation*. Nashville: Thomas Nelson.

Rainer, Thomas S. 1993. *The Book of Church Growth: History, Theology and Principles*. Nashville: Broadman Press.

Reeder, Harry L. 1986. Revitalizing a dying church. In *The Pastor-Evangelist: Preacher, Model and Mobilizer for Church Growth*, 162-181. Phillipsburg, NJ: Presbyterian and Reformed Publishing Company.

Reeves, Daniel R., and Ronald Jensen. 1984. *Always Advancing: Modern Strategies for Church Growth*. San Bernadino: Campus Crusade for Christ.

Reid, Clyde. 1967. *The Empty Pulpit.* New York: Harper and Row.

Roberts, Richard Owen. 1981. *Puritan Sermons 1659-1689: Being the Morning Exercises of Crippelgate, St. Giles in the Fields by Seventy Five Ministers of the Gospel in or Near London with Notes and Translations by James Nichols.* Wheaton: Richard Owen Roberts, Publishers.

Roberts, Richard Owen. 1982. *Revival.* Wheaton: Tyndale House Publishers.

Roberts, Richard Owen. 1994. ed. *Sanctify the Congregation: A Call to the Solemn Assembly and to Corporate Repentance.* Wheaton: International Awakening Press.

Robinson, Haddon W. 1980. *Biblical Preaching: The Development and Delivery of Expository Messages.* Grand Rapids: Baker Book House.

Ryken, Leland. 1986. *Worldly Saints: The Puritans As They Really Were.* Grand Rapids: Zondervan Publishing House.

Sands, Lord. 1923. *The Order and Conduct of Divine Services in the Church of Scotland.* Edinburgh: R and R Clark.

Sargent, Tony. 1994. *The Sacred Anointing: The Preaching of Dr. Martyn Lloyd-Jones.* Wheaton: Crossway Books.

Schaller, Lyle. 1996. Denominational or independent? Where are the advantages? *Clergy Journal*, August, 20-23.

Schuller, David S., Merton P. Strommen, and Milo L. Breeke. 1980. *Ministry in America: A Report and Analysis Based on an In-Depth Survey of 47 Denominations in the United States and Canada with Interpretation by 18 Experts.* San Francisco: Harper and Row.

Seaver, Paul S. 1970. *The Puritan Lectureships: The Politics of Religious Dissent: 1550–1662.* Stanford, CA: Stanford University Press.

Sewall, J. S. 1900. Expository preaching. In *Preachers and Preaching: Lectures Delivered Before the Maine Ministers' Institute at Cobb Divinity School, Lewiston, Maine, September 4-12, 1899*, 101-176. New York: Silver, Burdette and Company.

Sibbes, Richard. 1977. *The Complete Works of Richard Sibbes.* Edited by Alexander Balloch Grosart. Edinburgh: Banner of Truth Trust.

Spring, Gardiner. 1986. *Power in the Pulpit.* Edinburgh: Banner of Truth Trust.

Sproul, R. C. 1995. *Faith Alone: The Evangelical Doctrine of Justification.* Grand Rapids: Baker Book House.

Spurgeon, Charles H. n.d. *A Guide to Commentaries.* Edinburgh: Banner of Truth Trust.

Spurgeon, Charles H. 1986. *An All-Round Ministry*. Edinburgh: Banner of Truth Trust.

Spurgeon, Charles H. 1990. *Lectures to My Students*. Pasadena, TX: Pilgrim Publications.

Stephens, George T. 1961. *True Revival*. Abington: Bible Evangelism Books.

Stitzinger, James F. 1992. The history of expository preaching. In *Rediscovering Expository Preaching: Balancing the Science and Art of Biblical Exposition*, ed. Richard L. Mayhue, 36-62. Dallas, TX: Word Publishing.

Stott, John R.W. 1972. *Your Mind Matters: The Place of the Mind in the Christian Life*. Downers Grove, IL: InterVarsity Press.

Stott, John R.W. 1982. *Between Two Worlds: The Art of Preaching in the Twentieth Century*. Grand Rapids: Wm. B. Eerdmans Publishing Company.

Thielicke, Helmut. 1965. *The Trouble with the Church: A Call for Renewal*. New York: Harper and Row.

Thomas, Derek. 1996. *The Essential Commentaries for a Preacher's Library*. Greenville, SC: Reformed Academic Press.

Thompson, William D. 1981. *Preaching Biblically: Exegesis and Interpretation*. Nashville: Abingdon.

Truehart, Charles. 1996. Welcome to the next church. *Atlantic Monthly*, August, 37-58.

Turnbill, Ralph G. *A History of Preaching: Continuing the Works of Volumes 1 and 2 by Edwin C. Dargan*. Vol. 3. Grand Rapids: Baker Book House.

Wagner, C. Peter. 1984. *Leading Your Church to Growth: The Secret of Pastor-People Partnership in Dynamic Church Growth*. Ventura, CA: Regal Books.

Walter, Tony. 1985. *Need The New Religion: Exposing The Language of Need*. Downers Grove, IL: InterVarsity Press.

Warren, Rick. 1996. Preaching to the unchurched. *Preaching*, September-October, 4-11.

Webster, Douglas D. 1992. *Selling Jesus: What's Wrong with Marketing the Church*. Downers Grove, IL: InterVarsity Press.

Weener, Jay. 1990. Preaching and the artistic vision. *Reformed Review* (autumn): 3.

Wells, David F. 1993. *No Place for Truth; Or, Whatever Happened to Evangelical Theology?* Grand Rapids: Wm. B. Eerdmans Publishing Company.

Wells, David F. 1994. *God in the Wasteland: The Reality of Truth in a World of Fading Dreams*. Grand Rapids: Wm. B. Eerdmans Publishing Company.

Westminster Conference. 1986. *The Office and Work of the Minister.* Rowhedge, Colchester, England: Christian Design and Print.

Westminster Directory for the Public Worship of God. 1880. Philadelphia: Franklin.

Whitefield, George. 1854. *The Memoirs and Sermons of George Whitefield.* Edited by John Gillies. Philadelphia: Leary and Getz.

Wiersbe, Warren and David. 1986. *The Elements of Preaching: The Art of Biblical Preaching Clearly and Simply Presented.* Wheaton: Tyndale House Publishers.

Wigglesworth, Michael. 1895. *God's Controversy with New England.* Quoted in William DeLoss Love. *The Fasts and Thanksgiving Days of New England,* 190-191. Boston: Houghton, Mifflin and Company.

Wilson, Henry Steward. 1980. *The Speaking God: Luther's Theology of Preaching.* Ann Arbor: University Microfilms, International.